The Big Book of
Fat-Quarter Quilts

Martingale
Create with Confidence

The Big Book of Fat-Quarter Quilts
© 2016 by Martingale & Company®

Martingale®
19021 120th Ave. NE, Ste. 102
Bothell, WA 98011-9511 USA
ShopMartingale.com

Printed in China
21 20 19 18 17 16   8 7 6 5 4 3 2 1

Library of Congress Cataloging-in-Publication Data
is available upon request.

ISBN: 978-1-60468-807-8

MISSION STATEMENT

We empower makers who use fabric and yarn
to make life more enjoyable.

CREDITS

PUBLISHER AND
CHIEF VISIONARY OFFICER
Jennifer Erbe Keltner

CONTENT DIRECTOR
Karen Costello Soltys

DESIGN MANAGER
Adrienne Smitke

MANAGING EDITOR
Tina Cook

PRODUCTION MANAGER
Regina Girard

ACQUISITIONS EDITOR
Karen M. Burns

PHOTOGRAPHER
Brent Kane

COPY EDITOR
Melissa Bryan

What's your creative passion?

Find it at ShopMartingale.com

books • eBooks • ePatterns • daily blog • free projects
videos • tutorials • inspiration • giveaways

Contents

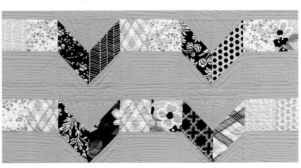

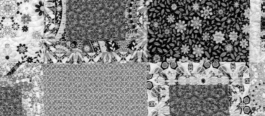

Introduction

What's your go-to fabric cut when you need a little fabric fix? You know, the one where you pet the bolt of fabric with no idea what you'll do with the piece, but you just *need* to own a little piece of it. Chances are, if you're like many quilters, it's a fat quarter. That 9" x 21" piece offers the possibility of cutting larger pieces or appliqué shapes than you can cut from a traditional quarter-yard cut.

There are also seemingly endless, always enticing shelves, bins, and bundles stacked high with precut fat quarters in a tempting variety. Who can resist the call of the orderly rows of fat quarters, neatly folded and beckoning quilters to imagine the possibilities? Frankly, the fat quarters in a quilt shop are equivalent to the candy bars at the checkout many of us faced off with as kids!

But once you get the fabrics home and stashed safely in your sewing space, it can be daunting to determine how to use those same fat quarters in a project. After all, many were accumulated with no pattern in mind.

Fret no more! *The Big Book of Fat-Quarter Quilts* is the solution. Inside you'll discover 66 patterns—all fat quarter friendly—ready to create with your treasured cuts of fabric. In fact, as you peruse the pages, your problem won't be what to make with the fat quarters you already have. It will be determining whether or not you have *enough* to make all the quilts you love. Enjoy!

It Takes Two

Two people falling in love and deciding to spend the rest of their lives together is a beautiful thing—so simple, yet so brave and full of significance. This quilt's union of brights and white may seem simplistic, but it boldly and playfully grabs your attention.

FINISHED QUILT: 60½" x 60½"
FINISHED BLOCK: 12" x 12"
Designed by Rachel Griffith; pieced by Lani Padilla; quilted by Darla Padilla

Materials

Yardage is based on 42"-wide fabric. Fat quarters are 18" x 21".

16 fat quarters of assorted dark solids for blocks
1⅜ yards of white solid for blocks and inner border
1⅛ yards of aqua solid for outer border
⅝ yard of fabric for binding
3¾ yards of fabric for backing
65" x 65" piece of batting

Cutting

From *each* of the dark fat quarters, cut:

1 square, 4¼" x 4¼"; cut the square in half diagonally
    to yield 2 triangles (32 total)
2 strips, 1¼" x 6¼" (32 total)
2 strips, 1¼" x 6¾" (32 total)
2 strips, 1¼" x 8½" (32 total)
2 strips, 2½" x 8½" (32 total)
2 strips, 2½" x 12½" (32 total)

From the white solid, cut:

2 strips, 4¼" x 42"; crosscut into 16 squares, 4¼" x 4¼".
    Cut the squares in half diagonally to yield 32
    triangles.
20 strips, 1¼" x 42"; crosscut into:
    32 strips, 1¼" x 6¼"
    32 strips, 1¼" x 6¾"
    32 strips, 1¼" x 8½"
5 strips, 1½" x 42"

From the aqua solid, cut:

6 strips, 5½" x 42"

From the binding fabric, cut:

7 strips, 2¼" x 42"

Making the Triangle Units

1 Sew a dark 1¼" x 8½" strip to the long side of a white triangle. Press the seam allowances toward the dark strip. Trim the ends of the dark strip even with the short sides of the white triangle.

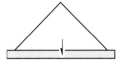 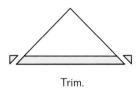

Trim.

2 Sew a matching dark 1¼" x 6¼" strip to one short side of the white triangle. Press the seam allowances toward the dark strip. Trim the end of the strip even with the strip along the bottom edge.

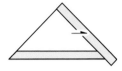 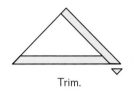

Trim.

3 Sew a matching dark 1¼" x 6¾" strip to the remaining side of the triangle as shown. Press the seam allowances toward the dark strip. Trim the end of the strip even with the strip along the bottom edge. Repeat the process to make a total of 32 triangle units with a white center.

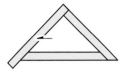 

Make 32.

4 Repeat steps 1–3 to make 32 triangle units with a dark center and white strips.

Make 32.

Making the Triangle Blocks

1 Lay out two matching triangles with white centers and two matching triangles with dark centers as shown. Join the triangles into pairs and press the seam allowances toward the dark strips. Join the triangle pairs to make a center unit. Press the seam allowances to one side. Trim the unit to measure 8½" x 8½". Make 16.

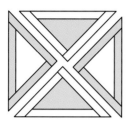 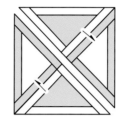

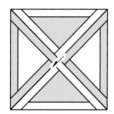

Make 16.

2 Select two matching 2½" x 8½" strips and two matching 2½" x 12½" strips that contrast with the block center. Sew the 8½" strips to the sides and the 12½" strips to the top and bottom. Press the seam allowances toward the just-added strips. Repeat to make a total of 16 blocks.

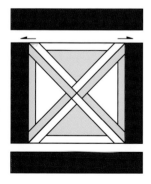 

Make 16.

Assembling the Quilt Top

1 Lay out the blocks in four rows of four blocks each, rotating the blocks as shown. Sew the blocks together in rows. Press the seam allowances in opposite directions from row to row. Sew the rows together and press the seam allowances in one direction.

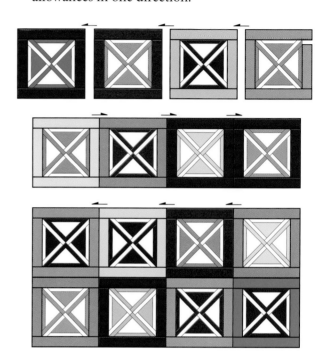

2 Sew the white 1½" x 42" strips together end to end. Measure the length of the quilt top. From the pieced strip, cut two white strips to this measurement and sew them to the sides of the quilt top. Press the seam allowances toward the inner border. Measure the width of the quilt top. From the remainder of the pieced strip, cut two white strips to this measurement and sew them to the top and bottom of the quilt top to complete the inner border. Press the seam allowances toward the inner border.

3 Sew the aqua 5½"-wide strips together end to end. Repeat step 2 to measure and cut the strips; then sew them to the quilt top for the outer border. Press all seam allowances toward the outer border.

Finishing the Quilt

For detailed information on finishing techniques, including layering, basting, and quilting, go to ShopMartingale.com/HowtoQuilt for free downloadable instructions. Use the 2¼"-wide strips to bind the quilt.

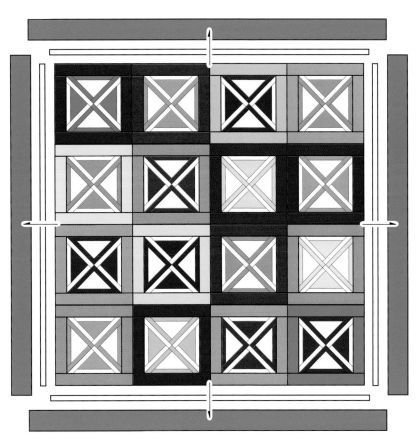

Quilt assembly

Country Haven

Create a haven meant for snuggling with this not-quite-traditional Log Cabin–style quilt. Strips of colorful prints and soothing neutrals combine with gently blooming daisies on the vine to bring a touch of easy, unassuming elegance to this easily stitched lap quilt.

FINISHED QUILT: 76½" x 76½"
FINISHED BLOCK: 10" x 10"

Designed, pieced, and machine appliquéd by Kim Diehl;
machine quilted by the staff at The Gathering Place in Rupert, Idaho

Materials

Yardage is based on 42"-wide fabric. Fat quarters are 18" x 21".

21 fat quarters of assorted prints for blocks, appliqués, and binding
½ yard *each* of 4 neutral prints for blocks
1¼ yards of black print for blocks and vines
2 yards of medium-green print for blocks and border
4⅔ yards of fabric for backing
84" x 84" piece of batting
Bias bar to fit appliqué vines

Cutting

Cut all strips across the width of the fabric in the order given unless otherwise noted. For greater ease in preparation, cutting instructions are provided separately for the appliqués.

From the *lengthwise* grain of the medium-green print, cut:

4 strips, 8½" x 60½"
Reserve the remainder of the medium-green print for the blocks.

From the 21 assorted print fat quarters and the remainder of the medium-green print, cut a *total* of:

104 rectangles, 1½" x 8½"
72 rectangles, 1½" x 6½"
72 rectangles, 1½" x 4½"
72 rectangles, 1½" x 2½"
Enough 2½"-wide random-length strips to make a 314" length of binding when pieced together end to end using straight, not diagonal, seams
Reserve the scraps for the appliqués.

From the neutral prints, cut a *total* of:

36 rectangles, 2½" x 8½"
36 rectangles, 2½" x 6½"
36 rectangles, 2½" x 4½"
36 squares, 2½" x 2½"

From the black print, cut:

12 strips, 2½" x 42"; crosscut into 180 squares, 2½" x 2½"
Enough 1¼"-wide bias strips to make 4 lengths measuring 60" each when pieced together end to end using straight, not diagonal, seams

Making the Blocks

1 Select two assorted print 1½" x 8½" rectangles. Join the pair along the long edges. Press the seam allowances to one side. Repeat for a total of 36 pieced 8½" units. Set aside the remainder of the 1½" x 8½" rectangles for the border pieced corner squares.

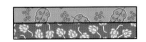

Make 36.

2 Repeat step 1 to make a total of 36 pieced rectangle units each in 6½", 4½", and 2½" lengths.

3 Lay out one pieced rectangle unit of each length, five black 2½" squares, one neutral print rectangle in each length, and one neutral print 2½" square in five horizontal rows as shown. Then join the pieces in each row. Press the seam allowances toward the black square. Join the rows. Press the seam allowances toward the 8½" pieced rectangle unit. Repeat for a total of 36 blocks measuring 10½" square, including the seam allowances.

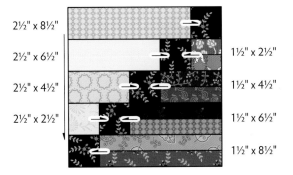

Make 36.

Assembling the Quilt Center

Lay out the blocks in six horizontal rows of six blocks each, turning every other block. Join the blocks in each row. Press the seam allowances of each row toward the blocks with the vertical strips. Join the rows. Press the seam allowances open.

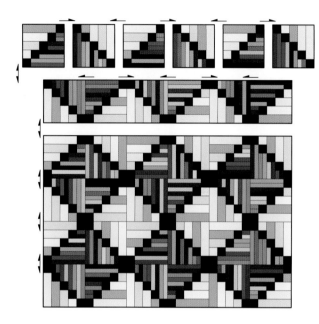

Appliquéing and Adding the Border

1. Using the patterns on page 13 and the assorted print scraps, prepare the following number of shapes for your favorite method of appliqué:

   - 48 leaves using pattern A
   - 20 flower petals using pattern A
   - 24 berries using pattern B
   - 4 flower centers using pattern B

Preparing Appliqué Points

For turned-edge appliqué (either by hand or machine), you may need to coax the seam allowance at a point to help it stay in place. If the seam allowance is lifting a bit and not firmly anchored to the back of the appliqué, dip the tip of an awl into a fabric glue stick and use it to add an extra little dollop where needed. Give the re-glued area a quick press with a hot iron, and the point will be sharp and crisp, with the seam allowance anchored perfectly in place.

2. Join the black bias strips end to end using straight, not diagonal, seams to make four 60" lengths. Use a bias bar to prepare four bias tubes for the vines. (For more information on using bias bars, download free "How to Appliqué" instructions from ShopMartingale.com/HowtoQuilt.)

3. Fold a green 8½" x 60½" strip in half lengthwise, right sides together, and use a hot, dry iron to press a center crease. Dot the seam of a prepared black stem with liquid basting glue at approximately ½" to 1" intervals. Beginning at the left-hand side of the strip, with the vine and border edges flush, press the prepared vine onto the cloth to make a serpentine shape along the center crease. Trim away any excess vine length to achieve the look you desire.

4. Using the quilt photo on page 10 as a guide, lay out 12 prepared leaf appliqués and six prepared berry appliqués along the vine. When you are pleased with your design, secure the appliqués in place. Work from the bottom layer to the top to position and secure five flower petal appliqués and one flower center, ensuring that any layered pieces are overlapped by at least ¼".

5. Repeat steps 3 and 4 to appliqué a total of four border strips.

6. Join eight assorted print 1½" x 8½" rectangles along the long edges. Press the seam allowances in one direction. Repeat for a total of four pieced corner squares.

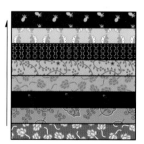

Make 4.

7 Referring to the photo, join appliquéd border strips to the right and left sides of the quilt center. Carefully press the seam allowances toward the border. Join a pieced corner square to each end of the remaining appliquéd border strips. Press the seam allowances toward the appliquéd border strips. Join these pieced border strips to the remaining sides of the quilt center. Press the seam allowances toward the border. The pieced and appliquéd quilt top should now measure 76½" square, including the seam allowances.

Finishing the Quilt

For detailed information on finishing techniques, including layering, basting, and quilting, go to ShopMartingale.com/HowtoQuilt for free downloadable instructions. Use the assorted 2½"-wide strips to bind the quilt.

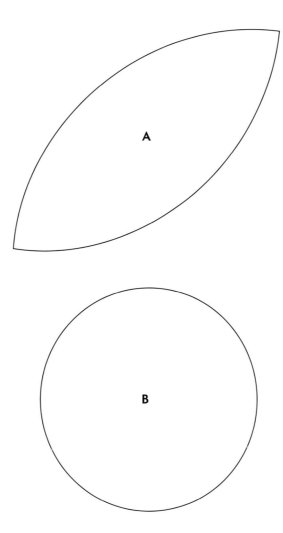

Appliqué patterns do not include seam allowances.

A

B

Floating Shoofly

Assembling Snowball blocks from strip-pieced squares creates a scrappy look. Add sashing and cornerstones to produce these floating Shoofly blocks, and encircle it all with a pieced border to complete the effect.

FINISHED QUILT: 68" x 78"

FINISHED BLOCK: 8" x 8"

Designed and pieced by Amy Smart; quilted by Emily Sessions

Materials

Yardage is based on 42"-wide fabric. Fat quarters are 18" x 21".

10 fat quarters of assorted orange prints for blocks and cornerstones

⅝ yard *each* of 10 different cream or neutral prints for blocks, sashing, and pieced outer border

1¼ yards of dark-orange print for inner border and binding

4⅝ yards of fabric for backing

72" x 82" piece of batting

Cutting

From *each* of the orange fat quarters, cut:

4 strips, 3½" x 21"; crosscut into 18 squares, 3½" x 3½" (180 total; 12 are extra)

1 strip, 2½" x 21"; crosscut into 5 squares, 2½" x 2½" (50 total; 8 are extra)

From *each* of the cream or neutral prints, cut:

2 strips, 2½" x 42" (20 total)

2 strips, 2" x 42" (20 total)

1 strip, 1½" x 42" (10 total)

1 strip, 8½" x 42"; crosscut into:

8 rectangles, 2½" x 8½" (80 total; 9 are extra)

3 rectangles, 3½" x 8½" (30 total; 8 are extra)

3 rectangles, 2½" x 3½" (30 total; 4 are extra)

From the remainder of the cream and neutral prints, cut a *total* of:

2 strips, 2½" x 42"

2 strips, 2" x 42"

1 strip, 1½" x 42"

4 squares, 3½" x 3½"

From the dark-orange print, cut:

8 strips, 1½" x 42"

9 strips, 2½" x 42"

Making the Blocks

1 Use the cream and neutral strips to make 11 strip sets. In each strip set, join two 2½" x 42" strips, two 2" x 42" strips, and one 1½" x 42" strip. Vary the order of widths and fabrics in each set. Press all of the seam allowances in one direction.

2 From *each* of 10 strip sets, cut three 8½" squares and three 4½" x 8½" rectangles.

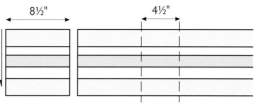

Make 11 strip sets.
Cut 3 squares and 3 rectangles from *each* of 10 of the strip sets.

3 Cut six 4½" x 8½" rectangles from the remaining strip set. You'll need a total of 30 pieced 8½" squares and 36 pieced 4½" x 8½" rectangles. Set the rectangles aside for the outer border.

4 Place an orange 3½" square on one corner of a pieced 8½" square, right sides together, and stitch from corner to corner as shown. Trim the excess fabric from the corner, leaving a ¼" seam allowance. Press the seam allowances toward the resulting orange triangle. Repeat on the remaining corners of the pieced square. Make 30.

Make 30.

5 In the same manner, stitch orange 3½" squares to two adjacent corners of 22 cream or neutral 3½" x 8½" rectangles to make 22 side blocks.

Make 22.

6 Lay a cream or neutral 3½" square on an orange 3½" square, right sides together. Draw a diagonal line from corner to corner on the wrong side of the lighter square and sew directly on the drawn line. Trim the excess fabric ¼" outside the seam. Press the seam allowances toward the orange fabric. Make four corner blocks.

Make 4.

Assembling the Quilt Top

1. Arrange the blocks, side blocks, corner blocks, sashing rectangles, and cornerstones as shown. Alternate the direction of the strips in the centers of the Snowball blocks.

2. Sew the pieces together in rows and press the seam allowances toward the sashing rectangles. Join the rows to complete the quilt top. Press the seam allowances in one direction.

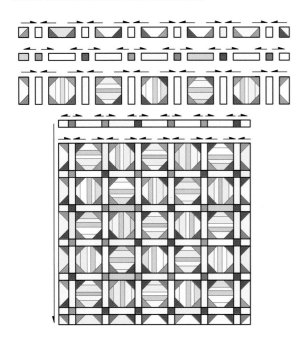

Adding the Borders

1. Sew two dark-orange 1½" x 42" strips together along their short edges; make four.

2. Measure the length of the quilt top. Trim two of the pieced strips to this measurement and sew them to the sides of the quilt top. Press the seam allowances toward the border.

3. Measure the width of the quilt top. Trim the remaining pieced strips to this measurement and sew them to the top and bottom edges. Press the seam allowances toward the border.

4. Sew nine 4½" x 8½" pieced rectangles together to create a border strip; make four. Measure the length of the quilt top, including the borders just added. Trim two pieced border strips and sew them to the quilt sides. Press the seam allowances toward the inner border.

5. Measure the width of the quilt top, including the borders just added. Trim the two remaining pieced border strips and add them to the top and bottom of the quilt. Press the seam allowances toward the inner border.

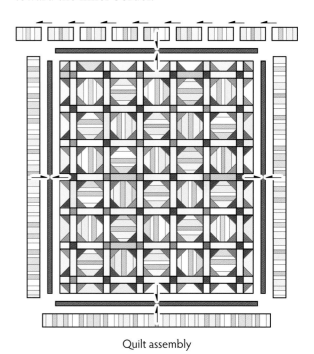

Quilt assembly

Finishing the Quilt

For detailed information on finishing techniques, including layering, basting, and quilting, go to ShopMartingale.com/HowtoQuilt for free downloadable instructions. Use the dark-orange 2½"-wide strips to bind the quilt.

Twirly Swirly

Designer Vickie Eapen says this basket quilt reminds her of Little Red Riding Hood, skipping through the forest with her basket of goodies for Grandma! Fortunately, these cheery prints are sure to soften the heart of any mischievous creatures that may be lurking.

FINISHED QUILT: 64½" x 64½"

FINISHED BLOCK: 16" x 16"

Designed and pieced by Vickie Eapen; machine quilted by Natalia Bonner

Materials

Yardage is based on 42"-wide fabric. Fat quarters are 18" x 21".

16 fat quarters of assorted primary prints for blocks*
2½ yards of white solid for background
¾ yard of brown houndstooth for blocks and binding
4 yards of fabric for backing
72" x 72" piece of batting

Vickie used 20 fat quarters for a bit more scrappiness, but 16 fat quarters is sufficient.

Cutting

From *each* of the primary-print fat quarters, cut:
1 strip, 4½" x 22"; crosscut into 4 squares, 4½" x 4½"
   (64 total; 6 are extra)
1 strip, 5" x 22"; crosscut into 3 squares, 5" x 5" (48 total)

From the brown houndstooth, cut:
1 strip, 4½" x 42"; crosscut into 6 squares, 4½" x 4½"
7 strips, 2¼" x 42"

From the white solid, cut:
6 strips, 5" x 42"; crosscut into 48 squares, 5" x 5"
4 strips, 8½" x 42"; crosscut into 32 rectangles, 4½" x 8½"
4 strips, 4½" x 42"; crosscut into 32 squares, 4½" x 4½"

Making the Blocks

1. Draw a diagonal line from corner to corner on the wrong side of the white 5" squares. Place a marked square on a primary-print 5" square with right sides together. Sew ¼" from the drawn line on both sides, and cut on the line to make two half-square-triangle units. Repeat to make a total of 96 half-square-triangle units (16 sets of six matching units). Press the seam allowances toward the print triangles. Trim each unit to 4½" x 4½".

Make 16 sets of
6 matching units.

2. Using pieces from the same print, arrange six half-square-triangle units, two matching 4½" squares, two contrasting 4½" squares, two white 4½" squares, and two white 4½" x 8½" rectangles. Sew the pieces together in rows as shown. Press the seam allowances in the directions indicated.

Join the rows, but do not press seam allowances yet. Repeat to make a total of 16 blocks.

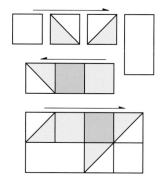 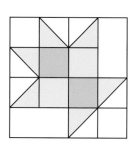

Make 16 blocks.

Assembling the Quilt Top

1. Arrange the blocks into four horizontal rows of four blocks each. Press the block seam allowances so that they alternate directions from block to block in each row.

2. Sew the blocks in each row together. Press the seam allowances in alternate directions from row to row. Sew the rows together. Press the seam allowances in one direction.

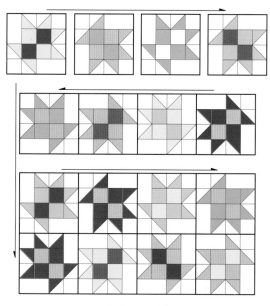

Quilt assembly

Finishing the Quilt

For detailed information on finishing techniques, including layering, basting, and quilting, go to ShopMartingale.com/HowtoQuilt for free downloadable instructions. Use the brown 2¼"-wide strips to bind the quilt.

Late Bloomers

Combine classic blocks and motifs with exuberant, colorful prints, toss in a bevy of whimsical appliquéd flowers, and what's the happy result? This cheerful lap quilt, positively brimming with modern tradition.

FINISHED QUILT: 65½" x 65½"
FINISHED BLOCK: 9" x 9"

Designed, pieced, and machine appliquéd by Kim Diehl; machine quilted by Deborah Poole

Materials

Yardage is based on 42"-wide fabric. Fat quarters are 18" x 21".

30 fat quarters of assorted prints (including some green) for blocks, border, and appliqués
1¾ yards of tan print for background
5 squares, 3½" x 3½", of assorted prints for Star block centers
⅝ yard of black print for binding
4 yards of fabric for backing
72" x 72" piece of batting
Bias bar to fit appliqué stem

Cutting

Cut all pieces across the width of fabric in the order given unless otherwise noted. For greater ease in preparation, cutting instructions are provided separately for the appliqués.

From the tan print, cut:
4 strips, 9½" x 42"; crosscut *each* strip into:
    1 rectangle, 9½" x 27½" (4 total)
    1 square, 9½" x 9½" (4 total)
10 squares, 4¼" x 4¼"; cut the squares in half diagonally to yield 20 triangles
20 squares, 3½" x 3½"

From *each* of the assorted print fat quarters, cut:
3 squares, 6¼" x 6¼"; cut the squares in half diagonally to yield 6 triangles (180 total)

From the remainder of the assorted print fat quarters, cut a *total* of:
8 squares, 9½" x 9½"
16 squares, 5¾" x 5¾"; cut the squares in half diagonally to yield 32 triangles
10 squares, 4¼" x 4¼"; cut the squares in half diagonally to yield 20 triangles
Reserve the scraps for the appliqués.

From the *bias* of one of the green fat quarters, cut:
8 strips, 1¼" x 8"
4 strips, 1¼" x 5"
Reserve the scraps for the appliqués.

From the black print, cut:
7 strips, 2½" x 42"

Making the Star Blocks

1 Layer together an assorted print 4¼" triangle and a tan 4¼" triangle. Stitch the pair together along the long diagonal edges. Press the seam allowances toward the assorted print triangle. Trim away the dog-ear points. Repeat for a total of 20 half-square-triangle units.

Make 20.

2 Cut each half-square-triangle unit in half as shown to make a total of 40 pieced triangles.

Make 40.

3 Select two pieced triangles sewn from different prints. Repeat step 1 to join the pieced triangles. Press the seam allowances to one side. Trim away the dog-ear points. Repeat for a total of 20 small pieced hourglass units measuring 3½" square, including the seam allowances.

Make 20.

4 Lay out four hourglass units, four tan 3½" squares, and one assorted print 3½" square in three horizontal rows as shown to form a Star block. Join the pieces in each row. Press the seam allowances toward the whole squares. Join the rows. Press the seam allowances away from the middle row. Repeat for a total of five pieced Star blocks measuring 9½" square, including the seam allowances.

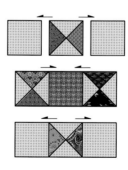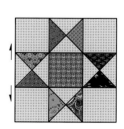

Make 5.

Making the Quilt-Center Hourglass Blocks

1 Join two assorted print 5¾" triangles along the long diagonal edges. Press the seam allowances to one side. Trim away the dog-ear points. Repeat for a total of 16 half-square-triangle units.

Make 16.

2 Cut each half-square-triangle unit in half as shown to make a total of 32 pieced triangles.

Make 32.

3 Select two pieced triangles sewn from different prints. Repeat step 1 to join the pieced triangles as shown. Press the seam allowances to one side. Trim away the dog-ear points. Repeat for a total of 16 pieced hourglass units measuring 5" square, including the seam allowances.

Make 16.

4 Lay out four hourglass units into two horizontal rows of two units each as shown. Join the pieces in each row. Press the seam allowances of each row in opposite directions. Join the rows. Press the seam allowances open. Repeat for a total of

four pieced Hourglass blocks measuring 9½" square, including the seam allowances.

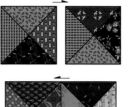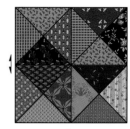

Make 4.

Making the Quilt-Center Star Points

1 Use a pencil and an acrylic ruler to draw a diagonal line from corner to corner on the wrong side of each assorted print 9½" square.

2 Layer a prepared 9½" square on one end of a tan 9½" x 27½" rectangle as shown. Stitch the pair together on the drawn line. Fold the inner corner of the assorted print square open to form a star point; press. Trim away the excess fabric layers beneath the top triangle, leaving a ¼" seam allowance. Repeat with the remaining end of the tan rectangle to form a mirror-image point. Repeat for a total of four pieced star-point units.

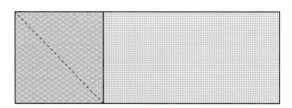

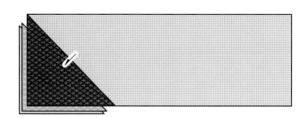

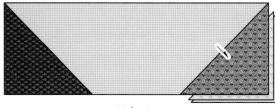

Make 4.

Preparing and Stitching the Appliqués

Using pattern pieces A–D on page 24 and the guidelines provided in the following steps, prepare shapes for your favorite method of appliqué.

1 Use the reserved scraps of assorted print fat quarters for the following appliqués:

- 12 flowers using pattern A. (The flower pattern isn't perfectly symmetrical; for added interest, Kim used a random mix of the flower pattern and the reversed flower pattern as she prepared her appliqués.)
- 12 flower centers using pattern B
- 16 berries using pattern D

Use the scraps from all of the green fat quarters, including those reserved from making the stems, to prepare:

- 12 leaves using pattern C
- 12 reversed leaves using pattern C

2 Use a bias bar to prepare the green 1¼"-wide bias strips for the stems. (For more information on using bias bars, download free "How to Appliqué" instructions from ShopMartingale.com/HowtoQuilt.)

3 Fold each pieced star-point unit in half crosswise and use a hot iron to lightly press a center crease.

4 Select one prepared star-point unit. Dot the seam allowance of a prepared 5"-long stem with liquid basting glue at approximately ½" to 1" intervals, and press it onto the star-point unit, centering it over the background crease with one end flush with the bottom of the unit as shown. Position a leaf appliqué and a reversed leaf appliqué along the stem, tucking the raw edges well to the center of the stem to prevent fraying; secure in place.

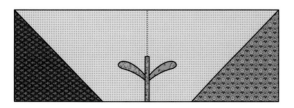

5 Working from the bottom layer to the top and using the quilt photo as a guide, lay out one flower, one flower center, and two berries on the center stem of the star-point unit, ensuring that any layered pieces are overlapped by at least ¼". Secure the appliqués in place. Remember to remove the paper pattern pieces before adding each new layer.

6 Using the quilt photo on page 19 as a guide, use two prepared 8"-long stems, two flowers, two flower centers, two leaves, two reversed leaves, and two berries to lay out the remainder of the appliqué design. When you are pleased with your arrangement, work from the bottom layer to the top to appliqué the shapes into place.

7 Repeat steps 4–6 for a total of four appliquéd star-point units.

Assembling the Quilt Center

1 Referring to the quilt photo, lay out the five Star blocks and four Hourglass blocks in three horizontal rows of three units each in alternating positions. Join the blocks in each row. Press the seam allowances open. Join the rows and press the seam allowances open.

2 Join appliquéd star-point units to the right and left sides of the quilt center. Carefully press the seam allowances toward the quilt center, taking care not to apply heat to the appliqués.

3 Join a tan 9½" square to each end of the remaining appliquéd star-point units. Press the seam allowances toward the squares. Join these pieced units to the remaining sides of the quilt center. Press the seam allowances toward the quilt center.

Making and Adding the Border

1 Following the steps for "Making the Quilt-Center Hourglass Blocks" on page 21, use the 180 assorted print 6¼" triangles to make 88 pieced hourglass border units measuring 5½" square, including the seam allowances. Please note that for added versatility as you assemble the units, there are four extra pieced triangles.

2 Select nine hourglass units from step 1; join the units end to end to make a pieced strip. Press the seam allowances to one side. Repeat for a total of four pieced strips.

3 Refer to the quilt assembly diagram below to join the long edges of two pieced strips, reversing the direction of one strip so the seam allowances nest together. Press the seam allowances open. Repeat for a total of two pieced border strips. Join these strips to the right and left sides of the quilt center. Press the seam allowances toward the quilt center.

4 Select 13 hourglass units from step 1 and join the units end to end to make a pieced strip. Press the seam allowances to one side. Repeat for a total of four pieced strips.

5 Join the long edges of two pieced strips, reversing the direction of one strip so the seam allowances nest together. Press the seam allowances open. Repeat for a total of two pieced border strips. Join these strips to the remaining sides of the quilt center. Press the seam allowances toward the quilt center. The pieced quilt top should now measure 65½" square, including the seam allowances.

Finishing the Quilt

For detailed information on finishing techniques, including layering, basting, and quilting, go to ShopMartingale.com/HowtoQuilt for free downloadable instructions. Use the black 2½"-wide strips to bind the quilt.

Quilt assembly

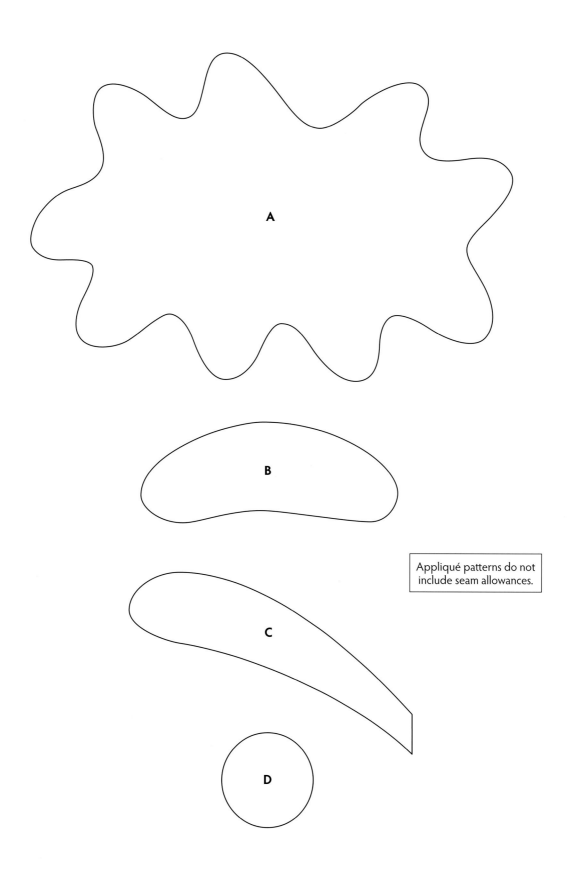

A

B

Appliqué patterns do not
include seam allowances.

C

D

The Big Book of Fat-Quarter Quilts

Flower Boxes

Log Cabin blocks are fun and easy to construct, and their versatility makes them a favorite of many quiltmakers. Depending on the fabrics you choose for this pattern, your quilt can have a primitive, contemporary, or traditional appearance.

FINISHED QUILT: 63½" x 72½"

Designed and made by Heather Mulder Peterson

Materials

Yardage is based on 42"-wide fabric. Fat quarters are 18" x 21".

14 fat quarters *or* 3½ yards *total* of assorted plaids for blocks and appliqué

2⅜ yards of black plaid for background

½ yard of green fabric for appliqué

⅜ yard of black fabric for block centers

¾ yard of black plaid for binding

4 yards of fabric for backing

68" x 77" piece of batting

1 yard of fusible web

Cutting

The plaid fabrics are cut in sets. Cut each set from 1 fabric for a consistent look within each block.

From the assorted plaids, cut:

20 sets of:
    1 strip, 2" x 8"
    2 strips, 2" x 6½"
    1 strip, 2" x 5"

88 sets of:
    1 strip, 2" x 5"
    2 strips, 2" x 3½"
    1 square, 2" x 2"

From the black fabric for block centers, cut:

5 strips, 2" x 42"; crosscut into 88 squares, 2" x 2"

From the black plaid for background, cut:

9 strips, 2" x 42"; crosscut into:
    12 strips, 2" x 8"
    24 strips, 2" x 6½"
    12 strips, 2" x 5"

3 strips, 6⅜" x 42"

3 strips, 5½" x 42"

4 squares, 12" x 12"; cut the squares into quarters diagonally to yield 16 side triangles (2 are extra)

2 squares, 6½" x 6½"; cut the squares in half diagonally to yield 4 corner triangles

From the black plaid for binding, cut:

2½"-wide bias strips to total 290" in length

Making the Blocks

1 Choose one of the 88 assorted plaid sets and sew the 2" plaid square to a 2" black square. Press the seam allowances toward the plaid. Continue adding the strips from the plaid set, working clockwise around the block. Press all the seam allowances outward and square up each block to 5" x 5".

Make 88.

2 Pick an assortment of 20 blocks from step 1. Choose one of the 20 assorted plaid sets and sew a 5" plaid strip to the top of a block. Press the seam allowances outward. Continue adding the strips from this set, working clockwise around the block. Press all the seam allowances outward and square up each block to 8" x 8".

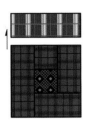

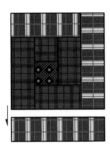
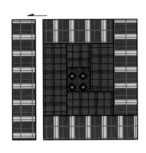

Make 20.

3 Pick an assortment of 12 blocks from step 1 and repeat step 2 using the 2"-wide black-plaid background strips. Square up each block to 8" x 8".

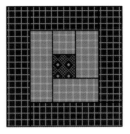

Make 12.

Assembling the Quilt Top

1 Lay out the blocks and the black side and corner setting triangles as shown. Sew the blocks and side triangles into rows. Press all seam allowances toward the black plaid. Sew the rows together and press the seam allowances in one direction. Add the corner triangles and press the seam allowances toward the triangles. Square up the quilt center to 42⅞" x 53½", trimming so the block points are ¼" from the edge.

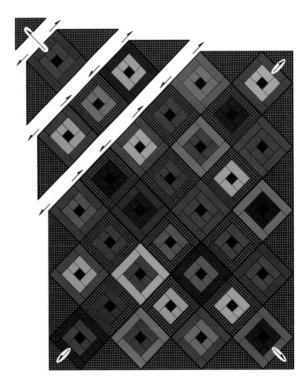

2 Sew the 6⅜"-wide black-plaid strips together end to end. Cut two strips, 53½" long, for the side borders. Sew the 5½"-wide black-plaid strips together end to end. Cut two strips, 54⅝" long, for the top and bottom borders.

3 Using the patterns on page 29, prepare the shapes for your favorite method of appliqué. Arrange the flowers on the border strips, as close to the strip edges as possible without overlapping the ¼" seam allowance. Lay each border strip next to the quilt-top center to make sure the flowers are centered and in the right place (about 10⅝" apart); you can also refer to the quilt photo on page 25 for placement. Secure the shapes to the border strips. Add the stem and leaf appliqués.

4 Sew the side borders to the quilt-top center, and then sew the top and bottom borders to the quilt top. Press all the seam allowances toward the black plaid border. Square up the quilt top to 54½" x 63½".

5 Using the remaining blocks from step 1 of "Making the Blocks," sew the blocks together into four strips of 14 blocks each. Sew two of these strips to the sides of the quilt top and the remaining two strips to the top and bottom. Press the seam allowances toward the black-plaid border.

Make 4.

Finishing the Quilt

For detailed information on finishing techniques, including layering, basting, and quilting, go to ShopMartingale.com/HowtoQuilt for free downloadable instructions. Use the black-plaid 2½"-wide bias strips to bind the quilt.

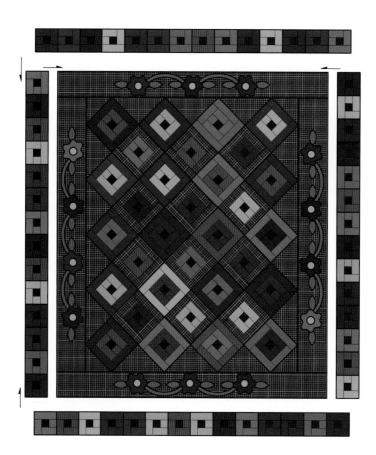

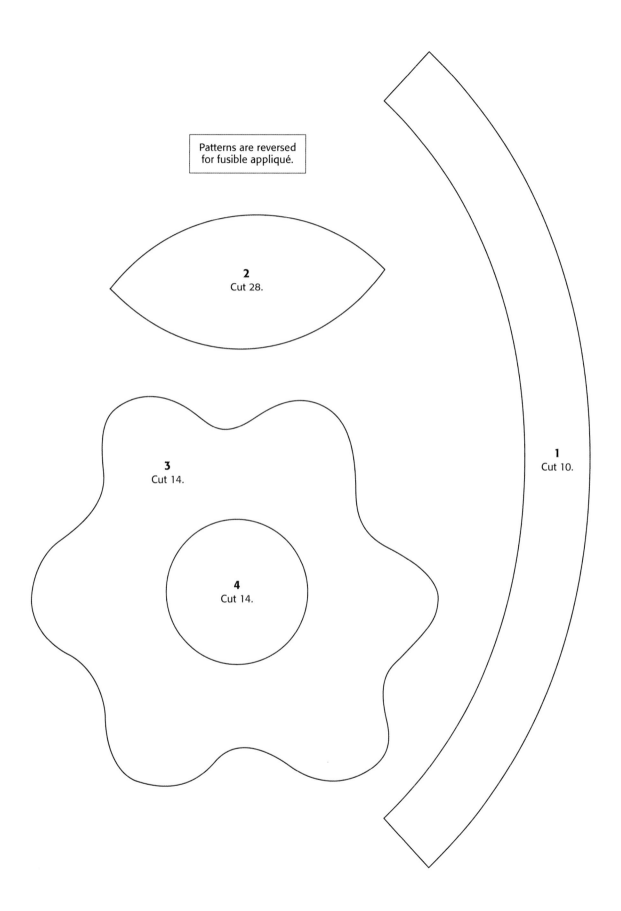

Patterns are reversed
for fusible appliqué.

2
Cut 28.

3
Cut 14.

4
Cut 14.

1
Cut 10.

Half Moon Bay

Sometimes the simplest quilt designs have the most impact. The blocks here are easily constructed from basic squares and rectangles, and the quilt assembly is uncomplicated. But the structured, geometric design and the deep, dark solid played against beach-themed prints combine for a statement that's quite dramatic.

FINISHED QUILT: 62½" x 82½"

FINISHED BLOCK: 8" x 8"

Designed by John Q. Adams; pieced by Kristen Danis; quilted by Angela Walters

Materials

Yardage is based on 42"-wide fabric. Fat quarters are 18" x 21".

12 fat quarters of assorted prints for blocks
2⅝ yards of dark-brown solid for blocks, sashing, and border
⅔ yard of fabric for binding
5¼ yards of fabric for backing
70" x 90" piece of batting

Cutting

From the dark-brown solid, cut:

24 strips, 2½" x 42"; crosscut *6 of the strips* into 96 squares, 2½" x 2½"
3 strips, 8½" x 42"; crosscut into 42 strips, 2½" x 8½"

From *each* of the assorted print fat quarters, cut:

8 rectangles, 4½" x 8½" (96 total)

From the binding fabric, cut:

8 strips, 2½" x 42"

Making the Blocks

1 Draw a diagonal line from corner to corner on the wrong side of each dark-brown 2½" square. Place a marked square on one corner of a print 4½" x 8½" rectangle. Sew along the marked line and trim away the corner fabric, leaving a ¼" seam allowance. Press the resulting triangle open. Repeat to make a mirror-image unit. Make 48 of each unit (96 total).

Make 48 of each.

Working with Directional Prints

If you're using directional prints, refer to the quilt assembly diagram on page 32 to determine which corner of the print rectangle to cover. You may want to place all of the rectangles on your floor or design wall to make sure they are oriented correctly before sewing any of the units.

2 Lay out two units from step 1 with the dark-brown triangles in the upper-right and bottom-left corners as shown. Sew the units together along the long edges to complete a block. Press the seam allowances toward the darker rectangle. Make 24 of block A.

Block A.
Make 24.

3 Lay out two units from step 1 with the dark-brown triangles in the upper-left and lower-right corners as shown. Sew the units together along the long edges to complete a block. Press the seam allowances toward the darker rectangle. Make 24 of block B.

Block B.
Make 24.

Assembling the Quilt Top

1 Join two dark-brown 2½" x 42" strips end to end to make a long strip. Press the seam allowances open. Make a total of nine long strips. Trim seven of the strips to measure 78½" long each. Trim the remaining two strips to each measure 62½" long.

2 Referring to the quilt assembly diagram for placement guidance, lay out six vertical columns with four A blocks, four B blocks, and seven dark-brown 2½" x 8½" sashing strips in each, alternating the blocks and sashing strips. Sew the blocks and strips together to make columns. Press the seam allowances toward the strips. The columns should measure 78½" long.

3 Sew the block columns and the 78½"-long pieced strips together, alternating them as shown in the assembly diagram. Press the seam allowances toward the sashing strips.

4 Sew the 62½"-long pieced strips to the top and bottom edges to complete the quilt top. Press the seam allowances toward the strips.

Finishing the Quilt

For detailed information on finishing techniques, including layering, basting, and quilting, go to ShopMartingale.com/HowtoQuilt for free downloadable instructions. Use the 2½"-wide strips to bind the quilt.

Quilt assembly

Yo-Yo

This is the ideal project for multitasking during a relaxing movie night at home. It involves the kind of repetition that doesn't demand a lot of concentration, so your hands can stay busy cutting fabric while your mind engages with the plot on-screen. Plus, a DVD is the perfect size to use as a pattern for these fun circles!

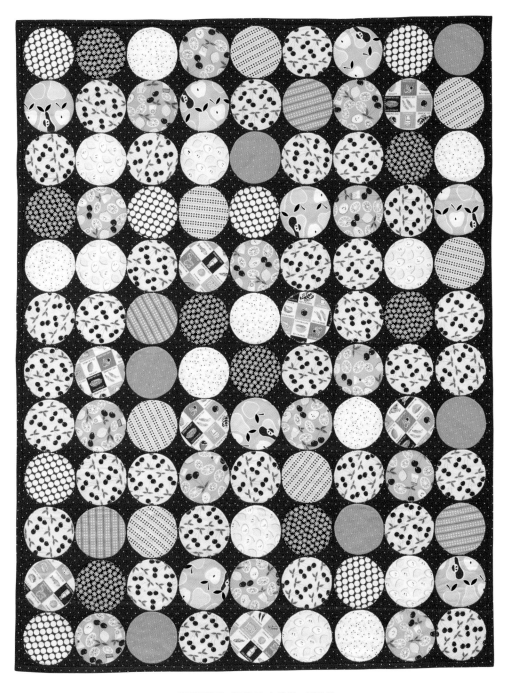

FINISHED QUILT: 44¾" x 59½"

FINISHED BLOCK: 14¾" x 14¾"

Designed and made by Barbara Brandeburg

Materials

Yardage is based on 42"-wide fabric. Fat quarters are 18" x 21".

3⅜ yards of red fabric for block backgrounds and
   binding
12 fat quarters of assorted fabrics for circles (the quilt
   shown uses 5 white or light prints, 3 green prints,
   2 yellow prints, 1 brown print, and 1 blue print)
3 yards of fabric for backing
51" x 66" piece of batting
2⅞ yards of lightweight nonwoven fusible interfacing

Cutting

From the assorted fat quarters, cut a *total* of:
108 squares, 5½" x 5½"

From the interfacing, cut:
108 squares, 5½" x 5½"

From the red fabric, cut:
12 squares, 15¼" x 15¼"
6 strips, 2½" x 42"

Making the Blocks

1 Using a fine-point, black permanent marker and
   the pattern on page 36 or a blank CD or DVD,
   center and mark a circle on the nonadhesive
   side of each interfacing square. **Note:** It may be
   necessary to use a contrasting bright-colored
   permanent marker to mark the interfacing used
   for the brown circles.

2 Place the adhesive side of each interfacing square
   on the right side of a 5½" fabric square. The
   marked side will be face up. Sew on the marked
   line, overlapping the stitches at the beginning and
   end. Trim ⅛" from the stitching.

3 Cut a 2½"-long slit in the center of the
   interfacing, being careful not to cut the fabric.
   Turn the circle right side out. Carefully run your
   thumb or finger along the inside seam line to
   push out the edges. Finger-press the outside edges
   to create a sharp edge. Do not iron the seam or
   you will melt the adhesive. It is not necessary to
   close the opening in the interfacing. Repeat for
   the remaining circles.

Make 108.

4 Position a circle in one corner of a red
   square, ⅜" from the edges. Follow the interfacing
   manufacturer's instructions and iron-temperature
   recommendations to fuse the shape in place.
   Repeat for the remaining corners.

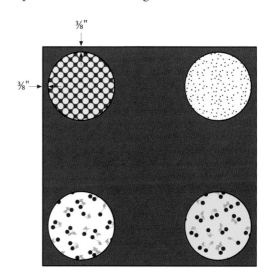

5 Position and press a circle between each of the corner circles on the red square. There should be approximately ⅛" of space between the shapes. Position and press the remaining circle in the center of the red square.

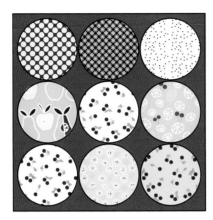

6 Repeat steps 4 and 5 to make a total of 12 blocks. Appliqué the edges of each circle with a narrow buttonhole stitch and coordinating thread. Using a sharp pair of scissors, carefully cut away the red backing and interfacing behind each circle, ¼" from the stitching.

Assembling the Quilt Top

1 Arrange the blocks into four rows of three blocks each.

2 Join the blocks in each row. Press the seam allowances in opposite directions from row to row. Join the rows. Press the seam allowances in one direction.

Finishing the Quilt

For detailed information on finishing techniques, including layering, basting, and quilting, go to ShopMartingale.com/HowtoQuilt for free downloadable instructions. Use the red 2½"-wide strips to bind the quilt.

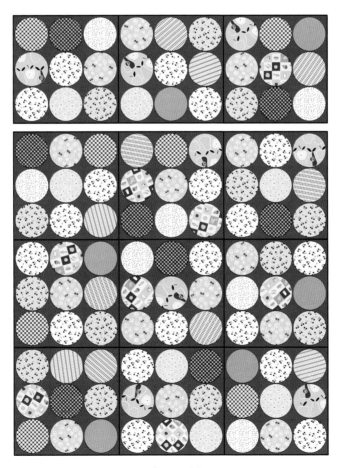

Quilt assembly

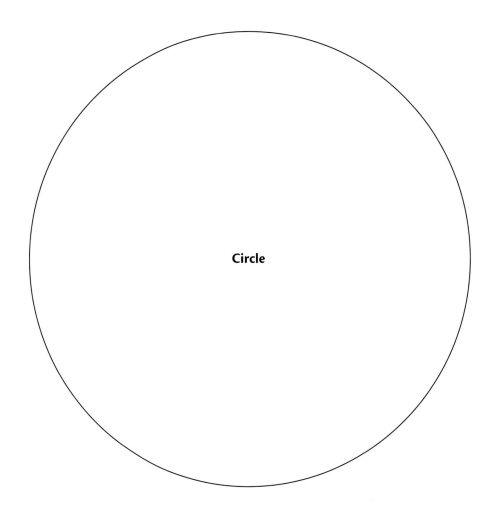

Circle

The Big Book of Fat-Quarter Quilts

Oak and Rose

Enjoy combining a vintage look with modern country colors.
To create an even stronger resemblance to "Grandma's old quilt,"
try using a variety of colors instead of the red.

FINISHED QUILT: 63½" x 63½"
FINISHED BLOCK: 15" x 15"

Designed and pieced by Jeanne Large and Shelley Wicks; machine quilted by Laila Nelson

Materials

Yardage is based on 42"-wide fabric. Fat quarters are 18" x 21".

11 fat quarters of assorted beige fabrics for blocks
2⅜ yards of dark-brown fabric for blocks, sashing, border, and binding
8 fat quarters of assorted red fabrics for blocks
4⅓ yards of fabric for backing
72" x 72" piece of batting

Cutting

From *each* of 3 of the assorted beige fat quarters, cut:
3 strips, 3⅞" x 21" (9 total); crosscut into 12 squares, 3⅞" x 3⅞" (36 total). Cut the squares in half diagonally to yield 24 triangles (72 total).
1 strip, 1½" x 21" (3 total)

From *each* of the 8 remaining beige fat quarters, cut:
10 strips, 1½" x 21" (80 total)

From the 8 assorted red fat quarters, cut a *total* of:
73 strips, 1½" x 21"

From the dark-brown fabric, cut:
4 strips, 3½" x 42"; crosscut into 36 squares, 3½" x 3½"
4 strips, 3⅞" x 42"; crosscut into 36 squares, 3⅞" x 3⅞". Cut the squares in half diagonally to yield 72 triangles.
3 strips, 3½" x 42"; crosscut into 12 rectangles, 3½" x 9½"
3 strips, 6½" x 42"; crosscut into 12 rectangles, 6½" x 9½"
7 strips, 2½" x 42"

Making the Blocks

1 Sew a beige 1½" x 21" strip to each long side of a red 1½" x 21" strip to make a strip set. Press the seam allowances toward the red strip. Repeat to make a total of 20 strip sets. Crosscut the strip sets into 100 rail-fence segments, 3½" wide.

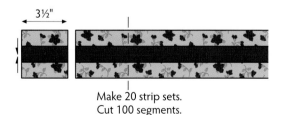

Make 20 strip sets.
Cut 100 segments.

2 Sew a red 1½" x 21" strip to each long side of a beige 1½" x 21" strip to make a strip set. Press the seam allowances toward the red strips. Repeat to make a total of 21 strip sets. Crosscut the strip sets into 250 segments, 1½" wide.

Make 21 strip sets.
Cut 250 segments.

3 Sew a beige 1½" x 21" strip to each long side of a red 1½" x 21" strip to make a strip set. Press the seam allowances toward the red strip. Repeat to make a total of 11 strip sets. Crosscut the strip sets into 125 segments, 1½" wide.

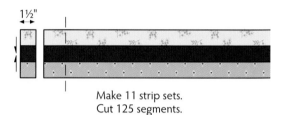

Make 11 strip sets.
Cut 125 segments.

4 Sew a segment from step 2 to each side of a segment from step 3 to make a nine-patch unit as shown. Press the seam allowances away from the center segment. Repeat to make a total of 125 nine-patch units.

Make 125.

5 Sew a beige 3⅞" triangle to a dark-brown 3⅞" triangle along the long edges as shown. Press the seam allowances toward the dark-brown triangle. Repeat to make a total of 72 half-square-triangle units.

Make 72.

6 Arrange four rail-fence segments from step 1, nine of the nine-patch units from step 4, eight half-square-triangle units from step 5, and four dark-brown 3½" squares into five horizontal rows as shown. Sew the pieces in each row together. Press the seam allowances as indicated. Sew the rows together. Press the seam allowances in one direction. Repeat to make a total of nine blocks. Set aside the remaining rail-fence segments and nine-patch units for the sashing and borders.

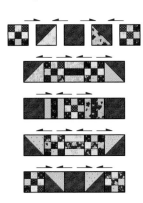 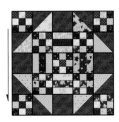

Make 9.

Assembling the Quilt Top

1 Sew a rail-fence segment to each end of a dark-brown 3½" x 9½" rectangle as shown. Press the seam allowances toward the rail-fence segments. Repeat to make a total of 12 sashing strips.

Make 12.

2 Alternately arrange three blocks and two sashing strips as shown to make a block row. Press the seam allowances toward the sashing strips. Repeat to make a total of three rows.

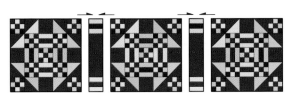

Make 3.

3 Sew a nine-patch unit to each end of a sashing strip. Press the seam allowances toward the sashing strip. Add a sashing strip to each end of this unit as shown. Press the seam allowances toward the sashing strips. Repeat to make a total of two sashing rows.

Make 2.

4 Alternately sew the block rows and sashing rows together as shown. Press the seam allowances toward the sashing rows.

5 Sew a rail-fence segment to a nine-patch unit as shown. Press the seam allowances toward the rail-fence unit. Repeat to make a total of 40 units.

Make 40.

6 Sew a unit from step 5 to each end of a dark-brown 6½" x 9½" rectangle as shown. Press the seam allowances toward the rectangle. Repeat to make a total of 12 border units.

Make 12.

7 Alternately sew together three border segments and two units from step 5 as shown. Be careful to alternate the direction of the units from step 5 so that the pattern is created. Press the seam allowances in one direction. Repeat to make a total of four border strips. Refer to the quilt assembly diagram below to sew border strips to opposite sides of the quilt top. Press the seam allowances toward the border.

Make 4.

8 Sew two units from step 5 together as shown to make a border corner block. Press the seam allowances as indicated. Repeat to make a total of two blocks. Make two additional blocks, arranging the units from step 5 as shown.

Make 2.   Make 2.

9 Refer to the assembly diagram to sew the blocks to the ends of the remaining two border strips, making sure the nine-patch units alternate with the border nine-patch units. Press the seam allowances toward the border strips. Sew these borders to the top and bottom of the quilt top. Press the seam allowances toward the border.

Finishing the Quilt

For detailed information on finishing techniques, including layering, basting, and quilting, go to ShopMartingale.com/HowtoQuilt for free downloadable instructions. Use the dark-brown 2½"-wide strips to bind the quilt.

Quilt assembly

Precious Stones

The patchwork squares create the look of an interlocking maze, inviting you to really have fun with a variety of fabric colors and print sizes. Elizabeth used a neutral background, but you could easily choose a subtle print that contrasts well with the other fabrics.

FINISHED QUILT: 60" x 70"
FINISHED BLOCK: 10" x 10"
Designed and made by Elizabeth Dackson

Materials

Yardage is based on 42"-wide fabric. Fat quarters are 18" x 21".

14 fat quarters of assorted prints for blocks
2¼ yards of white fabric for background
⅝ yard of medium-scale print for binding
3⅞ yards of fabric for backing
68" x 78" piece of batting

Cutting

From *each* of the assorted print fat quarters, cut:
42 squares, 2½" x 2½"

From the white fabric, cut:
29 strips, 2½" x 42"; crosscut into:
    126 squares, 2½" x 2½"
    84 rectangles, 2½" x 8½"

From the medium-scale print, cut:
7 strips, 2½" x 42"

Making the Blocks

Use a scant ¼" seam allowance and press seam allowances open after sewing each seam.

1 Sew three 2½" squares of assorted prints together into a column. Make 126 of these three-square units, chain piecing them for efficiency.

Make 126.

2 Sew a white 2½" square to each of the three-square units from step 1.

Make 126.

3 Sew three units from step 2 and two white 2½" x 8½" rectangles together, orienting the units from step 2 as shown. Make 42.

Make 42.

4 Sew five 2½" squares of assorted prints together to create a horizontal patchwork strip. Sew the strip to the top of a unit from step 3. Repeat to make a total of 42 blocks.

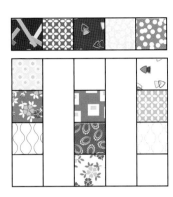

Make 42.

Assembling the Quilt Top

1 Arrange the blocks into seven rows of six blocks each. Sew the blocks in each row together, pressing seam allowances open as you go.

2 Sew the rows together to complete the quilt top. You may find it easiest to join the rows in pairs first and then sew the pairs together. Press.

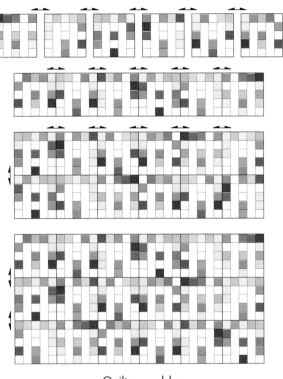

Quilt assembly

Finishing the Quilt

For detailed information on finishing techniques, including layering, basting, and quilting, go to ShopMartingale.com/HowtoQuilt for free downloadable instructions. Use the print 2½"-wide strips to bind the quilt.

Big Thicket

Composed of two simple-to-construct blocks, this quilt's repetitive structural pattern and eclectic fabric choices create an intriguing effect of geometry and architecture. Is it chain links? Circuitry? A garden maze? A blueprint? That's up to the fabric to imply, and the viewer to decide.

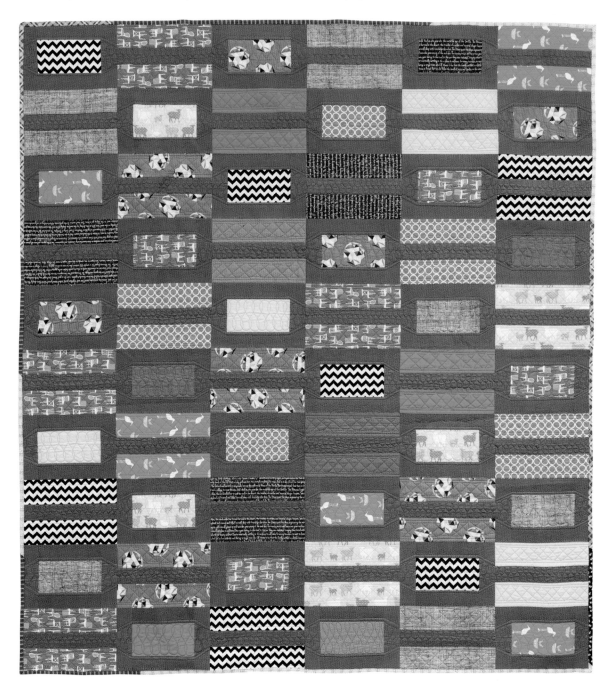

FINISHED QUILT: 72½" x 80½"
FINISHED BLOCK: 8" x 12"

Designed by John Q. Adams; pieced by Lucky Peterson; quilted by Angela Walters

Materials

Yardage is based on 42"-wide fabric. Fat quarters are 18" x 21".

15 fat quarters of assorted prints for blocks
3 yards of gray solid for blocks
⅔ yard of fabric for binding
5¼ yards of fabric for backing
80" x 88" piece of batting

Cutting

From the gray solid, cut:
8 strips, 8½" x 42"; crosscut into 120 rectangles, 2½" x 8½"
2 strips, 12½" x 42"; crosscut into 30 rectangles, 2½" x 12½"

From the assorted print fat quarters, cut a *total* of:
30 rectangles, 4½" x 8½"
60 rectangles, 3½" x 12½" (30 sets of 2 matching rectangles)

From the binding fabric, cut:
8 strips, 2½" x 42"

Assembling the Blocks

1 Sew gray 2½" x 8½" rectangles to the top and bottom of a print 4½" x 8½" rectangle. Press the seam allowances toward the gray rectangles. Sew gray 2½" x 8½" rectangles to opposite sides of the unit to complete block A. Press the seam allowances toward the gray rectangles. The block should measure 8½" x 12½". Make a total of 30 of block A.

Block A.
Make 30.

Quick and Easy

Use chain piecing to quickly piece the blocks in this pattern.

2 Sew together two matching print 3½" x 12½" rectangles and one gray 2½" x 12½" rectangle as shown to make block B. Press the seam allowances

toward the gray rectangle. The block should measure 8½" x 12½". Make a total of 30 of block B.

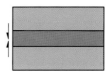

Block B.
Make 30.

Assembling the Quilt Top

1 Lay out the blocks in 10 rows of six blocks each, alternating the A and B blocks as shown in the quilt assembly diagram below and distributing your prints and colors in an eye-pleasing way.

2 When you are pleased with the arrangement, join the blocks into rows. Press the seam allowances toward the A blocks.

3 Join the rows and press the seam allowances in one direction. Trim and square up the quilt top as needed.

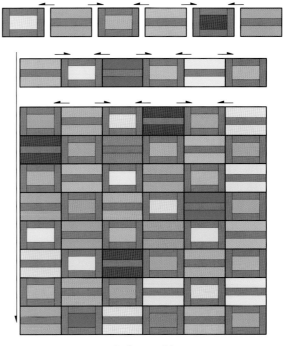

Quilt assembly

Finishing the Quilt

For detailed information on finishing techniques, including layering, basting, and quilting, go to ShopMartingale.com/HowtoQuilt for free downloadable instructions. Use the 2½"-wide strips to bind the quilt.

It's Hip to Be Square

Squares, squares, squares, and a few rectangles—that's what this design has, as well as some wonderful jewel-tone batiks. Each block has its own border, so in the end it's very simple to stitch them all together for a great, contemporary look.

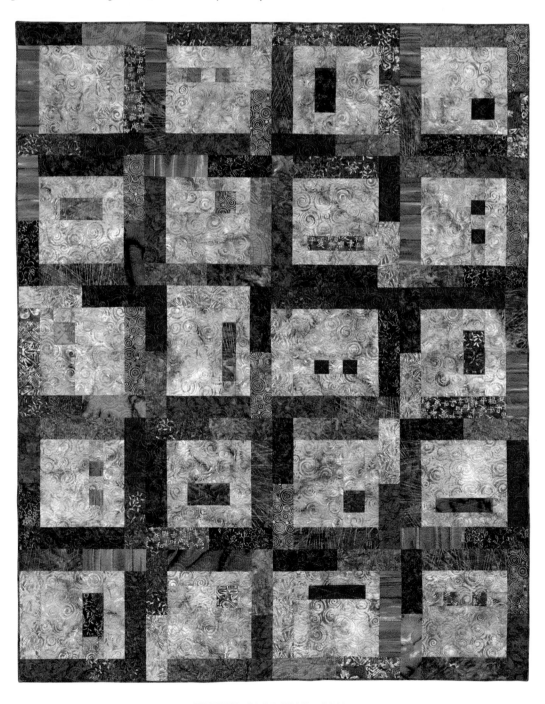

FINISHED QUILT: 72½" x 90½"
FINISHED BLOCK: 18" x 18"
Designed and made by Cheryl Brown

Materials

Yardage is based on 42"-wide fabric. Fat quarters are 18" x 21".

3⅛ yards of tan batik for blocks

18 fat quarters in assorted jewel-tone batiks (green, purple, blue, and burgundy) for block centers and block borders

¾ yard of purple tone-on-tone batik for binding

5¾ yards of fabric for backing

77" x 95" piece of batting

Cutting

From the tan batik, cut:

7 strips, 2½" x 42"; crosscut into:
    15 squares, 2½" x 2½"
    15 rectangles, 2½" x 3½"
    10 rectangles, 2½" x 12½"

6 strips, 3½" x 42"; crosscut into:
    10 squares, 3½" x 3½"
    5 rectangles, 3½" x 7½"
    10 rectangles, 3½" x 12½"

2 strips, 6½" x 42"; crosscut into 5 rectangles, 6½" x 12½"

4 strips, 7½" x 42"; crosscut into 10 rectangles, 7½" x 12½"

2 strips, 8½" x 42"; crosscut into 5 rectangles, 8½" x 12½"

From the assorted jewel-tone fat quarters, cut a *total* of:

5 pairs of matching squares, 2½" x 2½"

5 rectangles, 2½" x 8½"

5 squares, 3½" x 3½"

5 rectangles, 3½" x 6½"

80 rectangles, 3½" x 9½"

40 rectangles, 3½" x 12½"

From the purple tone-on-tone batik, cut:

2¼"-wide bias strips to total 340" in length

Making the Blocks

The quilt is composed of four different blocks, A through D, each easy to piece.

Block A

1 Sew a tan 2½" square to each end of an assorted 2½" x 8½" rectangle. Press the seam allowances toward the squares.

2 Sew a tan 2½" x 12½" rectangle to the left side of the unit from step 1, and then sew a gray-and-tan 8½" x 12½" rectangle to the right side of the unit. Press the seam allowances toward the tan rectangles. Make five blocks.

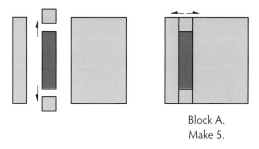

Block A.
Make 5.

Block B

1 Sew a tan 2½" x 3½" rectangle to the top of an assorted 3½" square. Then sew a gray-and-tan 3½" x 7½" rectangle to the bottom of the square. Press the seam allowances toward the rectangles.

2 Sew a tan 2½" x 12½" rectangle to the left side of the unit from step 1. Then sew a gray-and-tan 7½" x 12½" rectangle to the right side of the unit. Press the seam allowances toward the tan rectangles. Make five blocks.

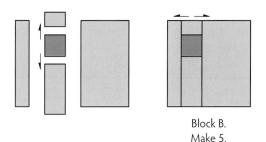

Block B.
Make 5.

Block C

1 Sew a tan 3½" square to each end of an assorted 3½" x 6½" rectangle. Press the seam allowances toward the squares.

2 Sew a tan 3½" x 12½" rectangle to the left side of the unit from step 1. Then sew a gray-and-tan 6½" x 12½" rectangle to the right side of the unit. Press the seam allowances toward the tan rectangles. Make five blocks.

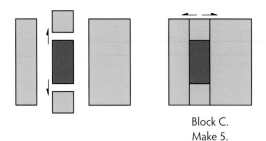

Block C.
Make 5.

Block D

1 Sew one of the assorted 2½" squares to the top of a tan 2½" square. Then sew the matching 2½" square to the bottom of the square.

2 Sew gray-and-tan 2½" x 3½" rectangles to the top and bottom of the unit from step 1. Press the seam allowances toward the tan pieces.

3 Sew a tan 3½" x 12½" rectangle to the left side of the unit. Then sew a gray-and-tan 7½" x 12½" rectangle to the right side of the unit. Press the seam allowances toward the tan rectangles. Make five blocks.

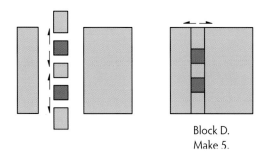

Block D.
Make 5.

Block Borders

1 Sew assorted 3½" x 12½" rectangles to the top and bottom of each block. Rotate the blocks so that the squares and rectangles are in different positions. Press the seam allowances toward the border.

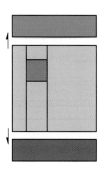

2 Pairing colors randomly, sew two of the assorted 3½" x 9½" rectangles together along the short ends. Press the seam allowances to one side. Make 40 side borders.

3 Sew the borders from step 2 to the sides of each block. Press the seam allowances outward.

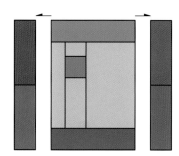

Assembling the Quilt Top

1 Arrange the blocks in five rows of four blocks each, rotating the blocks so that the borders with seams are adjacent to borders without seams. The squares and rectangles within the blocks should be in different positions as shown in the quilt assembly diagram. Refer also to the quilt photo on page 46 for placement guidance.

2 Sew the blocks in each row together; press the seam allowances toward the borders with two pieces. Sew the rows together; press the seam allowances in one direction.

Finishing the Quilt

For detailed information on finishing techniques, including layering, basting, and quilting, go to ShopMartingale.com/HowtoQuilt for free downloadable instructions. Use the purple 2¼"-wide bias strips to bind the quilt.

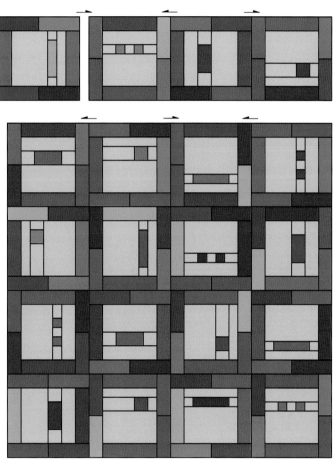

Quilt assembly

Pathways

Perfect for teens, grads, and anyone who loves a modern vibe, this playful quilt is sure to be cherished for years. The design hints at improvisation but is actually controlled.

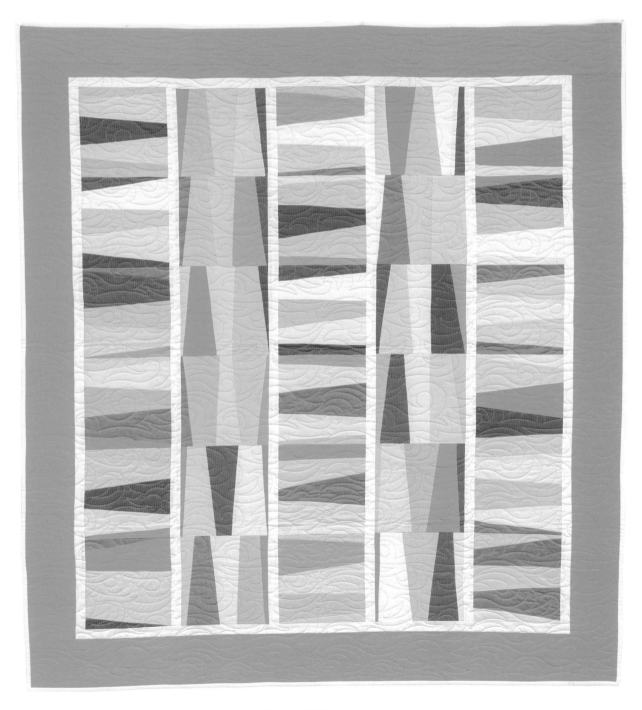

FINISHED QUILT: 59" x 63½"
FINISHED BLOCK: 8½" x 8½"
Designed by Rachel Griffith; pieced by KarrieLyne Winters; quilted by Darla Padilla

Materials

Yardage is based on 42"-wide fabric. Fat quarters are 18" x 21".

12 fat quarters of assorted solids for blocks
1⅛ yards of teal solid for outer border
1 yard of cream solid for sashing, inner border, and binding
3¾ yards of fabric for backing
63" x 68" piece of batting

Cutting

From *each* of the assorted solid fat quarters, cut:
2 strips, 11" x 18" (24 total)

From the cream solid, cut:
11 strips, 1½" x 42"
7 strips, 2¼" x 42"

From the teal solid, cut:
6 strips, 5½" x 42"

Making the Blocks

1 Using your rotary cutter and ruler, make six cuts on each 11" x 18" strip to yield seven wedges per strip (168 total). You don't need to measure; the wedges should be wonky in appearance but have straight edges. Aim to make the wedges about the same size. This will make the blocks look more balanced once the wedges are sewn together.

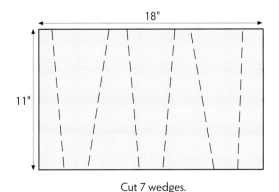

Cut 7 wedges.

Joining the Wedges

When making the blocks, switching the narrow and wide ends of the wedges will make the blocks appear balanced. If the first wedge has a narrow end at the top, position the second wedge with the wide end at the top.

2 Randomly join five different-color wedges to make a block. Press the seam allowances to one side. The block will be oversized. Use a square ruler to trim the block to measure 9" x 9". Repeat to make a total of 30 blocks.

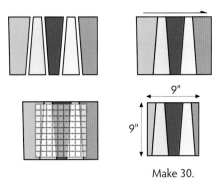

Make 30.

Making the Rows

The quilt is assembled in vertical rows with the blocks rotated 90° in two of the rows.

1 With the wedges positioned *horizontally*, lay out six blocks as shown. Join the blocks to make a row. Press the seam allowances in one direction. The row should measure 51½" long. Repeat to make a total of three of row A.

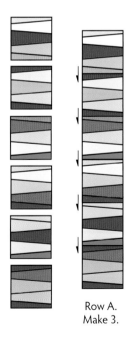

Row A.
Make 3.

2 With the wedges positioned *vertically*, lay out six blocks as shown. Join the blocks to make a row. Press the seam allowances in one direction. The row should measure 51½" long. Repeat to make a second row B.

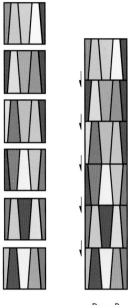

Row B.
Make 2.

Assembling the Quilt Top

1 Sew the cream 1½"-wide strips together end to end. From the pieced strip, cut four strips, 51½" long. Lay out the A and B rows and cream strips as shown. Sew the rows and strips together. Press the seam allowances toward the sashing strips.

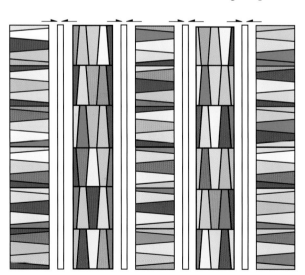

2 Measure the length of the quilt top. From the pieced cream strip, cut two strips to this measurement and sew them to the sides of the quilt top. Press the seam allowances toward the cream strips. Measure the width of the quilt top. From the remainder of the pieced cream strip, cut two strips to this measurement and sew them to the top and bottom of the quilt top to complete the inner border. Press the seam allowances toward the border.

3 Sew the teal 5½"-wide strips end to end. Repeat step 2 to measure and cut the strips; then sew them to the quilt top for the outer border. Press all seam allowances toward the outer border.

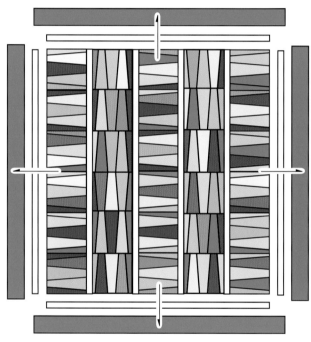

Quilt assembly

Finishing the Quilt

For detailed information on finishing techniques, including layering, basting, and quilting, go to ShopMartingale.com/HowtoQuilt for free downloadable instructions. Use the cream 2¼"-wide strips to bind the quilt.

Elephant Parade

Like many quilters, Dana had more fabric in her stash than she knew what to do with. When she realized that her stack of gray fabrics had grown so huge it was about to topple over, she was struck by the thought of elephants, and Elephant Parade was born.

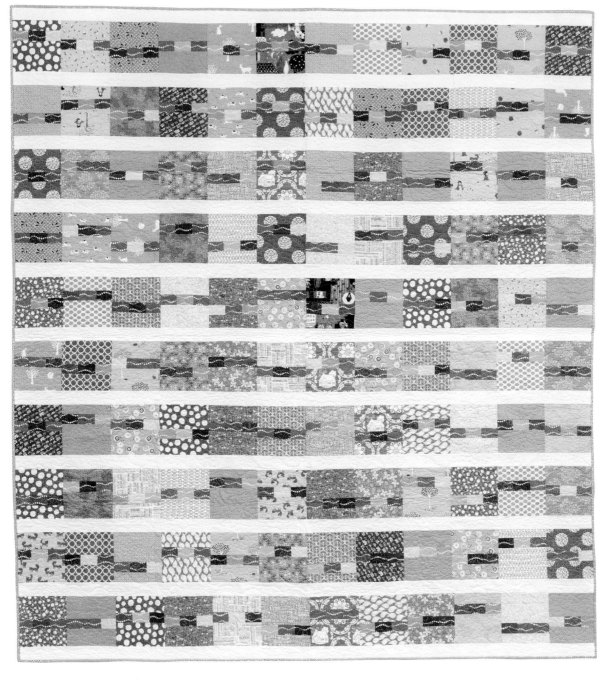

FINISHED QUILT: 84½" x 92½"
FINISHED BLOCK: 7" x 7"
Designed and pieced by Dana Bolyard; machine quilted by Russ Adams

Materials

Yardage is based on 42"-wide fabric. Fat quarters are 18" x 21".

30 fat quarters of assorted gray prints for blocks
9 fat quarters of assorted bright prints for blocks
1¾ yards of white solid for sashing
¾ yard of gray print for binding
7¾ yards of fabric for backing
92" x 100" piece of batting

Cutting

From *each* of the gray fat quarters, cut:
4 squares, 8" x 8" (120 total)

From *each* of the bright fat quarters, cut:
7 strips, 2" x 21"; crosscut into 40 rectangles, 2" x 3" (360 total)

From the white solid, cut:
24 strips, 2½" x 42"

From the gray print for binding, cut:
9 strips, 2½" x 42"

Making the Blocks

1 Sew three bright rectangles together end to end to make an 8" strip. Press the seam allowances in one direction. Make 120.

Make 120.

2 Select an 8" gray square and use a rotary cutter and ruler to cut the square randomly into two pieces. No measuring is necessary, and the square need not be cut perfectly in half. The angle can be slightly wonky (not parallel to an edge), but don't make it too extreme or you won't be able to square up the block. If the gray print is directional, keep that in mind when making this cut.

3 Sew a pieced strip of bright fabrics between the two parts of the gray square. Press the seam allowances toward the gray fabric.

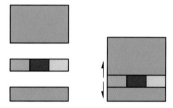

4 Repeat steps 2 and 3 to make 120 blocks. As you cut and sew the remaining blocks, vary the position of the cut across each gray square. Trim each block to 7½" x 7½".

Assembling the Quilt Top

1 Arrange 12 blocks into a row, varying the position of the brightly colored patchwork to achieve an irregular line of color across the row. Sew the blocks together, and press the seam allowances in one direction. Make 10 rows, pressing the seam allowances in alternate directions from row to row.

Make 10.

2 Remove the selvages and sew two white 2½"-wide strips together end to end to make a sashing strip; make 11. Measure the length of each sashing strip; they must be 84½" long to fit the pieced rows. If your sashing strips are shorter, use the remaining white 2½"-wide strips to add length as necessary.

3 Arrange the pieced rows and sashing strips as shown in the quilt assembly diagram.

4 Find the center of each sashing strip and pin it to the bottom of the adjacent pieced row, pinning at the seam between the sixth and seventh blocks in the row. Then pin each end of the sashing strip to the corresponding end of the pieced row, easing any extra fabric into place as necessary. Sew the pinned rows together, and press the seam allowances toward the sashing.

5 Sew the block-and-sashing rows together. Stitch the remaining sashing strip to the top edge of the top row to complete the quilt top.

Finishing the Quilt

For detailed information on finishing techniques, including layering, basting, and quilting, go to ShopMartingale.com/HowtoQuilt for free downloadable instructions. Use the gray 2½"-wide strips to bind the quilt.

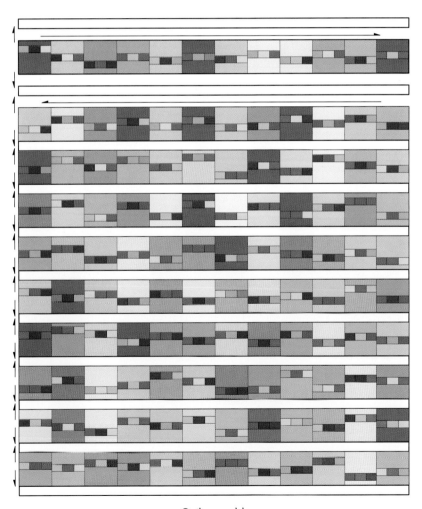

Quilt assembly

Little Charmer

Here's an opportunity to feature your favorite fat quarters or charm squares in a cheerful baby quilt. (Of course, you can always make it larger if you want.) It's double the fun with a coordinating print border.

FINISHED QUILT: 41" x 41"
FINISHED BLOCK: 9" x 9"
Designed and made by Barbara Groves and Mary Jacobson

Materials

Yardage is based on 42"-wide fabric. Fat quarters are 18" x 21".

10 fat quarters of assorted prints for blocks
1 yard of blue print for inner and outer borders
½ yard of green solid for blocks and middle border
⅜ yard of green print for binding
2¾ yards of fabric for backing
49" x 49" piece of batting

Cutting

From the assorted prints, cut a *total* of:
36 squares, 5" x 5"

From the green solid, cut:
3 strips, 2½" x 42"; crosscut into 36 squares,
    2½" x 2½"
4 strips, 1½" x 42"; crosscut into:
    2 strips, 1½" x 31½"
    2 strips, 1½" x 33½"

From the blue print, cut:
4 strips, 2½" x 42"; crosscut into:
    2 strips, 2½" x 27½"
    2 strips, 2½" x 31½"
4 strips, 4¼" x 42"; crosscut into:
    2 strips, 4¼" x 33½"
    2 strips, 4¼" x 41"

From the green print, cut:
5 strips, 2¼" x 42"

Making the Blocks

Use ¼"-wide seam allowances throughout and sew with a short stitch length (14 or 15 stitches per inch). Press all seam allowances open.

1. Draw a diagonal line on the wrong side of each green 2½" square. With right sides together, place a marked green square on the corner of each 5" square as shown. Stitch on the marked line. Trim the seam allowances to ¼". Flip the resulting green triangle open and press. Make 36 units.

Stitch.   Trim.   Make 36.

2. Arrange and sew four units from step 1 into a block as shown. Make nine blocks.

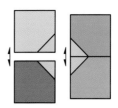 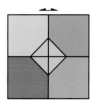

Make 9.

Assembling the Quilt Top

1. Arrange the blocks into three rows of three blocks each. Sew the blocks into rows, and then sew the rows together. The quilt center should measure 27½" x 27½".

2. Sew the blue 2½" x 27½" strips to opposite sides of the quilt center. Sew the blue 2½" x 31½" strips to the top and bottom of the quilt center.

3. Sew the green 1½" x 31½" strips to opposite sides of the quilt center. Sew the green 1½" x 33½" strips to the top and bottom of the quilt.

4. Sew the blue 4¼" x 33½" strips to opposite sides of the quilt center. Sew the blue 4¼" x 41" strips to the top and bottom of the quilt.

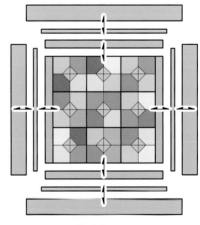

Quilt layout

Finishing the Quilt

For detailed information on finishing techniques, including layering, basting, and quilting, go to ShopMartingale.com/HowtoQuilt for free downloadable instructions. Use the green 2¼"-wide strips to bind the quilt.

Sugar

Sugar is a twin-size quilt made with 9" tulip-inspired blocks. For even more sweetness, whip up the coordinating crib-size version, called Sugar Sweet, which is constructed of 7½" blocks (see page 208). Both are pretty and cheerful, but each has its own personality.

FINISHED QUILT: 64" x 80"

FINISHED BLOCK: 9" x 9"

Designed and pieced by Amber Johnson

Materials

Yardage is based on 42"-wide fabric. Fat quarters are 18" x 21".

5 yards of white solid for blocks, sashing, and setting triangles

⅓ yard of yellow solid for blocks

8 fat quarters of assorted bright prints for blocks

1 fat quarter of yellow floral for sashing squares

⅔ yard of pink floral for binding

5 yards of fabric for backing

72" x 88" piece of white batting

Cutting

From the white solid, cut:

3 strips, 5½" x 42"; crosscut into 16 squares, 5½" x 5½"

4 strips, 5" x 42"; crosscut into 32 squares, 5" x 5"

29 strips, 2¾" x 42"; crosscut *26 of the strips* into:
   32 rectangles, 2¾" x 5"
   80 rectangles, 2¾" x 9½"
   18 squares, 2¾" x 2¾"

4 squares, 17½" x 17½"; cut the squares into quarters diagonally to yield 16 side triangles (2 are extra)

2 squares, 10½" x 10½"; cut the squares in half diagonally to yield 4 corner triangles

From *each* of the bright fat quarters, cut:

2 squares, 5½" x 5½" (16 total)

4 rectangles, 5" x 9½" (32 total)

From the yellow solid, cut:

3 strips, 2¾" x 42"

From the yellow-floral fat quarter, cut:

31 squares, 2¾" x 2¾"

From the pink floral, cut:

8 strips, 2½" x 42"

Making the Blocks

1 Draw a diagonal line from corner to corner on the wrong side of the white 5½" squares. Place a marked square on top of a bright 5½" square with right sides together. Pin the squares together and sew a scant ¼" from both sides of the drawn line. Cut on the drawn line to yield two half-square-triangle units. Press the seam allowances toward the bright triangles. Trim each half-square-triangle unit to 5". Make 32.

Make 32.

2 Draw a diagonal line from corner to corner on the wrong side of the white 5" squares. Place a marked square on the left end of a bright 5" x 9½" rectangle with right sides together. Pin the white square in place and sew on the drawn line. Trim ¼" from the stitching line. Press the seam allowances toward the rectangle. Make 32.

Make 32.

3 Sew a yellow-solid 2¾" x 42" strip to a white 2¾" x 42" strip with right sides together. Press the seam allowances toward the yellow strip. Make three strip sets. Cut a total of 32 segments, 2¾" wide.

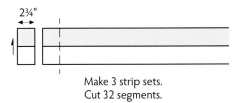

2¾"

Make 3 strip sets.
Cut 32 segments.

4 Sew a white 2¾" x 5" rectangle to one long edge of each segment from step 3, positioning the yellow square in the lower-right corner. Press the seam allowances toward the white rectangles.

Make 32.

5 Sew a unit from step 4 to a half-square-triangle unit from step 1. Press the seam allowances toward the rectangle unit. Sew a matching rectangle unit from step 2 to the bottom. Press the seam allowances toward the rectangle. The block should measure 9½" x 9½". Make 32 blocks.

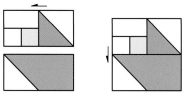

Make 32.

Assembling the Quilt Top

The quilt is assembled in diagonal rows. Refer to the quilt assembly diagram at right for guidance. Press all seam allowances toward the sashing rectangles and sashing rows.

1 Make sashing rows as shown using the white 2¾" squares, white 2¾" x 9½" rectangles, and yellow-floral 2¾" squares. (The white squares sewn to the sashing pieces make it easier to align the seams with the adjacent row.)

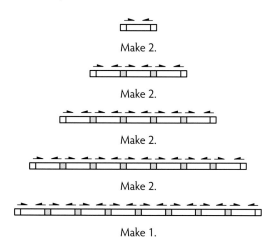

Make 2.

Make 2.

Make 2.

Make 2.

Make 2.

Make 1.

2 Arrange the blocks, sashing rectangles, sashing rows, and side setting triangles in diagonal rows as shown, rotating the blocks to create the design. (The setting triangles are cut oversized and will be trimmed later.) When you are happy with the color placement, sew the blocks, sashing strips, and side triangles into rows. Sew the rows together with the sashing rows. Add the corner triangles last, centering them on the sashing, and press seam allowances toward the triangles.

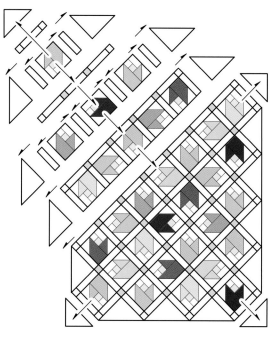

Quilt assembly

3 Trim around the quilt edges, cutting through the white sashing squares ¼" from their top and bottom points. Square up the corners. The quilt center should now measure approximately 64" x 80".

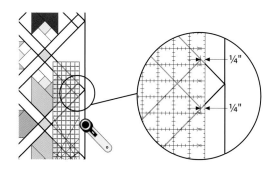

Finishing the Quilt

For detailed information on finishing techniques, including layering, basting, and quilting, go to ShopMartingale.com/HowtoQuilt for free downloadable instructions. Use the pink 2½"-wide strips to bind the quilt.

Juicy

Looking for a project that's perfect for sewing with friends? Here's the answer—a quilt that's enjoyable and simple without too many instructions, allowing you to participate in all the juicy chatter with your pals and still be able to sew without having to focus too much.

FINISHED QUILT: 60½" x 84½"

FINISHED BLOCK: 6" x 6"

Designed and made by Monica Solorio-Snow

Materials

Yardage is based on 42"-wide fabric. Fat quarters are 18" x 21".

10 fat quarters of assorted prints for blocks
2⅜ yards of gray solid for flying-geese border, Hourglass blocks, and binding
2¼ yards of white solid for background and Hourglass blocks
5¼ yards of fabric for backing
66" x 90" piece of batting

Cutting

From *each* of 9 assorted print fat quarters, cut:
6 squares, 6½" x 6½" (54 total)

From the 1 remaining fat quarter, cut:
5 squares, 6½" x 6½"

From the white solid, cut:
6 strips, 7¼" x 42"; crosscut into 29 squares, 7¼" x 7¼". Cut the squares into quarters diagonally to yield 116 triangles.
9 strips, 3½" x 42"; crosscut into:
    20 rectangles, 3½" x 6½"
    52 squares, 3½" x 3½"

From the gray solid, cut:
6 strips, 7¼" x 42"; crosscut into 29 squares, 7¼" x 7¼". Cut the squares into quarters diagonally to yield 116 triangles.
4 strips, 3½" x 42"; crosscut into 24 rectangles, 3½" x 6½"
8 strips, 2½" x 42"

Making the Blocks

The fun part about this pattern is that it looks complicated, but it's constructed of two basic units: squares and rectangles.

Flying-Geese Units

1 Place a white square on one corner of a gray rectangle, right sides together. Stitch a diagonal line from corner to corner as shown. Trim the excess corner fabric, leaving a ¼" seam allowance. Press the seam allowances toward the resulting white triangle.

2 Repeat step 1, sewing a white square on the other end of the gray rectangle. Trim and press to complete a flying-geese unit. Make 24 units.

Make 24.

Hourglass Blocks

1 With right sides together, sew a gray triangle and a white triangle together along their short edges as shown. Press the seam allowances toward the gray triangle. Make 116.

Make 116.

2 Join two units to make an Hourglass block, using the opposing seam allowances to nest the units into place for a nice, snug fit. Press the seam allowances to one side. Make 58 blocks.

Make 58.

Assembling the Quilt Top

1 Sew two white squares, five flying-geese units, and four white rectangles together as shown to make the top row. Press the seam allowances toward the white squares and rectangles. Repeat to make the bottom row.

2 Sew two flying-geese units, five assorted print squares, and four Hourglass blocks together as shown. Press the seam allowances toward the assorted squares. Make seven rows.

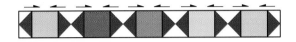

3 Sew two white rectangles, five Hourglass blocks, and four assorted print squares together as

shown. Press the seam allowances toward the white rectangles and assorted squares. Make six rows.

4 Referring to the assembly diagram, join the rows to complete the quilt top. Press the seam allowances in one direction.

Finishing the Quilt

For detailed information on finishing techniques, including layering, basting, and quilting, go to ShopMartingale.com/HowtoQuilt for free downloadable instructions. Use the gray 2½"-wide strips to bind the quilt.

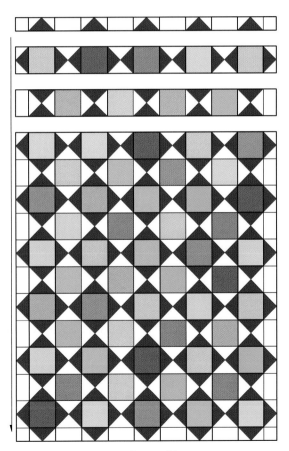

Quilt assembly

Starflower

Modern quilters often talk about negative space. Here, Angela reversed the concept, using white for the wonky white stars and letting them fade into the background. As a result, the bright prints in the background areas emerge as fun flowers.

FINISHED QUILT: 60" x 60"

FINISHED BLOCK: 8½" x 8½"

Designed and made by Angela Nash

Materials

Yardage is based on 42"-wide fabric. Fat quarters are 18" x 21".

3½ yards of white solid for blocks
5 fat quarters of assorted pink prints for blocks
3 fat quarters of assorted yellow prints for blocks
3 fat quarters of assorted orange prints for blocks
⅝ yard of deep-pink solid for binding
3¾ yards of fabric for backing
66" x 66" piece of batting

Cutting

From the white solid, cut:
49 squares, 9" x 9"; cut *40 of the squares* in half diagonally to yield 80 triangles

From *each* of the 11 fat quarters, cut:
4 squares, 9" x 9" (44 total; 2 pink and 2 yellow are extra)

From the deep-pink solid, cut:
7 strips, 2½" x 42"

Assembling the Blocks

1. Choose 10 yellow squares, 18 pink squares, and 12 orange squares.

2. Place a white triangle on one corner of a yellow, pink, or orange square at any angle you like. Make sure the triangle hangs over the edge at least ½" so that the corner is fully covered.

Fixing a Short Fat Quarter

If you have a fat quarter that isn't quite 18" wide, some of your squares will be a tad smaller than 9". You can make up for it with the white triangles by positioning the triangles so that their bottoms extend past the edge of the square. Then the completed block can be squared up to the correct size.

Chain Piecing

Once you have a feel for what angles appeal to you in the star points, you can position the white triangles on the assorted squares and chain piece them, sewing all the units first. Then trim and press all 40 units.

3. Flip the white triangle along the diagonal edge as shown and stitch using a ¼" seam allowance.

4. Open the triangle and make sure the corner of the square is fully covered. Fold the triangle back and trim the excess corner fabric, cutting along the edge of the white triangle.

5. Press the seam allowances open. Do not trim the extra white fabric yet. Make 40 units. Vary the size and angle of the white triangles for fun, wonky interest.

Make 40.

6. Repeat steps 2–5, stitching a white triangle to an adjacent corner of each unit from step 5. Make 40 blocks and trim each block to measure 9" x 9".

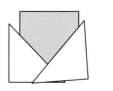

Make 40.

Assembling the Quilt Top

1 Lay out the nine white 9" squares and the star-point blocks as shown in the assembly diagram, paying attention to the orientation of the star points on each block.

2 Being careful to keep the blocks in order and oriented correctly, sew them together in rows. Press the seam allowances open. Join the rows; press the seam allowances open.

Finishing the Quilt

For detailed information on finishing techniques, including layering, basting, and quilting, go to ShopMartingale.com/HowtoQuilt for free downloadable instructions. Use the deep-pink 2½"-wide strips to bind the quilt.

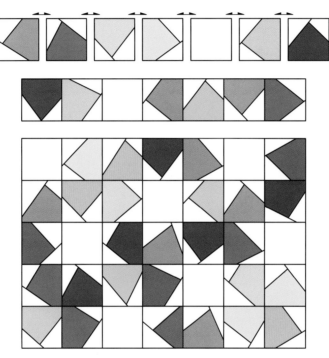

Quilt assembly

The Big Book of Fat-Quarter Quilts

Easy Peasy

Reminiscent of the blocks found in one of your grandmother's "everyday" quilts, these old-fashioned Churn Dash blocks boast a serving of modern style as they seem to float above a field of scrappy plaid. Show off your own personal flair as you piece this contemporary take on a tried-and-true classic.

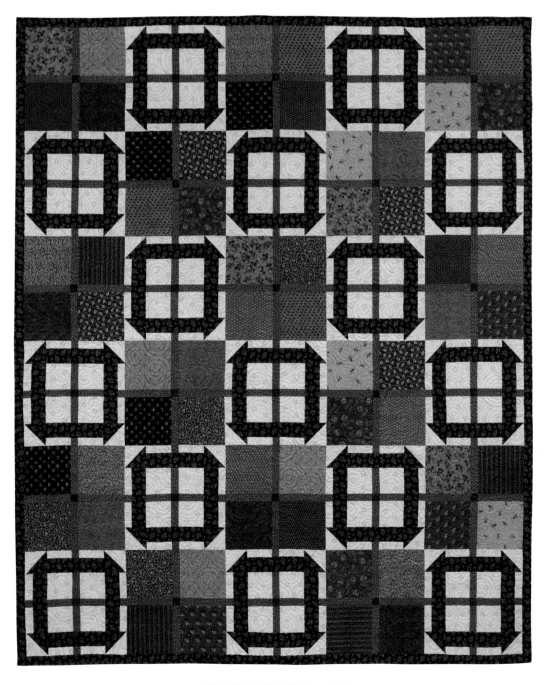

FINISHED QUILT: 72½" x 86½"
FINISHED BLOCK: 14½" x 14½"

Designed and pieced by Kim Diehl; machine quilted by Deborah Poole

Materials

Yardage is based on 42"-wide fabric. Fat quarters are 18" x 21"; a fat eighth is 9" x 21".

15 fat quarters of assorted prints for setting squares
2⅝ yards of black print for blocks, border, and binding
1⅞ yards of cream print for blocks
1⅛ yards of dark-tan print for plaid patchwork
1 fat eighth of cranberry print for plaid center squares
5¼ yards of fabric for backing
79" x 93" piece of batting

Cutting

From the cream print, cut:
12 strips, 4" x 42"
3 strips, 3⅞" x 42"; crosscut into 30 squares, 3⅞" x 3⅞". Cut the squares in half diagonally to yield 60 triangles.

From the dark-tan print, cut:
24 strips, 1½" x 42"; crosscut *18 of the strips* into:
 60 rectangles, 1½" x 7"
 30 rectangles, 1½" x 4"
 Reserve the remaining 6 strips for the strip-set patchwork.

From the black print, cut:
24 strips, 2½" x 42"; crosscut *15 of the strips* into 60 rectangles, 2½" x 8½". Reserve the remaining 9 strips for the binding.
3 strips, 3⅞" x 42"; crosscut into 30 squares, 3⅞" x 3⅞". Cut the squares in half diagonally to yield 60 triangles.
8 strips, 1½" x 42"

From the *length* of the cranberry-print fat eighth, cut:
3 strips, 1½" x 21"; crosscut into 30 squares, 1½" x 1½"

From *each* of the assorted print fat quarters, cut:
4 squares, 7" x 7" (60 total)

Making the Blocks

1 Join a cream 4" x 42" strip to each long edge of a dark-tan 1½" x 42" strip. Press the seam allowances toward the dark-tan print. Repeat for

a total of six strip sets. Crosscut the strip sets into 30 segments, 4" wide, and 60 segments, 1½" wide.

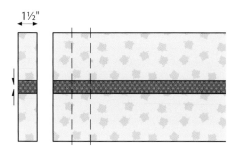

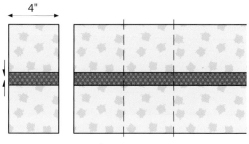

Make 6 strip sets.
Cut 30 segments, 4" wide,
and 60 segments, 1½" wide.

2 Join a cream 3⅞" triangle and a black 3⅞" triangle along the long bias edges. Press the seam allowances toward the black print. Trim away the dog-ear points. Repeat for a total of 60 half-square-triangle units measuring 3½" square, including the seam allowances.

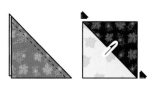

Make 60.

3 Join a small strip-set segment from step 1 to a black 2½" x 8½" rectangle as shown. Press the seam allowances toward the black print. Repeat for a total of 60 pieced units.

Make 60.

4 Join a half-square-triangle unit from step 2 to each end of a pieced unit from step 3 as shown. Press the seam allowances toward the pieced unit. Repeat for a total of 30 pieced Churn Dash units. Reserve the remaining pieced units.

Make 30.

5 Join dark-tan 1½" x 4" rectangles to opposite sides of a cranberry-print 1½" square. Press the seam allowances toward the dark-tan print. Repeat for a total of 15 pieced dark-tan strips.

Make 15.

6 Join a large strip-set segment from step 1 to each long side of a pieced dark-tan strip from step 5. Press the seam allowances toward the dark-tan strip. Repeat for a total of 15 pieced block center units.

Make 15.

7 Join reserved pieced units from step 4 to opposite sides of a pieced block center unit. Press the seam allowances toward the black print. Repeat for a total of 15 pieced center block rows.

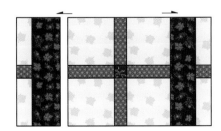

Make 15.

8 Lay out two pieced Churn Dash units from step 4 and a pieced center block row from step 7 to form a Churn Dash block. Join the rows. Press the seam allowances toward the center row. Repeat for a total of 15 Churn Dash blocks measuring 14½" square, including the seam allowances.

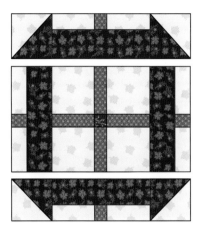

Make 15.

Making the Setting Squares

1 Join assorted print 7" squares to opposite sides of a dark-tan 1½" x 7" rectangle. Press the seam allowances toward the dark-tan print. Repeat for a total of 30 pieced setting square units.

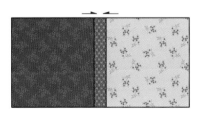

Make 30.

2 Join dark-tan 1½" x 7" rectangles to opposite sides of a cranberry-print 1½" square. Press the seam allowances toward the dark-tan print. Repeat for a total of 15 pieced dark-tan strips.

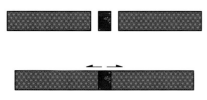

Make 15.

3 Lay out two pieced setting square units from step 1 and one pieced dark-tan strip from step 2 in three horizontal rows as shown. Join the rows. Press the seam allowances toward the dark-tan strip. Repeat for a total of 15 pieced setting squares measuring 14½", including the seam allowances.

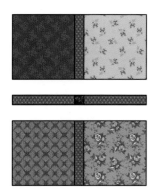

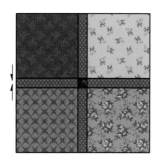

Make 15.

Assembling the Quilt Center

1 Lay out three Churn Dash blocks and two pieced setting squares in alternating positions as shown. Join the pieces to form row A. Press the seam allowances toward the setting squares. Repeat to make a total of three A rows.

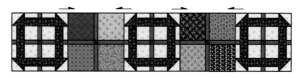

Row A. Make 3.

2 In the same manner, lay out three pieced setting squares and two Churn Dash blocks. Join the pieces to form row B. Press the seam allowances toward the setting squares. Repeat to make a total of three B rows.

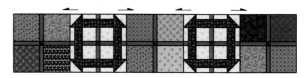

Row B. Make 3.

3 Lay out the A and B rows in alternating positions to form the quilt center. Join the rows. Press the seam allowances toward the B rows. The pieced quilt center should measure 70½" x 84½", including the seam allowances.

Adding the Border

1 Join two black print 1½" x 42" strips end to end to form a pieced border strip. Press the seam allowances to one side. Repeat for a total of four pieced border strips.

2 Fold the longest side of the quilt center in half to find the center. Align the center seam of a pieced border strip with the midpoint of the quilt center; pin the strip in place, working from the center outward to each end. Stitch the pinned border strip in place. Press the seam allowances toward the border strip. Repeat with the remaining long side of the quilt center. Trim away the excess border lengths so the strips are flush with the top and bottom edges of the quilt center.

3 Repeat step 2 with the remaining sides of the quilt center. The pieced quilt top should now measure 72½" x 86½", including the seam allowances.

Finishing the Quilt

For detailed information on finishing techniques, including layering, basting, and quilting, go to ShopMartingale.com/HowtoQuilt for free downloadable instructions. Use the remaining black 2½"-wide strips to bind the quilt.

Stella

"Stella! Hey, Stella!" cried Marlon Brando on the silver screen, immortalizing the name for all time. With an abundance of flowers and offset quirkiness, this quilt's a looker whose rich colors will remain timeless in any season.

FINISHED QUILT: 70" x 72"
FINISHED BLOCK: 4" x 8"

Designed and made by Jeanne Large and Shelley Wicks; machine quilted by Craig and Colleen Lawrence

Materials

Yardage is based on 42"-wide fabric. Fat quarters are 18" x 21".

15 fat quarters of assorted gold, red, purple, and rust fabrics for blocks and flower appliqués

10 fat quarters of assorted beige fabrics for blocks

1⅝ yards of red print for outer border and binding

1⅛ yards of black tone on tone for sashing and first and third borders

1 yard of beige tone on tone for second border

1 fat quarter of gold print for flower-center appliqués

1 fat quarter of green print for leaf appliqués

4⅓ yards of fabric for backing

78" x 80" piece of batting

1½ yards of 18"-wide lightweight paper-backed fusible web

3⅓ yards of 1½"-wide green rickrack for vine

Matching threads for appliqué

Cutting

From *each* of the 10 assorted beige fat quarters, cut:

3 strips, 4½" x 21"; crosscut into 12 squares, 4½" x 4½" (120 total)

From *each* of the 15 assorted gold, red, purple, and rust fat quarters, cut:

1 strip, 8½" x 21"; crosscut into 4 rectangles, 4½" x 8½" (60 total)

From the black tone on tone, cut:

17 strips, 2" x 42"

From the beige tone on tone, cut:

3 strips, 8½" x 42"

3 strips, 2" x 42"

From the red print, cut:

7 strips, 4½" x 42"

8 strips, 2½" x 42"

Making the Flying-Geese Rows

1 Use a pencil and a ruler to lightly draw a diagonal line from corner to corner on the wrong side of each beige 4½" square.

2 Layer one of the marked squares on one end of an assorted 4½" x 8½" rectangle as shown, right sides together. Sew from corner to corner directly on the drawn line. Fold the top corner back and align it with the corner of the rectangle beneath it; press. Trim away the excess layers of fabric beneath the top triangle, leaving a ¼" seam allowance. Repeat to make a total of 60 units. In the same manner, layer a marked beige square on the opposite end of each rectangle as shown, right sides together. Stitch, press, and trim as before to make 60 Flying Geese blocks.

 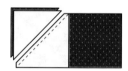

Make 60.

3 Join 12 Flying Geese blocks along the long edges to make a row. Press the seam allowances as shown. Repeat to make a total of five rows.

Make 5.

Assembling the Quilt Top

1 Sew the black 2" x 42" strips together end to end to make one long strip. From this strip, cut six strips, 2" x 48½"; two strips, 2" x 49½"; two strips, 2" x 61"; and two strips, 2" x 62".

2 Alternately sew the black 2" x 48½" sashing/first-border strips and flying-geese rows together side by side. Press the seam allowances toward the

black strips. Sew the black 2" x 49½" first-border strips to the top and bottom of the quilt top. Press the seam allowances toward the first border.

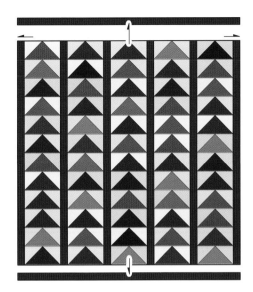

3 Sew the beige 8½" x 42" second-border strips together end to end to make one long strip. From this strip, cut one strip, 8½" x 51½"; one strip, 8½" x 49½"; and one square, 8½" x 8½".

4 Lay the beige 8½" x 51½" strip along the left side of the quilt top and the beige 8½" x 49½" strip along the top. Position the beige 8½" square in the corner between the two strips as shown. Using the illustration as a guide, arrange the rickrack along the length of the beige strips but not into the corner square. Stitch the rickrack into place.

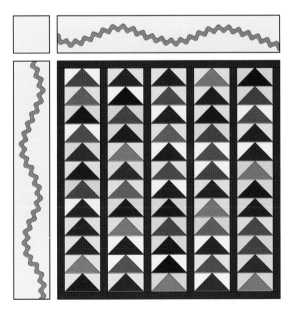

5 Use the patterns on pages 75 and 76 to prepare the shapes for your favorite method of appliqué from the fabrics indicated.

6 Use the placement diagram below and the quilt photo on page 71 as guides to arrange the appliqué shapes on the beige second-border strips and secure them in place. If attaching fusible-web shapes, be careful not to scorch the rickrack with your iron.

7 Sew the left-side appliquéd second-border strip to the left side of the quilt top. Press the seam allowances toward the second border. Sew the 8½" square to the left end of the top appliquéd strip. Press the seam allowances toward the appliquéd strip. Sew the appliquéd second-border strip to the top of the quilt top. Press the seam allowances toward the second border. Appliqué the remaining large flower and leaves to the corner square, being sure to cover the ends of the rickrack with the flower.

Appliqué placement

8 Sew the beige 2" x 42" second-border strips together end to end to make one long strip. From this strip, cut one strip, 2" x 59½", and one strip, 2" x 59". Sew the 2" x 59½" strip to the right side of the quilt. Press the seam allowances toward the second border. Sew the 2" x 59" strip to the bottom of the quilt. Press the seam allowances toward the second border.

9 Sew the black 2" x 61" third-border strips to the sides of the quilt top. Press the seam allowances toward the third border. Sew the black 2" x 62" strips to the top and bottom of the quilt top. Press the seam allowances toward the third border.

10 Sew the red 4½" x 42" outer-border strips together end to end to make one long strip. From this strip, cut two strips, 4½" x 64", and two strips, 4½" x 70". Sew the 4½" x 64" strips to the sides of the quilt top. Press the seam allowances toward the outer border. Sew the 4½" x 70" strips to the top and bottom of the quilt top. Press the seam allowances toward the outer border.

Finishing the Quilt

For detailed information on finishing techniques, including layering, basting, and quilting, go to ShopMartingale.com/HowtoQuilt for free downloadable instructions. Use the red 2½"-wide strips to bind the quilt.

Quilt assembly

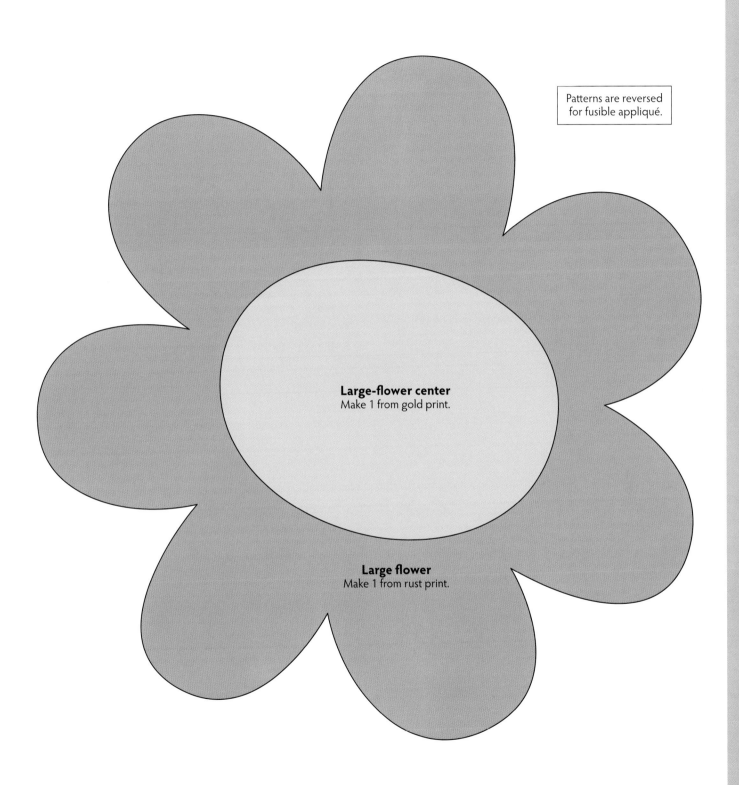

Patterns are reversed
for fusible appliqué.

Large-flower center
Make 1 from gold print.

Large flower
Make 1 from rust print.

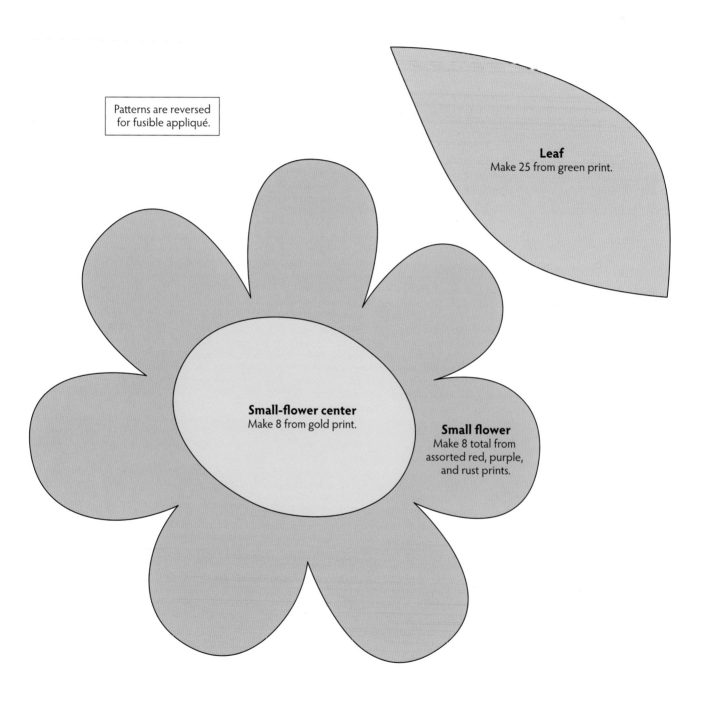

Patterns are reversed for fusible appliqué.

Leaf
Make 25 from green print.

Small-flower center
Make 8 from gold print.

Small flower
Make 8 total from assorted red, purple, and rust prints.

Moonlight

Twinkling stars dance across a Log Cabin-style background of soothing neutrals, evoking the image of a clear, tranquil night when stars and moonlight illuminate the homes below.

FINISHED QUILT: 78½" x 78½"

FINISHED BLOCK: 8" x 8"

Designed and pieced by Gerri Robinson; machine quilted by Rebecca Segura

Materials

Yardage is based on 42"-wide fabric. Fat quarters are 18" x 21".

21 fat quarters of assorted tan prints for blocks and sashing

2⅞ yards of cream solid for blocks and sashing

¾ yard of dark-tan print for binding

7¾ yards of fabric for backing

88" x 88" piece of batting

Cutting

From the cream solid, cut:

28 squares, 4½" x 4½"

405 squares, 2½" x 2½"

104 squares, 1½" x 1½"

From the assorted tan fat quarters, cut a *total* of:

8 rectangles, 2½" x 18½"

4 rectangles, 2½" x 10½"

92 rectangles, 2½" x 8½"

72 rectangles, 2½" x 6½"

184 rectangles, 2½" x 4½"

184 squares, 2½" x 2½"

From the dark-tan print, cut:

9 strips, 2½" x 42"

Making the Chain Blocks

1 Sew two cream 2½" squares and two tan squares together to make a four-patch unit. Press the seam allowances as indicated. The unit should measure 4½" square. Make a total of 36 units.

Make 36.

2 Sew tan 2½" x 4½" rectangles to opposite sides of a four-patch unit to make a center unit. Press the seam allowances toward the tan rectangles. The unit should measure 4½" x 8½". Make 36.

   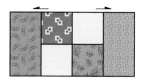

Make 36.

3 Sew a cream 2½" square to one end of a tan 2½" x 6½" rectangle to make a 2½" x 8½" strip. Press the seam allowances toward the tan rectangle. Make 72.

Make 72.

4 Sew two pieced strips from step 3 and one center unit from step 2 together to complete a Chain block. Press the seam allowances toward the pieced strips. The block should measure 8½" square. Make a total of 36 blocks.

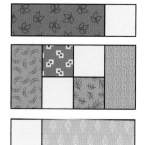 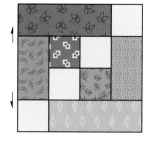

Make 36.

Making the Star Blocks

1 Use two cream 2½" squares and one tan 2½" x 4½" rectangle to make a flying-geese unit. The unit should measure 2½" x 4½". Make a total of 112 units.

Make 112.

2 Sew two flying-geese units from step 1 to opposite sides of a cream 4½" square as shown to make a center unit. Press the seam allowances toward the center. The unit should measure 4½" x 8½". Make a total of 28 units.

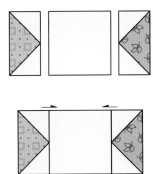

Make 28.

3 Sew a tan square to each end of the remaining flying-geese units to make 2½" x 8½" strips. Press the seam allowances toward the tan squares. Make a total of 56 strips.

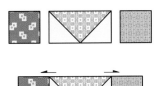

Make 56.

4 Sew two pieced strips from step 3 and one center unit from step 2 together to complete a Star block. Press the seam allowances toward the center. The block should measure 8½" square. Make a total of 28 blocks.

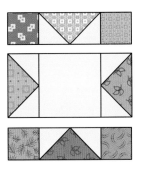
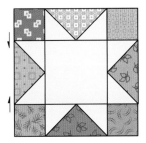

Make 28.

Assembling the Quilt Center

1 Sew cream 1½" squares to adjacent corners on one end of a tan 2½" x 8½" rectangle to make a pieced sashing unit. The unit should measure 2½" x 8½". Make 52 units.

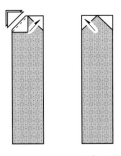

Make 52.

2 Lay out the Chain blocks, pieced sashing units, tan 2½" x 8½" rectangles, and cream 2½" squares as shown in the quilt assembly diagram below, making sure to orient the sashing units as shown. The triangle corners should form small stars when the strips are positioned correctly. Once you're satisfied with the arrangement, sew the pieces together into rows. Press the seam allowances toward the pieced sashing units.

3 Join the rows and press the seam allowances as indicated. The quilt top should measure 58½" square.

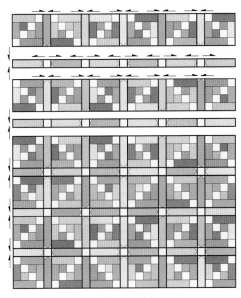

Quilt assembly

Adding the Borders

1 Lay out two tan 2½" x 8½" rectangles, two tan 2½" x 18½" rectangles, and three cream squares as shown. Sew the pieces together to make the top inner-border strip. Press the seam allowances toward the tan rectangles. The strip should measure 2½" x 58½". Repeat to make the bottom inner-border strip.

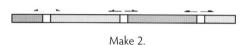

Make 2.

2 Lay out two tan 2½" x 10½" rectangles, two tan 2½" x 18½" rectangles, and three cream squares as shown. Sew the pieces together to make a side inner-border strip. Press the seam allowances toward the tan rectangles. The strip should measure 2½" x 62½". Repeat to make a second side inner-border strip.

Make 2.

3 For the outer border, sew six Star blocks and seven tan 2½" x 8½" rectangles together as shown to make the top border. Press the seam allowances toward the tan rectangles. The strip should measure 8½" x 62½". Repeat to make the bottom border.

Top/bottom border
Make 2.

4 Sew eight Star blocks and seven tan 2½" x 8½" rectangles together as shown to make a side border. Press the seam allowances toward the tan rectangles. The strip should measure 8½" x 78½". Repeat to make a second side border.

Side border
Make 2.

5 Sew the top and bottom inner-border strips to the quilt center, and then sew the side inner-border strips to the quilt center. Press all the seam allowances toward the inner border.

6 Sew the top, bottom, and side outer-border strips to the quilt top. Press all seam allowances toward the inner border.

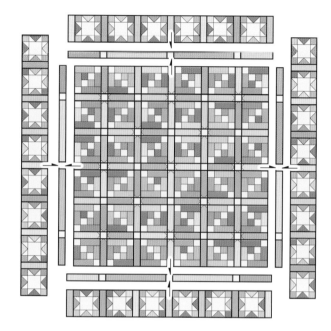

Finishing the Quilt

For detailed information on finishing techniques, including layering, basting, and quilting, go to ShopMartingale.com/HowtoQuilt for free downloadable instructions. Use the dark-tan 2½"-wide strips to bind the quilt.

Love Blooms

Appliquéing a completed Log Cabin quilt can be cumbersome and intimidating, but adding a touch of appliqué to the blocks before putting them together is an easier process that's much more inviting.

FINISHED QUILT: 97" x 97"
FINISHED BLOCK: 10½" X 10½"
Designed and made by Heather Mulder Peterson

Materials

Yardage is based on 42"-wide fabric. Fat quarters are 18" x 21".

2⅝ yards of black floral for outer border

10 fat quarters of assorted dark fabrics for blocks

10 fat quarters of assorted cream fabrics for blocks and sashing

1⅓ yards of black print for blocks, sashing, and inner border

⅞ yard of red fabric for pieced border and appliqué

¾ yard of gold fabric for pieced border and appliqué

¾ yard of blue fabric for middle border and appliqué

⅓ yard of green fabric for appliqué

⅛ yard of purple fabric for appliqué

1 yard of black stripe for binding

9 yards of fabric for backing

101" x 101" piece of batting

1¼ yards of fusible web

Cutting

From the black print, cut:

18 strips, 2" x 42"; crosscut *10 of the strips* into:
    28 strips, 2" x 11"
    24 squares, 2" x 2"

2 strips, 3⅞" x 42"; crosscut into 18 squares, 3⅞" x 3⅞"

From the assorted cream fabrics, cut:

32 strips, 2" x 11"

36 strips, 2" x 9½"

36 strips, 2" x 8"

36 strips, 2" x 6½"

36 strips, 2" x 5"

18 squares, 3⅞" x 3⅞"

1 square, 2" x 2"

From the assorted dark fabrics, cut:

36 strips, 2" x 11"

36 strips, 2" x 9½"

36 strips, 2" x 8"

36 strips, 2" x 6½"

36 strips, 2" x 5"

36 strips, 2" x 3½"

From the gold fabric, cut:

5 strips, 4⅜" x 42"; crosscut into 44 squares, 4⅜" x 4⅜"

From the red fabric, cut:

5 strips, 4⅜" x 42"; crosscut into 44 squares, 4⅜" x 4⅜"

From the blue fabric, cut:

9 strips, 1½" x 42"

From the black floral, cut:

10 strips, 7½" x 42"

From the black stripe, cut:

2½"-wide bias strips to total 400" in length

Making the Blocks

1 Draw a diagonal line from corner to corner on the wrong side of each 3⅞" cream square. Place a marked square on top of a 3⅞" black-print square, right sides together, and sew ¼" from the drawn line on both sides. Cut on the drawn line to yield two half-square-triangle units. Press the seam allowances toward the black print. Make 36 units and square them up to 3½" x 3½".

2 Sew the strips of cream and dark fabrics to the half-square-triangle units as shown. Start with the smallest dark strip on the bottom and add strips in a clockwise rotation, pressing all of the seam allowances outward. Make 36 blocks and square up each block to 11" x 11".

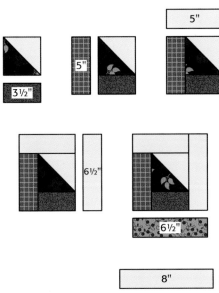

 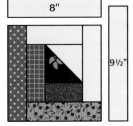

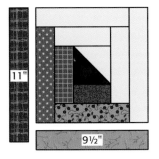 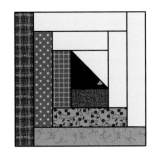

Make 36.

3 Using the patterns on page 85 and referring to the quilt photo on page 81 for color choices, prepare the shapes for your preferred method of appliqué. Attach shapes 1 through 4 to make the single flower design on 12 of the Log Cabin blocks, and attach shapes 5 through 11 to make the double flower design on 12 more of the Log Cabin blocks. Refer to the photo and the assembly diagram on page 84 for placement, and keep the shapes close to the outer edge of each block without overlapping the ¼" seam allowance.

4 Machine appliqué the blue daisies using a blanket stitch with matching thread. Use a zigzag stitch with matching thread for the other shapes.

Assembling the Quilt Center

1 Lay out the 36 blocks, the 11" black-print strips, the 11" cream strips, the 2" black-print squares, and the 2" cream square as shown.

2 Sew the blocks and other fabric strips into rows, pressing all seam allowances toward the sashing. Sew the rows together and press the seam allowances toward the sashing. Square up the quilt center to 71" x 71".

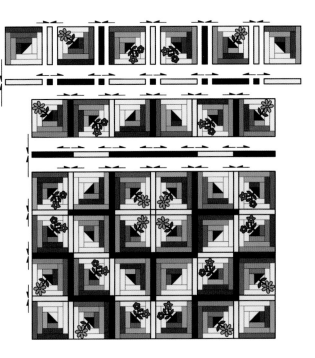

Adding the Borders

1 Sew the 2" black-print strips together end to end. Cut two strips, 71" long, and sew them to the sides of the quilt-top center. Cut two strips, 74" long, and sew them to the top and bottom of the quilt top. Press all seam allowances toward the black border.

2 Referring to step 1 of "Making the Blocks," sew the 4⅜" gold squares and the 4⅜" red squares together to make 88 half-square-triangle units. Press the seam allowances toward the red and square up each unit to 4" x 4". Sew 21 of the units together as shown, pressing the seam allowances in one direction, and trim each strip to a length of 74". Sew these strips to the sides of the quilt top and press the seam allowances toward the black inner border. Sew the remaining units together as shown, pressing the seam allowances in one direction, and trim each strip to a length of 81". Sew these strips to the top and bottom of the quilt top and press the seam allowances toward the black inner border.

Side border.
Make 2.

Top/bottom border.
Make 2.

3 Sew the blue strips together end to end. Cut two strips, 81" long, and sew them to the sides of the quilt top. Cut two strips, 83" long, and sew them to the top and bottom of the quilt top. Press the seam allowances toward the blue border.

4 Sew the black floral strips together end to end. Cut two strips, 83" long, and sew them to the sides of the quilt top. Cut two strips, 97" long, and sew them to the top and bottom of the quilt top. Press the seam allowances toward the black floral border.

Finishing the Quilt

For detailed information on finishing techniques, including layering, basting, and quilting, go to ShopMartingale.com/HowtoQuilt for free downloadable instructions. Use the black-striped 2½"-wide bias strips to bind the quilt.

4
Cut 12.

3
Cut 12.

Patterns are reversed
for fusible appliqué.

1
Cut
12.

2
Cut 24.

8
Cut 12.

9
Cut 12.

10
Cut 12.

11
Cut 12.

7
Cut 36.

6
Cut 12.

5
Cut
12.

Happily Ever After

Whether celebrating a wedding or the 25th or 50th anniversary of a special pair, this design is a perfect way to honor the commitment and joy of time spent together.

FINISHED QUILT: 54½" x 54½"
FINISHED BLOCK: 9" x 9"
Designed and pieced by Rachel Griffith; quilted by Darla Padilla

Materials

Yardage is based on 42"-wide fabric. Fat quarters are 18" x 21".

9 fat quarters of assorted light-gray prints for sashing
1⅛ yards of gray solid for blocks
4 fat quarters of assorted dark-gray prints for sashing
3 fat quarters of assorted yellow prints for blocks
½ yard of fabric for binding
3½ yards of fabric for backing
59" x 59" piece of batting

Cutting

From the gray solid, cut:
18 strips, 2" x 42"; crosscut into:
    32 rectangles, 2" x 6½"
    48 rectangles, 2" x 9½"
    4 squares, 2" x 2"

From the assorted yellow fat quarters, cut a *total* of:
16 squares, 6½" x 6½"

From the assorted dark-gray fat quarters, cut a *total* of:
200 squares, 2" x 2"
25 squares, 3½" x 3½"

From the assorted light-gray fat quarters, cut a *total* of:
40 rectangles, 3½" x 9½"
20 rectangles, 2" x 3½"

From the binding fabric, cut:
6 strips, 2¼" x 42"

Making the Blocks

Sew gray 2" x 6½" rectangles to opposite sides of a yellow square. Press the seam allowances toward the gray rectangles. Sew gray 2" x 9½" rectangles to the top and bottom of the unit to complete the block. Press the seam allowances toward the gray rectangles. Repeat to make a total of 16 blocks.

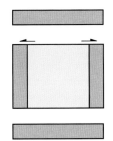
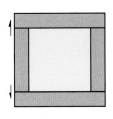

Make 16.

Making the Sashing

1 Draw a line from corner to corner on the wrong side of each dark-gray 2" square. Place a marked square on one end of a light-gray 2" x 3½" rectangle, right sides together, and sew on the line as shown. Trim away the corner fabric, leaving a ¼"-wide seam allowance. Press the seam allowances toward the resulting triangle.

2 Place a second marked square on the opposite end of the rectangle, right sides together. Sew on the marked line and trim as before. Press the seam allowances toward the resulting triangle. Repeat to make a total of 20 flying-geese units.

Make 20.

3 Place marked dark-gray squares from step 1 on two corners of a light-gray 3½" x 9½" rectangle, right sides together, and sew on the marked lines as shown. Trim away the corner fabric, leaving a ¼"-wide seam allowance. Press the seam allowances toward the resulting triangles.

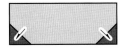

4 Place marked squares on the remaining two corners of the rectangle, right sides together. Sew on the marked lines and trim as before. Press the seam allowances toward the resulting triangles. Repeat to make a total of 40 sashing units.

Make 40.

Assembling the Quilt Top

1 Lay out five flying-geese units, four gray 2" x 9½" rectangles, and two gray 2" squares as shown. Join the pieces to make the top row and press the seam allowances toward the gray rectangles and squares. Repeat to make the bottom row.

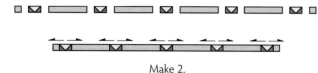

Make 2.

2 Lay out five dark-gray 3½" squares, four sashing units, and two flying-geese units as shown. Join the pieces to make a sashing row and press the seam allowances toward the dark-gray squares. Repeat to make a total of five rows.

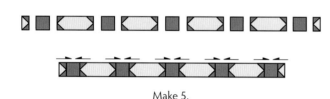

Make 5.

3 Lay out five sashing units, four blocks, and two gray 2" x 9½" rectangles as shown. Join the pieces to make a block row and press the seam allowances toward the blocks and gray rectangles. Repeat to make a total of four rows.

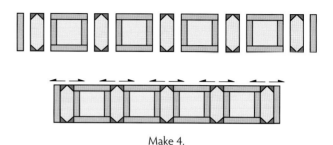

Make 4.

4 Lay out the rows as shown in the quilt assembly diagram. Sew the rows together to complete the quilt top. Press the seam allowances toward the sashing rows.

Finishing the Quilt

For detailed information on finishing techniques, including layering, basting, and quilting, go to ShopMartingale.com/HowtoQuilt for free downloadable instructions. Use the 2¼"-wide strips to bind the quilt.

Quilt assembly

Monterey Square

Named for one of the picturesque public squares in Savannah, Georgia, this quilt is a fabulous way to feature big, bold prints that don't lend themselves well to patterns with tiny pieces. In this design, you can showcase those large-scale florals and paisleys by pairing them with coordinating solids.

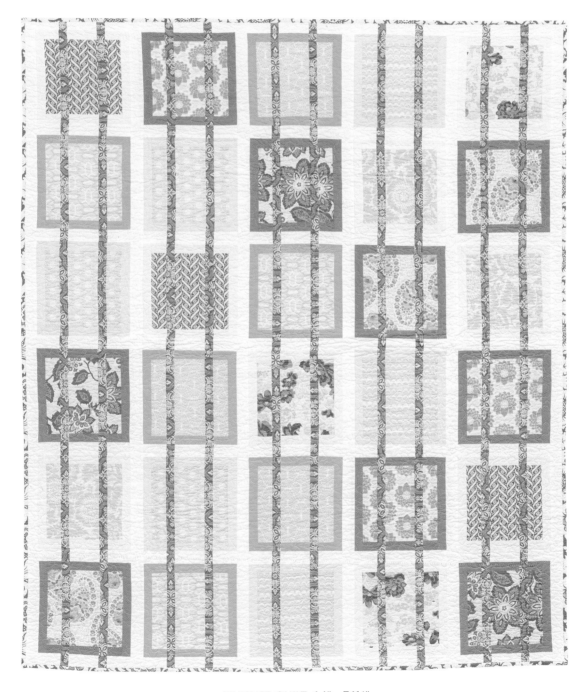

FINISHED QUILT: 64" x 76½"
FINISHED BLOCK: 11" x 11"
Designed and made by Elizabeth Dackson

Materials

Yardage is based on 42"-wide fabric. Fat quarters are 18" x 21".

10 fat quarters of assorted large-scale prints for blocks*
⅜ yard *each* of 5 coordinating solids for blocks
1⅜ yards of white solid for sashing
1⅛ yards of small- or medium-scale print for
   vertical strips
⅔ yard of print for binding
4⅔ yards of fabric for backing
72" x 84" piece of batting

You can also use 30 precut squares, 10" x 10".

Cutting

Refer to the cutting diagram below when cutting the fat quarters.

From *each* of the large-scale print fat quarters, cut:
3 rectangles, 8½" x 9½" (30 total)

From *each* of the coordinating solids, cut:
12 rectangles, 1½" x 8½" (60 total)
12 rectangles, 1½" x 11½" (60 total)

From the small- or medium-scale print, cut:
24 strips, 1½" x 42"; crosscut into:
   70 rectangles, 1½" x 2"
   60 rectangles, 1½" x 11½"

From the white solid, cut:
22 strips, 2" x 42"; crosscut *10 of the strips* into:
   70 rectangles, 2" x 3¼"
   35 rectangles, 2" x 4"

From the binding fabric, cut:
8 strips, 2½" x 42"

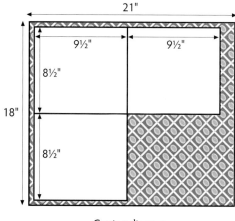

Cutting diagram

Piecing the Blocks

Use a scant ¼" seam allowance and press seam allowances open after sewing each seam.

1 Pair the print 8½" x 9½" rectangles with the solid rectangles in your desired color combinations.

2 Sew a solid 1½" x 8½" rectangle to each 8½"-long side of a large-scale print rectangle. Sew matching solid 1½" x 11½" rectangles to the top and bottom of the unit. Press.

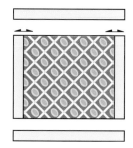 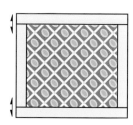

3 Place the block from step 2 on your cutting mat, rotating it so that the shorter side is closest to you. Using your ruler, measure 3¼" from the left side of the block, and make a vertical cut along that line.

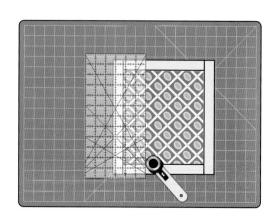

4 Rotate the cutting mat 180° and measure 3¼" from the opposite side of the block. Make a second vertical cut along that line. You now have three sections for your block.

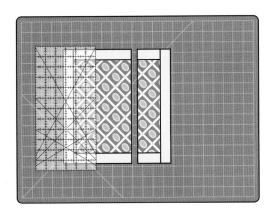

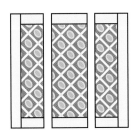

You Can Do It!

The first time you cut into a constructed block can be awfully nerve-racking—what if I cut wrong? Cut with confidence. Measure twice, and cut once. Cut firmly, while holding your ruler in place.

5 Place the small- or medium-scale print 1½" x 11½" rectangles between the sections and sew them together as shown. Press the seam allowances open. The block should measure 11½" x 11½".

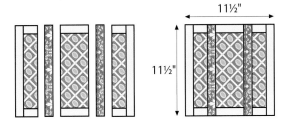

6 Repeat steps 2–5 to make a total of 30 blocks.

Assembling the Quilt Top

You'll piece the quilt top in columns rather than rows. Pieced horizontal sashing strips go between the blocks, and unpieced sashing strips go between the columns.

1 To make the pieced sashing strip, sew a print 1½" x 2" rectangle to each end of a white 2" x 4" rectangle, matching up the 2"-long raw edges. Press the seam allowances open. Sew a white 2" x 3¼" rectangle to each end of the unit as shown. Make 35.

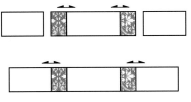

Make 35.

2 Arrange the 30 blocks into five columns of six blocks each in an order that is pleasing to your eye. You can arrange the blocks with the same solid together, or distribute them randomly throughout the quilt top as Elizabeth did. Place a pieced sashing strip between the blocks in each column and at the top and bottom of the columns.

3 Working with one column at a time, sew the sashing pieces and blocks together, taking care to match up the seams of the print fabrics to create the illusion that one piece of fabric runs the

length of the quilt. Press seam allowances open. The columns should measure 76½" in length. Make five columns.

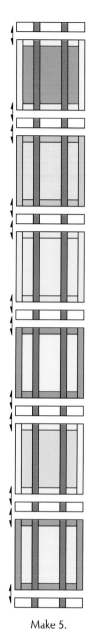

Make 5.

4 Piece the 12 white 2" x 42" strips together in pairs for the vertical sashing. Cut each sewn pair to measure 2" x 76½". Sew the block columns and sashing strips together as shown. Press the seam allowances open.

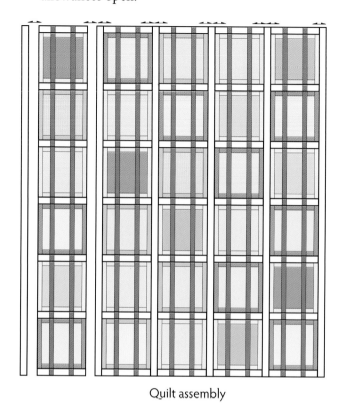

Quilt assembly

Finishing the Quilt

For detailed information on finishing techniques, including layering, basting, and quilting, go to ShopMartingale.com/HowtoQuilt for free downloadable instructions. Use the print 2½"-wide strips to bind the quilt.

Old Architectural Stars

Easy patchwork blocks are paired with appliqué stars in this quilt that's based on an antique. The red stars with holes in the center are reminiscent of architectural stars seen on the sides of early homes along the East Coast. Here, as in architecture, the stars are purely decorative, giving a bright red punch to the overall design.

FINISHED QUILT: 75½" x 75½"

FINISHED BLOCK: 15" x 15"

Designed, pieced, and appliquéd by Karen Costello Soltys; machine quilted by Krista Moser

Materials

Yardage is based on 42"-wide fabric unless otherwise noted. Fat quarters are 18" x 21".

8 to 12 fat quarters of assorted dark reproduction prints (brown, navy blue, medium blue) for pieced blocks*

3 fat quarters of assorted light shirting prints for pieced blocks

3 yards of unbleached muslin for appliqué and pieced blocks

2 yards of red solid for appliqué stars, pieced blocks, and binding**

⅝ yard of cheddar solid for appliqué blocks

2½ yards of 90"-wide fabric for quilt backing***

81" x 81" piece of batting

Template plastic or freezer paper for appliqué template

Fine-point permanent marker

Karen used 10 fat quarters for the quilt shown. Each fat quarter is sufficient to make one and a half blocks. If you don't want to mix the dark fabrics within a block, start with 12 fat quarters.

**If you prefer to cut your binding strips 2½" wide rather than 2", you'll need a total of 2¼ yards of red solid.*

***In keeping with the vintage theme of the quilt, Karen used unbleached muslin for the quilt backing. Using 90"-wide muslin makes a backing without a seam.*

Cutting

Using the pattern on page 97, make a star template from template plastic or freezer paper.

From *each* of the dark fat quarters, cut:
At least 12 squares, 3½" x 3½" (144 total). You need 12 squares per block; if using fewer than 12 fat quarters, cut more squares from each and cobble together renegade blocks from a mix of colors.

From *each* of the light shirting fat quarters, cut:
20 squares, 3½" x 3½" (60 total)

From the muslin, cut:
13 squares, 10" x 10"
52 rectangles, 3½" x 9½"
48 squares, 3½" x 3½"

From the red solid, cut:
48 squares, 3½" x 3½"
8 strips, 2" x 42"

From the cheddar solid, cut:
5 strips, 3½" x 42"; crosscut into 52 squares, 3½" x 3½"

Making the 25 Patch Blocks

Instructions are for one block.

1. Choose 12 matching dark 3½" squares. (After you get the hang of it, you can start mixing and matching dark squares, if desired.) You'll also need five matching light-print squares, four muslin 3½" squares, and four red squares. Lay out the squares as shown, with the red squares in the four corners and the muslin squares in the middle position on each edge of the block.

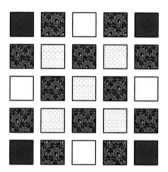

2. Sew the squares together into rows and press the seam allowances toward the dark squares. Sew the rows together and press the seam allowances in one direction. Chain piece the squares if you like.

3. Repeat to make 12 blocks that measure 15½" x 15½", including the outer seam allowances.

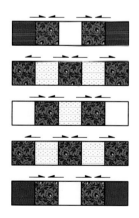
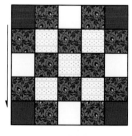

25 Patch block.
Make 12.

Making the Appliqué Blocks

The quilt shown features needle-turn appliqué; if you prefer a faster method, use fusible appliqué.

1 Cut out the center circle in the star template. Trace 13 stars onto the red fabric using a fine-point permanent marker, such as a Pigma pen. Be sure to leave ½" between stars for seam allowances. Cut out the stars roughly ¼" from the marked lines. Don't cut out the center circle at this time.

2 Fold a 10" muslin square in half vertically and horizontally and crease to mark placement guidelines. Position a star on the background so that the vertical points align with one fold line and the other fold line intersects the space between the remaining points as shown. Pin the star to the muslin square.

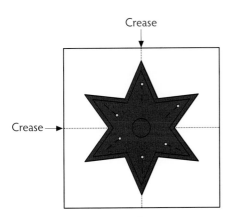

Crease

Crease

Align top and bottom points
with vertical crease.
Horizontal crease should
intersect star as shown.

3 Use embroidery scissors to snip into the inner corner between two star points so that you can fold under the seam allowance along one edge. Begin appliquéing along that edge.

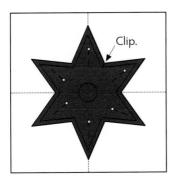

Clip.

4 When you reach the tip of the star point, stitch exactly to the marked point. Take one more tiny stitch at the point to secure, and then fold under the star point as shown. Take another stitch at the point to secure. Then fold the seam allowance the rest of the way under. If necessary, trim the seam allowance to ⅛". (The star points are narrow, so fitting a lot of bulk under them can be difficult unless you trim the seam allowance.)

Take extra stitch.

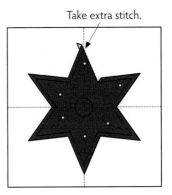

5 Clip into the next inner point so you can easily turn under the second edge of the star point. Continue stitching until you reach the inner point. Take a second stitch at the innermost point for security, and then sweep under the edge of the adjacent star point to continue stitching.

Clip.

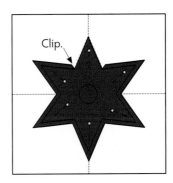

6 Repeat steps 4 and 5 until you've worked your way around the entire star. Insert the needle and pull the thread through to the back of the block. Take a few tiny stitches through the muslin, inside the area of the star, to secure; clip the thread.

7 Pull the center of the star away from the muslin so that you can make a snip in it without cutting the muslin. Then slip the tip of your embroidery scissors into the slit and trim the circle approximately ⅛" inside the marked line, leaving a narrow seam allowance. Make small perpendicular snips around the circle so that you'll be able to turn under the edges easily.

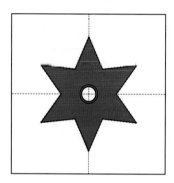

Trim circle, leaving
⅛" seam allowance.

8 Appliqué your way around the circle and fasten off as for the star.

9 Press the star block from the back, and then square up and trim the block to 9½" x 9½", centering the star. (The 4¾" lines on your ruler should run through the center of the star.)

10 Arrange four cheddar squares, four muslin rectangles, and one Star block into three rows. Join the pieces and press the seam allowances as shown. Join the rows. Press the seam allowances away from the center.

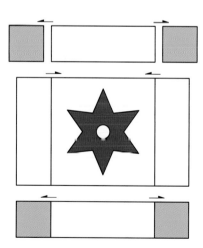

11 Repeat to make a total of 13 Star blocks. The blocks should measure 15½" x 15½".

Assembling the Quilt Top

1 Starting with a Star block, lay out the Star blocks and pieced blocks in alternating positions to make five rows of five blocks each.

2 Sew the blocks together into rows, pressing the seam allowances away from the Star blocks. Join the rows, pressing the seam allowances in one direction.

Quilt assembly

Finishing the Quilt

For detailed information on finishing techniques, including layering, basting, and quilting, go to ShopMartingale.com/HowtoQuilt for free downloadable instructions. Use the red 2"-wide strips to bind the quilt.

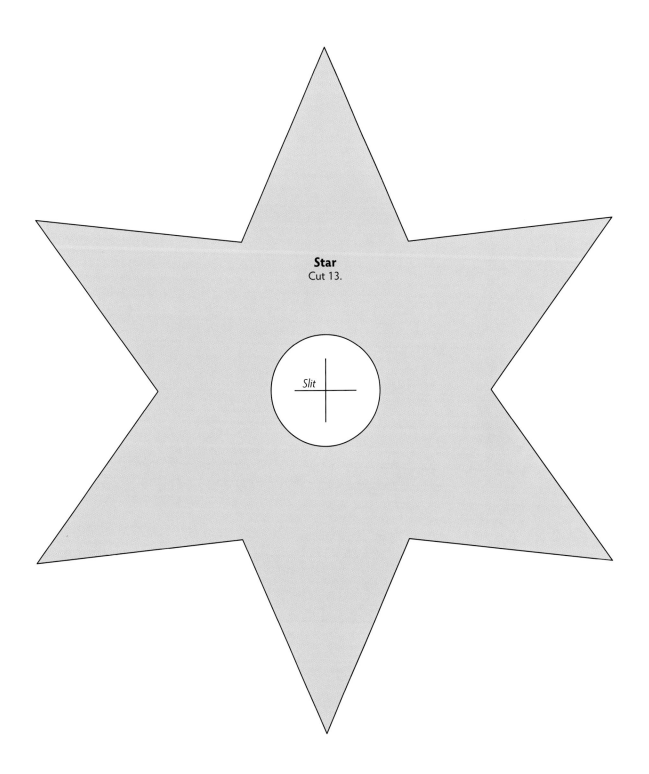

Star
Cut 13.

Slit

Square Deal

Use a fabulous stack-and-shuffle method to cut and piece the blocks really fast. There's a lot of freedom with this block, so put any thoughts of precision piecing aside.

FINISHED QUILT: 67" x 81" (approximately)
FINISHED BLOCK: 14" x 14"
Designed and pieced by Amy Smart; quilted by Melissa Kelley

Materials

Yardage is based on 42"-wide fabric. Fat quarters are 18" x 21".

20 fat quarters of assorted prints for blocks and pieced outer border
⅝ yard of yellow solid for inner border
⅝ yard of red solid for binding
5 yards of fabric for backing
73" x 87" piece of batting

Cutting

From *each* of the assorted print fat quarters, cut:
1 square, 17" x 17" (20 total)
1 rectangle, 4" x 18"* (20 total). Crosscut *1 of the rectangles* into 4 squares, 3" x 3". Set the remaining rectangles aside for the outer border (1 is extra).

From the yellow solid, cut:
7 strips, 3" x 42"

From the red solid, cut:
8 strips, 2½" x 42"

*If the fat quarter is too small to cut a full 4" x 18" rectangle, cut the largest rectangle possible. Standardize the rectangles so that all are the same width; variations in length are acceptable.

Cutting the Block Pieces

These blocks are cut by stacking the 17" squares in groups of four and cutting through all the layers as shown. As you cut the fabric, arrange the pieces as shown in the block layout on page 100 so that it's easy to shuffle the fabrics without losing track of placement. A flat cookie sheet makes a wonderful stacking surface.

1 Stack four 17" print squares, right side up and matching the raw edges. From the left side of the stack, cut a 2" x 17" rectangle. Cut a 2¼" x 17" rectangle from the right side.

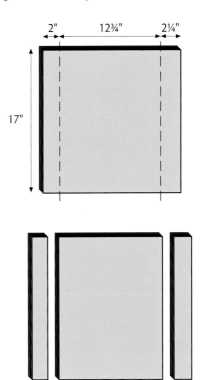

2 From the top edge of the remaining stack, cut a 2¼" x 12¾" rectangle. Cut a 2¾" x 12¾" rectangle from the bottom edge of the stack.

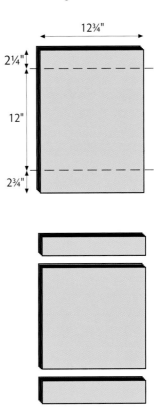

3 From the left side of the remaining stack, cut a 1¾" x 12" rectangle. Cut a 4" x 12" rectangle from the right side.

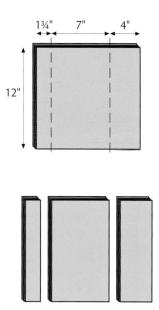

4 Cut a 2" x 7" rectangle from the top edge of the remaining stack and a 3" x 7" rectangle from the bottom edge. This leaves a 7" square for the center.

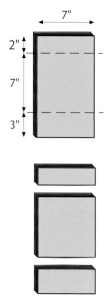

Making the Blocks

1 Arrange the sliced group of four fabrics as shown. Leave the stack of 7" center squares as is. Move the top fabric from each of the four stacks surrounding the center square to the bottom of the stack. Move the top two fabrics from the four outer stacks to the bottom. As each block is assembled, a pattern of three concentric squares will emerge.

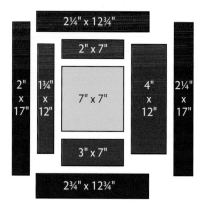

2 Working with the top fabric in each shuffled stack, sew the 2" x 7" and 3" x 7" rectangles to the top and bottom of the center square. Press the seam allowances away from the center.

3 Sew the 1¾" x 12" and 4" x 12" rectangles to the sides of the center section, matching one end of each new rectangle to a raw edge of the assembled section. Press the seam allowances away from the center. Trim the excess fabric from the new rectangles.

Align strips to top of block.
Trim excess.

4 Sew the 2¼" x 12¾" rectangle to the top and the 2¾" x 12¾" rectangle to the bottom of the assembled unit. Press the seam allowances away from the center. Trim the excess fabric.

Align strips to left side of block. Trim excess.

5 Sew the 2" x 17" and 2¼" x 17" rectangles to the sides of the assembled unit. Press the seam allowances away from the center. Trim the rectangle ends and square up the block to measure 14½" x 14½".

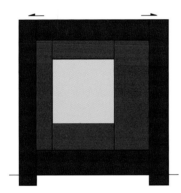

Align strips to top of block. Trim excess.

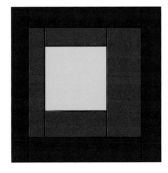

6 Repeat steps 1–5 with the remaining fabrics in the four-fabric group; use the fabrics at the top of each stack to create a block. Repeat the entire cutting and sewing process to make a total of 20 blocks, each including three different fabrics.

Assembling the Quilt Top

1 Arrange the blocks in five rows of four blocks as shown in the quilt assembly diagram on page 102. Rotate individual blocks so that the center square "floats" in different directions in adjacent blocks.

2 Sew the blocks together into rows, pressing the seam allowances to the right in rows 1, 3, and 5 and to the left in rows 2 and 4. Sew the rows together and press the seam allowances in one direction.

Adding the Borders

1 Sew two yellow strips together along their short edges; make two.

2 Measure the length of the quilt top and trim the pieced border strips to this measurement. Sew them to the sides of the quilt top and press the seam allowances toward the border.

3 Cut one of the remaining yellow strips in half. Sew a half strip to one end of each remaining yellow strip. Measure the width of the quilt top between the border seams and add ½" for seam allowances. Trim each pieced yellow strip to this measurement. Sew a 3" square to each end of each strip and press the seam allowances toward the yellow strips.

4 Sew the assembled border units to the top and bottom edges of the quilt top. Press the seam allowances toward the border.

5 Trim 18 of the fat-quarter 4" x 18" rectangles to a consistent width, as close to 4" as possible. Sew four rectangles together end to end; make two. Sew the remaining rectangles together in two groups of five each to make the longer border units.

6 Measure and trim one of the shorter border units to match the quilt width and sew it to the bottom edge of the quilt. Press.

7 Measure and trim one of the longer border units to match the quilt length, including the border just added, and sew it to the right side of the quilt. Press.

8 Add the remaining short border unit to the top and the final long border unit to the left side of the quilt in the same way. Press.

Finishing the Quilt

For detailed information on finishing techniques, including layering, basting, and quilting, go to ShopMartingale.com/HowtoQuilt for free downloadable instructions. Use the red 2½"-wide strips to bind the quilt.

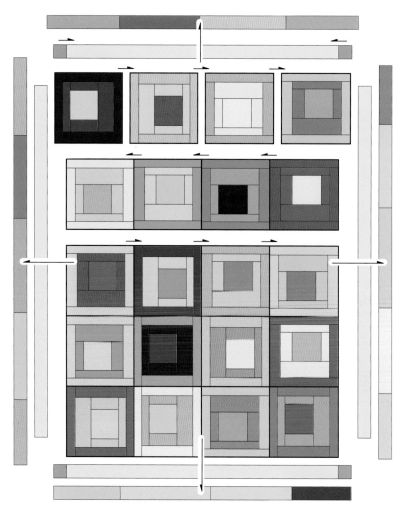

Quilt assembly

Rugby Stars

Rugby Stars was inspired by the classic rugby stripe of the 1970s—strong horizontal rows creating a very distinct and iconic striped pattern. Adapt the color scheme to match your own '70s-era memories.

FINISHED QUILT: 84½" x 76½"
FINISHED BLOCKS: 16" x 16" and 8" x 8"
Designed and pieced by Gerri Robinson; machine quilted by Rebecca Segura

Materials

Yardage is based on 42"-wide fabric. Fat quarters are 18" x 21".

12 fat quarters of assorted red prints for blocks
12 fat quarters of assorted cream and tan prints for blocks
½ yard of cream solid for small Star blocks
⅔ yard of blue solid for inner border
3⅛ yards of red print for outer border and binding
7½ yards of fabric for backing
86" x 94" piece of batting

Cutting

A different set of red, cream, and/or tan fabrics is used for each large Star block. Before cutting, determine the placement of the fabrics in each large Star block. Cut the pieces for all the large Star blocks before cutting the pieces for the small Star blocks. The small Star blocks are cut from the remainder of the fat quarters. Repeat the cutting directions to make 12 large Star blocks and 8 small Star blocks, keeping the fabrics for each block separate.

For 1 Large Star Block

From the assorted red, cream, and tan fat quarters, cut:

1 square, 4½" x 4½" (center star)
8 squares, 2½" x 2½" (center star)
8 squares, 4½" x 4½" (outer star)
4 rectangles, 2½" x 4½" (outer star)
4 squares, 2½" x 2½" (outer star)
4 rectangles, 4½" x 8½" (background)
4 squares, 4½" x 4½" (background)

For 1 Small Star Block

From the remaining assorted red, cream, and tan fat quarters, cut:

1 square, 4½" x 4½"
8 squares, 2½" x 2½"

For Small Star Background

From the cream solid, cut:

32 rectangles, 2½" x 4½"
32 squares, 2½" x 2½"

For Borders and Binding

From the blue solid, cut:

7 strips, 2½" x 42"

From the *lengthwise* grain of the red print, cut:

2 strips, 8½" x 73"
2 strips, 8½" x 80"

From the remaining red print, cut:

9 strips, 2½" x 42"

Making the Large Star Blocks

Instructions are for making one block, using the pieces cut for one large Star block.

1. Place a center-star 2½" square on one corner of an outer-star 2½" x 4½" rectangle, right sides together. Stitch a diagonal line from corner, and then trim the excess corner fabric, leaving a ¼" seam allowance. Press the seam allowances toward the resulting triangle. Repeat with a second, matching center-star 2½" square to make a flying-geese unit. Make four matching units.

Make 4.

2. Sew flying-geese units from step 1 to opposite sides of a matching center-star 4½" square. Press the seam allowances toward the center. The unit should measure 4½" x 8½".

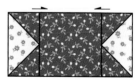

Make 1.

3 Sew matching outer-star 2½" squares to both ends of each remaining flying-geese unit to make two 2½" x 8½" strips. Press the seam allowances toward the cream squares.

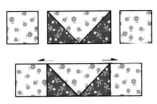

Make 2.

4 Sew the strips from step 3 to the center unit from step 2 as shown. Press the seam allowances toward the center. The star unit should measure 8½" square.

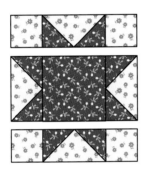

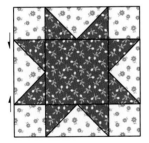

Make 1.

5 Sew two matching outer-star 4½" squares and one background 4½" x 8½" rectangle together to make a large flying-geese unit. Make four matching units.

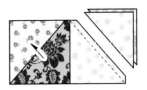

Make 4.

6 Sew two flying-geese units from step 5 to opposite sides of the star unit from step 4 to make a center unit. Press the seam allowances toward the star unit. The unit should measure 8½" x 16½".

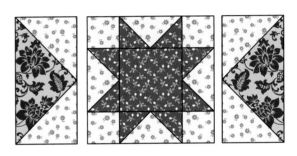

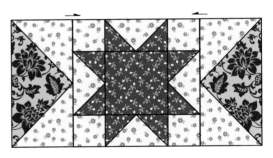

Make 1.

7 Sew background 4½" squares to both ends of the remaining flying-geese units to make two 4½" x 16½" strips. Press the seam allowances toward the background squares.

Make 2.

8 Sew the strips from step 7 to the unit from step 6 to complete the large Star block. Press the seam allowances toward the center. The block should measure 16½" square. Repeat to make a total of 12 blocks.

Make 12.

Making the Small Star Blocks

Instructions are for making one block, using the pieces cut for one small Star block and the cream background pieces.

1 Use two matching small-star 2½" squares and one cream 2½" x 4½" rectangle to make a flying-geese unit. The unit should measure 2½" x 4½". Make four matching units.

Make 4.

2 Sew two flying-geese units from step 1 to opposite sides of a matching small-star 4½" square to make a center unit. Press the seam allowances toward the center. The unit should measure 4½" x 8½".

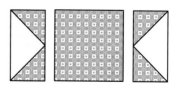

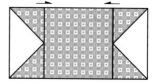

Make 1.

3 Sew cream 2½" squares to both ends of the remaining flying-geese units to make two 2½" x 8½" strips. Press the seam allowances toward the cream squares.

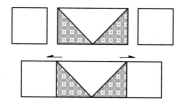

Make 2.

4 Sew two strips from step 3 and one center unit from step 2 together to complete a small Star block. Press the seam allowances toward the center. The block should measure 8½" square. Repeat to make a total of eight blocks.

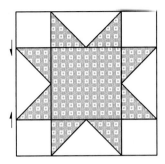

Make 8.

Assembling the Quilt Top

1 Sew four large Star blocks together to make a row. Press the seam allowances in one direction. The row should measure 16½" x 64½". Make three rows.

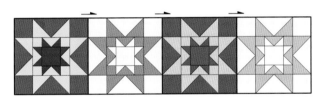

Make 3.

2 Sew the small Star blocks together to make a row. Press the seam allowances in one direction. The row should measure 8½" x 64½".

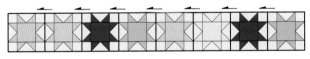

Make 1.

3 Lay out the rows from steps 1 and 2 as shown in the quilt assembly diagram below. Join the rows to complete the quilt center. Press the seam allowances in one direction. The quilt center should measure 64½" x 56½".

4 Join the blue 2½"-wide strips end to end to make a long strip. Measure and cut the inner-border strips; then sew them to the quilt top. Press the seam allowances toward the inner border.

5 Repeat to add the red 8½"-wide outer-border strips. Press the seam allowances toward the outer border.

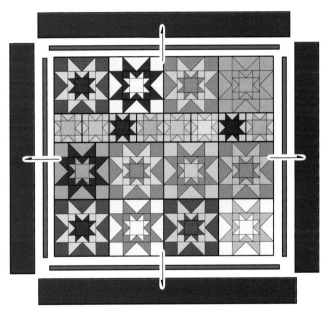

Quilt assembly

Finishing the Quilt

For detailed information on finishing techniques, including layering, basting, and quilting, go to ShopMartingale.com/HowtoQuilt for free downloadable instructions. Use the red 2½"-wide strips to bind the quilt.

Dancing Daisy

Is it ever possible to have too many daisies? Absolutely not! And *red* daisies? Why, they're absolutely irresistible. You can make as many as you like and choose any color you like—use your imagination!

FINISHED QUILT: 56" x 72½"

Designed and pieced by Shelley Wicks and Jeanne Large; machine quilted by Colleen Lawrence

Materials

Yardage is based on 42"-wide fabric. Fat quarters are 18" x 21"; a fat eighth is 9" x 21".

22 fat quarters of assorted brown prints for blocks

⅓ yard *each* of 4 red prints for daisies

⅜ yard of blue check for dots

1 fat eighth of light-green fabric for flower centers

⅝ yard of brown print for binding

3⅝ yards of fabric for backing

63" x 80" piece of batting

2 yards of 17"-wide lightweight fusible web for appliqué

18" x 30" piece of lightweight fusible interfacing for appliqué

Matching thread for appliqués

Cutting

From *each* of the assorted brown fat quarters, cut:

2 strips, 6" x 20"; crosscut each strip into 3 squares, 6" x 6" (132 total; 2 are extra)

From the blue check, cut:

2 strips, 5½" x 42"; crosscut each strip into 7 squares, 5½" x 5½" (14 total)

From the brown print for binding, cut:

7 strips, 2½" x 42"

Assembling the Quilt Top

1 Lay out the brown 6" squares into 13 rows of 10 squares each.

2 Sew the squares together into rows. Press the seam allowances in opposite directions from row to row.

3 Join the rows to form the quilt top. Press all seam allowances in one direction.

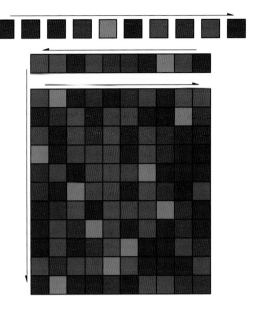

4 Using the patterns on page 110, prepare the following pieces for your favorite method of appliqué.

- 15 petals from each of the four red fabrics (60 total)

- 12 flower centers from the light-green fabric

- 14 blue dots from the squares

5 Using the quilt photo on page 108 as a guide, arrange the shapes on the quilt top. Trim the daisies and dots that are dancing off the quilt even with the quilt edge. Secure the appliqués in place.

Finishing the Quilt

For detailed information on finishing techniques, including layering, basting, and quilting, go to ShopMartingale.com/HowtoQuilt for free downloadable instructions. Use the brown-print 2½"-wide strips to bind the quilt.

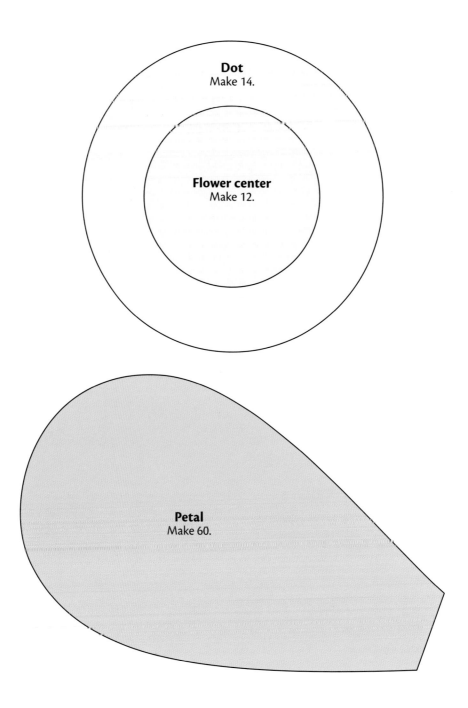

Dot
Make 14.

Flower center
Make 12.

Petal
Make 60.

Blooms for Annabelle

Vicki first designed this pattern for her friend Annabelle using charm squares (precut 5" squares), but then converted the original pattern to use with fat quarters. Yardage is provided for both options, so choose charms or fat quarters and stitch your own beautiful quilt.

FINISHED QUILT: 71½" x 81"

FINISHED BLOCK: 8" x 8"

Designed and made by Vicki Bellino

Materials

Yardage is based on 42"-wide fabric. Fat quarters are 18" x 21".

3⅜ yards of light small-scale print for blocks and sashing

1⅝ yards of red-and-gray print for outer border

1½ yards of gray solid for vines, leaves, inner border, and binding

6 fat quarters *or* 55 squares, 5" x 5", of assorted red prints for blocks and flowers

6 fat quarters *or* 55 squares, 5" x 5", of assorted gray prints for blocks and flowers

4⅞ yards of fabric for backing

76" x 86" piece of batting

Freezer paper

9½" square ruler

Cutting

Use the patterns on page 115 to cut and prepare the appliqués for your favorite appliqué method. Vicki used freezer paper to prepare her appliqués and machine stitched them in place.

From the light small-scale print, cut:

11 strips, 5" x 42"; crosscut into 84 squares, 5" x 5"

25 strips, 2" x 42"; crosscut 12 strips into 48 rectangles, 2" x 8½"

From *each* of the fat quarters of assorted red prints, cut:

7 squares, 5" x 5" (42 total)

From *each* of the fat quarters of assorted gray prints, cut:

7 squares, 5" x 5" (42 total)

From the gray solid, cut:

7 strips, 1" x 42"

8 strips, 2" x 42"

1½"-wide bias strips to total 200" of bias vine

From the red-and-gray print, cut:

8 strips, 6½" x 42"

From the remainder of the fat quarters of assorted red prints, cut:

9 large flowers

9 small flower centers

From the remainder of the fat quarters of assorted gray prints and gray solid fabric, cut:

9 small flowers

9 large flower centers

18 large leaves

18 medium leaves

10 small leaves

Making the Blocks

1 Draw a diagonal line on the wrong side of each light-print 5" square. With right sides together, place one light square on top of each of the red and gray 5" squares and sew ¼" from each side of the drawn line. Cut apart on the drawn line to make a total of 168 half-square-triangle units. Press the seam allowances of the red units toward the red fabrics. Press the seam allowances of the gray units toward the light print. Doing this allows your seam allowances to nestle together nicely when you sew the blocks together. Square up each half-square-triangle unit to 4½" x 4½".

Make 84.   Make 84.

2 Each block will consist of two red and two gray half-square-triangle units. Sew blocks together as shown, pressing the seam allowances as indicated. Make 42 blocks.

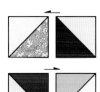 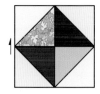

Make 42.

Assembling the Quilt Top

1 Arrange the blocks in six vertical rows of seven blocks each. Sew a light-print 2" x 8½" sashing rectangle to the top of each block, pressing seam allowances toward the sashing. Sew a sashing rectangle to the bottom of the last block in each vertical row. Sew the blocks into rows.

2 Sew the light-print 2" x 42" strips together end to end and from this long strip, cut seven 68½"-long strips. (Measure your vertical rows before cutting, and adjust the length of the strips if needed.) Sew the sashing strips to the vertical rows in three sections as shown and press seam allowances toward the sashing.

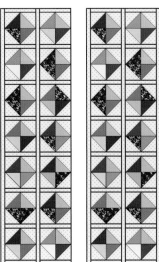

Make 2.   Make 1.

3 Prepare vines from the gray bias strips and position the vines down the sashing strip between each of the block rows, curving them as shown in the quilt photo on page 111. Apply a few drops of appliqué glue to the wrong side of the vine and press down with your fingers to hold it in place. Add the flowers and leaves in the same manner using the photo for placement guidance, or arrange them to your liking. Hand or machine appliqué everything in place.

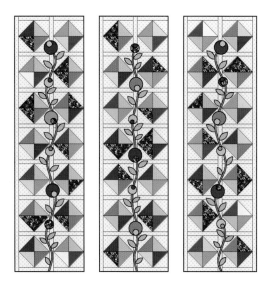

4 Sew the three sections together and press.

Adding the Borders

1 Sew the gray 1" x 42" strips together end to end and cut two 59"-long strips for the top and bottom inner borders. Sew these strips to the quilt, pressing the seam allowances toward the border. Cut two side borders 69½" long and sew them to the sides of the quilt.

2 Sew the red-and-gray 6½" x 42" strips together end to end, cut two 60"-long strips, and sew them to the top and bottom of the quilt, pressing seam allowances toward the outer border. For the side borders, cut two 81½"-long strips and sew them to the sides of the quilt.

Finishing the Quilt

For detailed information on finishing techniques, including layering, basting, and quilting, go to ShopMartingale.com/HowtoQuilt for free downloadable instructions. Use the gray 2"-wide strips to bind the quilt.

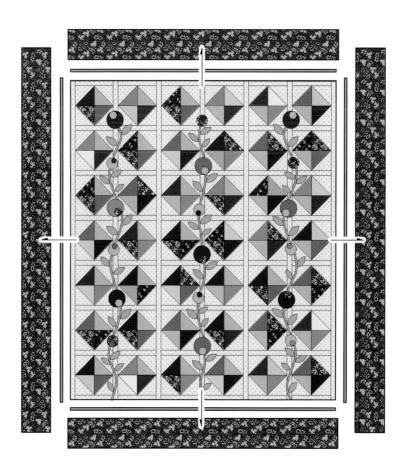

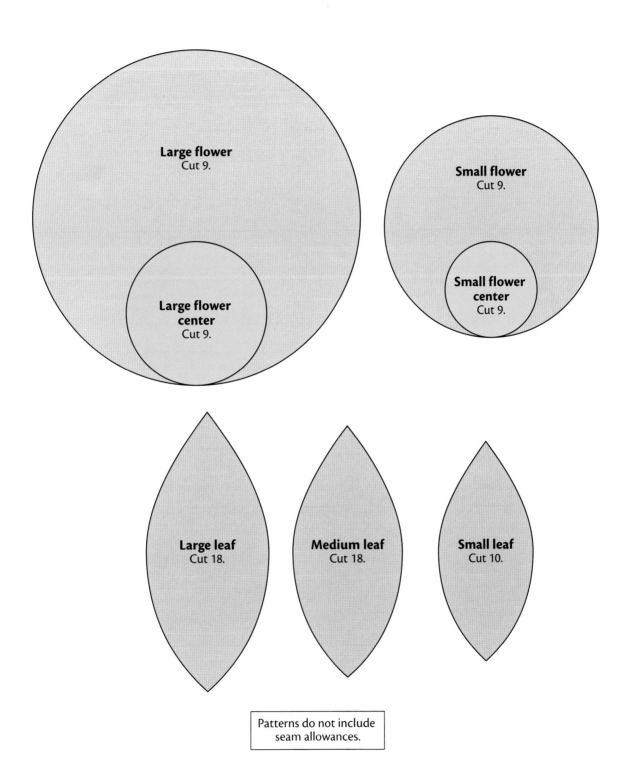

Large flower
Cut 9.

Large flower center
Cut 9.

Small flower
Cut 9.

Small flower center
Cut 9.

Large leaf
Cut 18.

Medium leaf
Cut 18.

Small leaf
Cut 10.

Patterns do not include
seam allowances.

On a Whim

If you are on a tight schedule, here's the quilt pattern for you. It goes together quickly and is easy enough for a beginner. As a bonus, it looks good in many different color combinations, so let the fabric do the work and save yourself time by avoiding intricate piecing.

FINISHED QUILT: 53¼" x 67¼"

Designed and made by Heather Mulder Peterson

Materials

Yardage is based on 42"-wide fabric. Fat quarters are 18" x 21".

11 fat quarters of assorted prints for blocks and
  border corner posts
⅞ yard of yellow print for outer border
½ yard of dark-pink fabric for inner border
⅝ yard of blue plaid for binding
3½ yards of fabric for backing
58" x 72" piece of batting

Cutting

From the assorted prints, cut:
48 pairs* of 2 strips, 1⅞" x 7½" (96 total)
48 rectangles, 4¾" x 7½"
4 squares, 1⅞" x 1⅞"

From the dark-pink fabric, cut:
6 strips, 1⅞" x 42"

From the yellow print, cut:
6 strips, 4½" x 42"

From the blue plaid, cut:
2½"-wide bias strips to total 250" in length

*Cut each pair from 1 fabric for a consistent look
within each block.*

Making the Blocks

Sew pairs of colored strips to the long edges of
colored rectangles in pleasing color combinations.
Press the seam allowances toward the strips. Make 48.
Square up each block to 7½" x 7½".

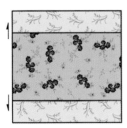

Make 48.

Assembling the Quilt Top

1 Sew the blocks into eight rows of six blocks each.
   Press the seam allowances as indicated in the
   diagram on page 118. Sew the rows together and
   press the seam allowances in either direction.
   Square up the quilt top to 42½" x 56½".

2 Sew the dark-pink strips together end to end. Cut
   two lengths at 56½", two lengths at 42½", and
   eight pieces at 4½". Sew the yellow strips together
   end to end. Cut two lengths at 56½", two lengths
   at 42½", and four squares, 4½" x 4½".

3 Sew a 1⅞" colored square, two 4½" dark-pink
   pieces, and one yellow square together as shown.

  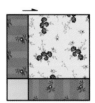

Make 4.

4 Sew the matching lengths of dark-pink and yellow strips together in pairs; press toward the dark pink. Sew the 56½"-long strip pairs to the sides of the quilt top and press the seam allowances toward the dark pink. Sew the corner units from step 3 to the ends of the 42½"-long strip pairs as shown, pressing the seam allowances toward the strip pairs. Sew these border strips to the top and bottom of the quilt top and press the seam allowances as directed.

Finishing the Quilt

For detailed information on finishing techniques, including layering, basting, and quilting, go to ShopMartingale.com/HowtoQuilt for free downloadable instructions. Use the blue-plaid 2½"-wide bias strips to bind the quilt.

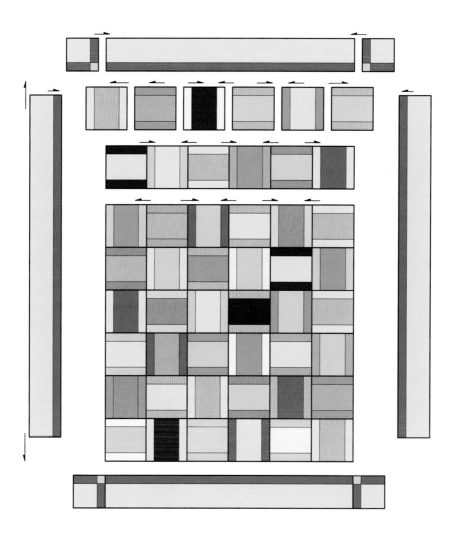

The Big Book of Fat-Quarter Quilts

Interwoven Strips

Try starting with a pretty fat-quarter pack of prints, and then supplement with fat quarters from your stash or from the fat-quarter bins at your local quilt shop. Choose three to five brown or tan fabrics for every turquoise one.

FINISHED QUILT: 62½" x 72½"

FINISHED BLOCK: 5" x 5"

Designed and pieced by Robin Strobel; machine quilted by Karen M. Burns

Materials

Yardage is based on 42"-wide fabric. Fat quarters are 18" x 21".

18 fat quarters of assorted tan and brown prints for blocks

6 fat quarters of assorted turquoise prints for blocks

1¾ yards of dark-turquoise print for outer border and binding

⅜ yard of tan print for inner border

3¾ yards of fabric for backing (crosswise seam)

68" x 78" piece of batting

Cutting

From *each* of the fat quarters, cut:

5 rectangles, 3½" x 5½" (120 total)

10 rectangles, 1½" x 5½" (240 total)*

From the tan print, cut:

6 strips, 1½" x 42"

From the dark-turquoise print, cut:

7 strips, 5½" x 42"

7 strips, 2½" x 42"

Keep rectangles of the same fabric together.

Piecing the Blocks

Sew matching 1½" x 5½" rectangles to both long sides of a 3½" x 5½" contrasting rectangle. Press the seam allowances toward the darker fabric. Make 120 blocks.

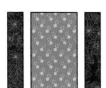 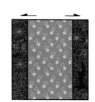

Make 120.

Assembling the Quilt Top

1 Arrange and sew the blocks into 12 rows of 10 blocks per row, alternating the direction of each block as shown. Press the seam allowances in opposite directions from row to row. Sew the rows together. Press the seam allowances in one direction.

2 Piece the 1½" tan-print strips end to end to make one long strip. From this, cut two side borders, 60½" long, and sew them to the quilt sides. Press the seam allowances toward the borders. From the remainder of the long tan strip, cut top and bottom borders, 52½" long, and sew them to the top and bottom of the quilt. Press the seam allowances toward the borders.

3 Piece the 5½" dark-turquoise strips end to end to make one long strip. From this strip, cut four strips, 62½" long, for the outer borders. Sew to the quilt.

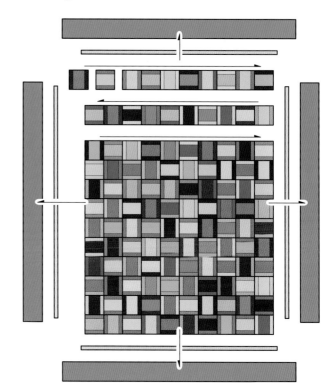

Finishing the Quilt

For detailed information on finishing techniques, including layering, basting, and quilting, go to ShopMartingale.com/HowtoQuilt for free downloadable instructions. Use the 2½"-wide dark-turquoise strips to bind the quilt.

Wonky Fences

Improvisational piecing is quite popular within the modern quilting movement, but many quilters are hesitant to give it a try. This pattern, a skewed variation of the traditional Rail Fence block, invites you to get your feet wet with wonky piecing in a somewhat planned, calculated way.

FINISHED QUILT: 50" x 60"

FINISHED BLOCK: 10" x 10"

Designed and made by Elizabeth Dackson

Materials

Yardage is based on 42"-wide fabric. Fat quarters are 18" x 21".

16 fat quarters of assorted prints for blocks
½ yard of print for binding
3¼ yards of fabric for backing
58" x 68" piece of batting

If Bigger Is Better

So you want to make a queen-size quilt? You'll need to make 90 blocks, set 9 x 10, for a 90" x 100" finished size.

Materials

46 fat quarters of assorted prints for blocks
⅞ yard of print for binding
8¼ yards of fabric for backing
98" x 108" piece of batting

Cutting

From *each* of the assorted print fat quarters, cut:
2 rectangles, 10½" x 13"

From the binding fabric, cut:
6 strips, 2½" x 42"

Piecing the Blocks

Use a scant ¼" seam allowance and press seam allowances open after sewing each seam.

1 Choose four different 10½" x 13" rectangles. This group of fabrics will make four blocks, so be sure your rectangles have variety and work well together. Stack the rectangles right side up on your cutting mat, aligning the raw edges and lining up the stack with the grid lines on the mat.

2 Using the cutting mat's grid lines, place your ruler 3" from the bottom-right corner of the rectangle stack and 2" from the upper-right corner of the stack. Make your first cut along the right edge of the ruler. Do not move the fabric layers.

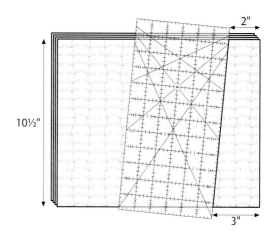

3 To make the second cut, place your ruler 6" from the bottom-right corner of the rectangle stack and 7½" from the upper-right corner. Cut along the right edge of the ruler, keeping the layers in position.

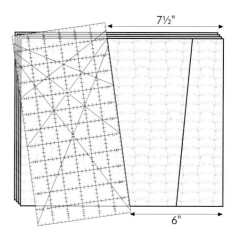

4 For the third cut, place your ruler 12" from the bottom-right corner of the rectangle stack and 10" from the upper-right corner. Cut along the right edge of the ruler. You should have four wedge-shaped pieces.

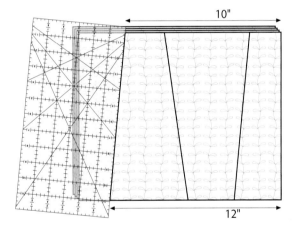

5 Separate the first stack of wedges and make four separate piles. Separate the second stack of wedges and place one with each of the piles you just created, mixing up the fabrics. Repeat for the

remaining two stacks and you should have four blocks, each with a different arrangement of fabrics.

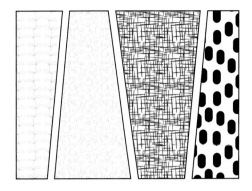

6 Sew the wedges together, offsetting the angled ends just slightly. Press all seam allowances open.

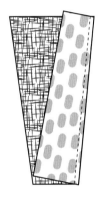 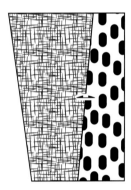

7 Place the pressed block on your cutting mat and trim to 10½" x 10½".

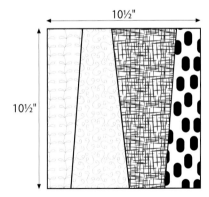

8 Repeat steps 1–7 to make a total of 30 blocks. You'll have enough pieces for 32 blocks if you want to have extras to choose from.

Assembling the Quilt Top

1 Arrange the blocks into six rows of five blocks. Rotate every other block to create more movement and visual interest.

2 Once you're happy with the layout, sew the blocks in each row together, pressing the seam allowances open as you go. Sew the rows together. Press the seam allowances open.

Finishing the Quilt

For detailed information on finishing techniques, including layering, basting, and quilting, go to ShopMartingale.com/HowtoQuilt for free downloadable instructions. Use the 2½"-wide strips to bind the quilt.

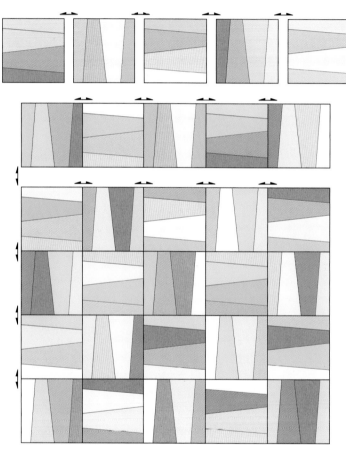

Quilt assembly

Joy

Joy is defined as a feeling of great pleasure and happiness—a feeling often associated with the holidays, but how lovely life would be if we could find that pleasure all year long. Piecing together a pile of colorful strips and scraps is bound to bring a bit of joy!

FINISHED QUILT: 68" x 82¼"
FINISHED BLOCK: 10" x 10"

Designed and pieced by Cindy Lammon; machine quilted by Candy Grisham

Materials

Yardage is based on 42"-wide fabric. Fat quarters are 18" x 21".

20 fat quarters of assorted red, green, and aqua prints for blocks

2⅛ yards of white solid for blocks and setting triangles

1⅝ yards of large-scale floral for blocks and outer border

⅜ yard of aqua tone on tone for inner border

⅔ yard of multicolored stripe for binding

5½ yards of fabric for backing

74" x 88" piece of batting

Cutting

From *each* of the assorted fat quarters, cut:

1 strip, 2" x 21" (20 total); crosscut into:
  2 rectangles, 2" x 3½" (40 total)
  2 rectangles, 2" x 6½" (40 total)
2 strips, 1¾" x 21" (40 total); crosscut each strip into:
  1 rectangle, 1¾" x 6½" (40 total)
  1 rectangle, 1¾" x 9" (40 total)
2 strips, 1¼" x 21" (40 total); crosscut each strip into:
  1 rectangle, 1¼" x 9" (40 total)
  1 rectangle, 1¼" x 10½" (40 total)
1 square, 3½" x 3½" (20 total)

From the large-scale floral, cut:

2 strips, 5½" x 42"; crosscut into 12 squares, 5½" x 5½"
8 strips, 5" x 42"

From the white solid, cut:

12 strips, 3" x 42"; crosscut each strip into:
  2 rectangles, 3" x 5½" (24 total)
  2 rectangles, 3" x 10½" (24 total)
2 strips, 15⅜" x 42"; crosscut each strip into 2 squares, 15⅜" x 15⅜". Cut the squares into quarters diagonally to yield 16 side triangles (2 are extra).
2 squares, 8" x 8"; cut the squares in half diagonally to yield 4 corner triangles

From the aqua tone on tone, cut:

7 strips, 1½" x 42"

From the multicolored stripe, cut:

8 strips, 2½" x 42"

Making the Square-in-a-Square Blocks

After sewing each seam, press the seam allowances as indicated by the arrows, or press them open.

1. Sort the pieces cut from the fat quarters into 20 piles, one for each block. Each pile should include the following:

   Center: 1 square, 3½" x 3½"

   First round: 1 matching set of 2 rectangles, 2" x 3½", and 2 rectangles, 2" x 6½"

   Second round: 1 matching set of 2 rectangles, 1¾" x 6½", and 2 rectangles, 1¾" x 9"

   Third round: 1 matching set of 2 rectangles, 1¼" x 9", and 2 rectangles, 1¼" x 10½"

2. Select one set of pieces. Sew the 2" x 3½" rectangles to opposite sides of the center square; press. Sew the matching 2" x 6½" rectangles to the top and bottom of the square; press.

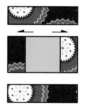

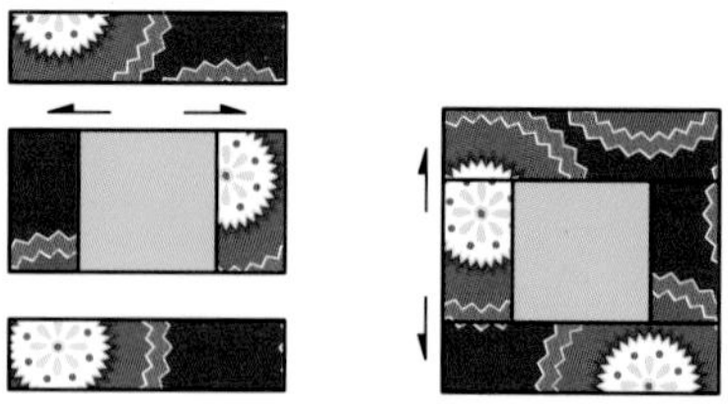

3. In the same manner, sew the 1¾" x 6½" rectangles and the matching 1¾" x 9" rectangles to the unit from step 2.

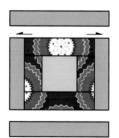 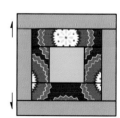

4 In the same manner, sew the 1¼" x 9" rectangles and the matching 1¼" x 10½" rectangles to the unit from step 3.

5 Repeat steps 2–4 to make a total of 20 blocks.

Making the Alternate Blocks

Sew white 3" x 5½" rectangles to opposite sides of a floral 5½" square; press. Sew white 3" x 10½" rectangles to the top and bottom of the square; press. Repeat to make a total of 12 blocks.

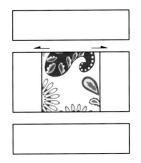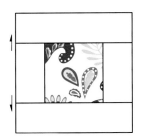

Make 12.

Assembling the Quilt Top

1 Refer to the quilt assembly diagram at right to arrange the blocks in diagonal rows as shown. Add the white side setting triangles along the sides and the white corner setting triangles to the corners. Sew the blocks and side setting triangles in each row together. Press the seam allowances toward the Square-in-a-Square blocks. Join the rows. Press the seam allowances away from the center row. Add the corner triangles last. Press the seam allowances toward the triangles.

2 Sew the seven aqua tone-on-tone 1½"-wide strips together end to end to make one long strip. From the pieced strip, cut two strips the length of the quilt top. Sew the strips to the sides of the quilt top. Press the seam allowances toward the border. From the remainder of the pieced strip, cut two strips the width of the quilt top. Sew these strips to the top and bottom of the quilt top. Press the seam allowances toward the border.

3 Repeat step 2 with the floral 5"-wide strips for the outer border.

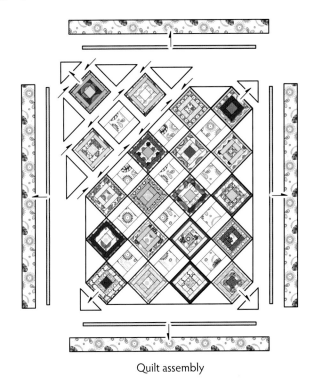

Quilt assembly

Finishing the Quilt

For detailed information on finishing techniques, including layering, basting, and quilting, go to ShopMartingale.com/HowtoQuilt for free downloadable instructions. Use the multicolored 2½"-wide strips to bind the quilt.

Shasta Daisy

For a quiltmaker who lives near Lake Shasta and Mount Shasta, making Shasta Daisy blocks just comes naturally! Whatever landscape *you* see out your window, this fresh, colorful twist on a traditional block is sure to inspire a cheery outlook.

FINISHED QUILT: 53½" x 53½"
FINISHED BLOCK: 12" x 12"
Designed and made by Barbara Brandeburg

Materials

Yardage is based on 42"-wide fabric. Fat quarters are 18" x 21".

1 fat quarter *each* of 4 blue fabrics, 3 orange fabrics, 3 green fabrics, 2 red fabrics, 2 gray fabrics, 1 yellow fabric, and 1 pink fabric for block backgrounds

8 to 9 fat quarters of assorted white fabrics for daisy appliqués

¾ yard of white print for sashing and border

1 fat quarter of yellow fabric for daisy-center appliqués

½ yard of blue print for binding

3⅜ yards of fabric for backing

60" x 60" piece of batting

5½ yards of fusible web

Cutting

From *each* of the fat quarters for block backgrounds, cut:

1 square, 12½" x 12½" (16 total)

From the white print for sashing and border, cut:

14 strips, 1½" x 42"; crosscut *4 of the strips* into 12 rectangles, 1½" x 12½"

From the blue print for binding, cut:

6 strips, 2½" x 42"

Making the Blocks

1 Using the patterns on pages 130 and 131, prepare the shapes for your favorite method of appliqué. Make 16 sets of daisies, with each set cut from the same white fat quarter and consisting of one large daisy and four corner daisies. Make 16 large-daisy centers and 64 corner-daisy centers from the yellow fabric.

2 Fold a background square in half and finger-press the fold. Repeat in the opposite direction to mark the block center.

3 Using the daisy appliqués from one set, position the large daisy in the center of the square. Secure in place. Position a corner daisy in each corner of the square, aligning the raw edges. Secure.

4 Position a daisy center on each flower, and appliqué into position.

5 Repeat steps 2–4 to make a total of 16 blocks.

Assembling the Quilt Top

1 Referring to the quilt photo on page 128 for color placement, sew four blocks and three white 1½" x 12½" rectangles together as shown. Repeat to make a total of four rows.

Make 4.

2 Sew the 10 white 1½"-wide strips together end to end to make one long piece. From this piece cut five sashing/border strips, 51½" long, and two border strips, 53½" long.

3 Join the rows and three of the 51½"-long strips. Sew the remaining 51½"-long strips to the sides, and then sew the 53½"-long strips to the top and bottom of the quilt top.

Finishing the Quilt

For detailed information on finishing techniques, including layering, basting, and quilting, go to ShopMartingale.com/HowtoQuilt for free downloadable instructions. Use the blue 2½"-wide strips to bind the quilt.

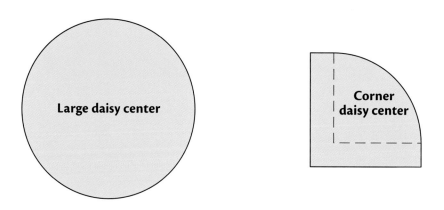

Large daisy center

Corner daisy center

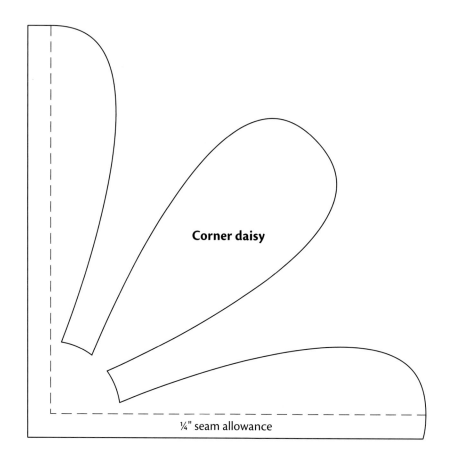

Corner daisy

¼" seam allowance

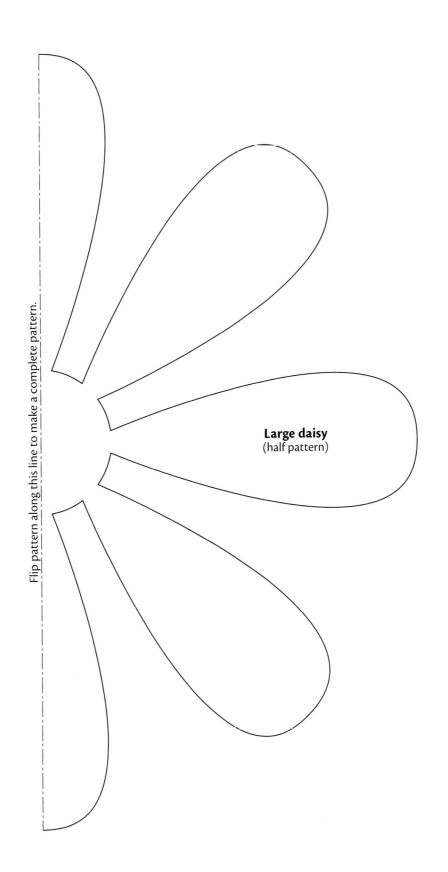

Flip pattern along this line to make a complete pattern.

Large daisy
(half pattern)

White Stars

Julie loves the creative challenge of playing with negative space. By swapping the usual value placement of colored stars and white backgrounds, she made a star quilt that shines.

FINISHED QUILT: 48½" x 64½"
FINISHED BLOCK: 16" x 16"
Designed and pieced by Julie Herman; machine quilted by Angela Walters

Materials

Yardage is based on 42"-wide fabric. Fat quarters are 18" x 21".

2½ yards of white solid for stars
12 fat quarters of assorted prints for background
¾ yard of teal-and-white print for bias binding
3⅓ yards of fabric for backing
54" x 70" piece of batting

Cutting

Refer to the cutting diagram below when cutting the fat quarters.

From *each* of the assorted print fat quarters, cut:
4 rectangles, 4½" x 8½" (48 total)
4 squares, 4½" x 4½" (48 total)

From the white solid, cut:
3 strips, 8½" x 42"; crosscut into 12 squares,
   8½" x 8½"
12 strips, 4½" x 42"; crosscut into 96 squares,
   4½" x 4½"

From the teal-and-white print, cut:
2¼"-wide bias strips to total 240" in length

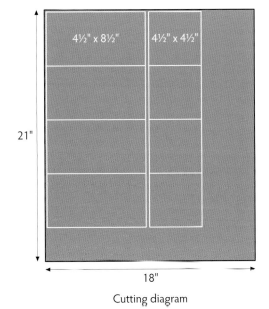

Cutting diagram

Making the Blocks

1 Draw a diagonal line on the wrong side of the 4½" white squares. Place a marked square on one end of an assorted rectangle, right sides together, and sew along the marked line as shown. Trim away the corner fabric, leaving a ¼" seam allowance. Press the seam allowances open.

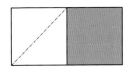 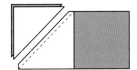

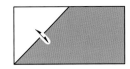

2 Place a second marked square on the opposite end of the rectangle, right sides together. Sew along the marked line and trim as before. Press the seam allowances open. Make a total of 48 flying-geese units.

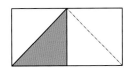 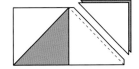

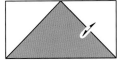

Make 48.

3 Arrange four matching flying-geese units, four assorted squares that match the flying-geese units, and one 8½" white square as shown.

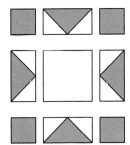

4 Sew the pieces together in rows; press the seam allowances open. Sew the rows together to complete the block. Press the seam allowances open. Repeat to make a total of 12 blocks.

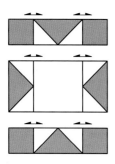

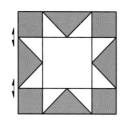

Make 12.

Assembling the Quilt Top

1 Lay out the blocks in four rows of three blocks each.

2 Sew the blocks together in rows and press the seam allowances open. Sew the rows together; press.

Finishing the Quilt

For detailed information on finishing techniques, including layering, basting, and quilting, go to ShopMartingale.com/HowtoQuilt for free downloadable instructions. Use the teal-and-white 2¼" wide bias strips to bind the quilt.

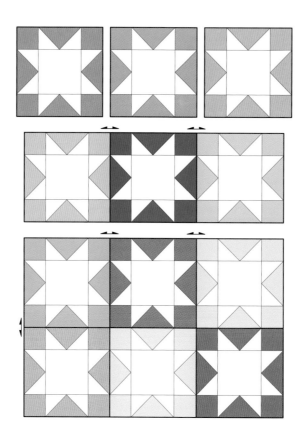

Heat Wave

Simple piecing leads to a stunning design, and changing hues offer opportunities to play. Blend from dark to light, cool to warm, bright to muted, or solids to prints. Here, black-and-white prints contrast a rich transition from red to orange to yellow.

FINISHED QUILT: 62½" x 72½"
FINISHED BLOCK: 10" x 10"

Designed, pieced, and machine quilted by Abbi Barden; quilting motif created by Lorraine Torrence

Materials

Yardage is based on 42"-wide fabric. Fat quarters are 18" x 21".

20 fat quarters of red, red-orange, orange, yellow-orange, and yellow batiks in textured solids and tone-on-tone prints for blocks and outer border

6 fat quarters of black-and-white prints for blocks and inner border

⅝ yard of black fabric for binding

3¾ yards of fabric for backing (crosswise seam)

69" x 79" piece of batting

Cutting

From *each* of the 2 darkest red fat quarters and the 2 lightest yellow fat quarters, cut:

2 rectangles, 5½" x 6½" (8 total)

From *all* of the analogous fat quarters, cut a *total* of:

160 squares, 5½" x 5½"

From *each* of the black-and-white fat quarters, cut:

2 strips, 1½" x 21" (12 total)

20 squares, 2⅜" x 2⅜" (120 total)

From the black fabric, cut:

7 strips, 2½" x 42"

Making the Blocks

1 With right sides together, place a 2⅜" black-and-white square on a corner of one of the 5½" colored squares that will be the upper-left corner of the block interior. Stitch from corner to corner, and then trim the excess corner fabric, leaving a ¼" seam allowance. Fold the resulting black-and-white triangle open. Repeat with three more 5½" colored squares. Press the seam allowances outward on diagonally opposing squares and inward on the remaining squares.

Color Flow

Before assembling the blocks, arrange the colored pieces on a design wall or other flat surface, including the outer-border squares and rectangles, until you're pleased with the flow of the colors from one piece to the next.

Heat Wave uses a palette of colors that lie next to each other on the color wheel, known as an analogous combination. Five warm colors—red, red-orange, orange, yellow-orange, and yellow—provide the "heat." Black-and-white scrappy diamonds create the surface pattern. To make this pattern in different colors, choose a color on the wheel and count in either direction for three to five colors. For example, you can use blue-purple, blue, blue-green, green, and yellow-green for a cooler scheme. Purple, red-purple, red, red-orange, and orange also work.

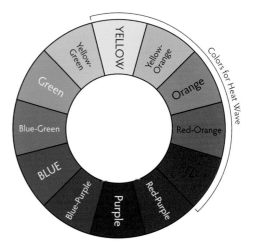

2 Sew the four units from step 1 together into a block. Working across the top row, make a total of five blocks, alternating the pressing direction of the horizontal seam allowances from block to block as shown.

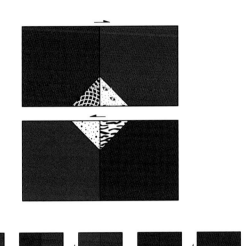

3 Repeat to make a total of 30 blocks.

Keeping the Blocks in Order

Return the assembled blocks to your design surface as you complete them, or label each one with its location—for example, "row 3, block 5."

Assembling the Quilt Top

1 Arrange the blocks in six horizontal rows of five blocks each.

2 Sew the blocks together in rows. Press the seam allowances in opposite directions from row to row. Join the rows. Press the seam allowances in one direction. The quilt top should measure 50½" x 60½".

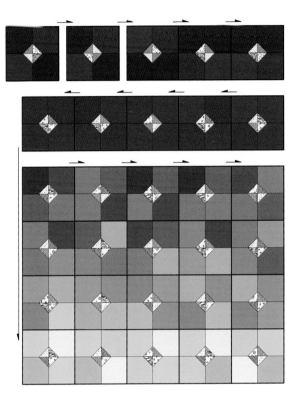

Adding the Borders

1 Stitch the 1½"-wide black-and-white strips together end to end in random order to make one long strip. Cut two strips, 60½" long, and attach them to the sides of the quilt top. Press the seam

allowances toward the inner borders. Cut two strips, 52½" long, and attach them to the top and bottom. Press the seam allowances toward the borders.

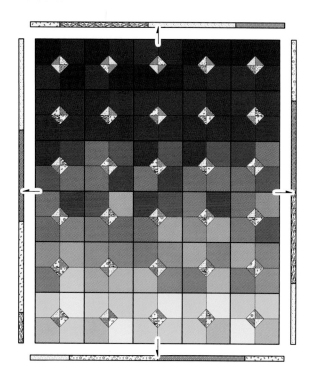

2 For the top outer border, join eight 5½" squares and add a 5½" x 6½" rectangle (marked with an "R" in the diagram) at each end as shown. The border should measure 52½" long. Repeat for the bottom outer border. Attach the top and bottom borders to the quilt top. Press the seam allowances toward the inner borders.

3 For each side border, join two 5½" x 6½" rectangles (marked with an "R" in the diagram) and 12 squares, with one square at each end as shown. These borders should measure 72½" long. Attach the side borders. Press the seam allowances toward the outer borders.

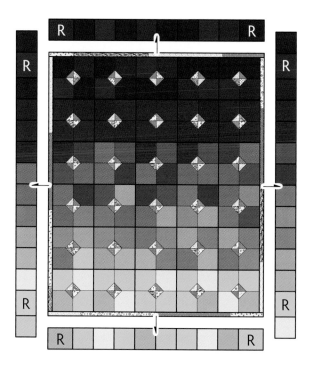

Finishing the Quilt

For detailed information on finishing techniques, including layering, basting, and quilting, go to ShopMartingale.com/HowtoQuilt for free downloadable instructions. Use the black 2½"-wide strips to bind the quilt.

Crosswalk

When it's time to welcome winter, why not whip together something quick and easy? The design looks more complicated than it really is, plus the quilt is just as appealing in many different colorways, so it's a perfect go-to project that you can make many times over.

FINISHED QUILT: 56½" x 70½"

FINISHED BLOCK: 14" x 14"

Designed and pieced by Jeanne Large and Shelley Wicks; machine quilted by Wendy Findlay

Materials

Yardage is based on 42"-wide fabric. Fat quarters are 18" x 21".

14 fat quarters of assorted red prints for blocks
2 yards of beige print for block background
⅝ yard of red print for binding
3⅔ yards of fabric for backing
65" x 79" piece of batting

Cutting

From *each* of the red fat quarters, cut:
5 strips, 3" x 21"; crosscut into 29 squares, 3" x 3" (406 total; 6 are extra)

From the beige print, cut:
5 strips, 8⅜" x 42"; crosscut into 20 squares, 8⅜" x 8⅜". Cut the squares into quarters diagonally to yield 80 triangles.
5 strips, 4½" x 42"; crosscut the strips into 40 squares, 4½" x 4½". Cut the squares in half diagonally to yield 80 triangles.

From the red print, cut:
7 strips, 2½" x 42"

Piecing the Blocks

1. Sew four different red 3" squares together in pairs. Press the seam allowances in opposite directions for each. Sew the pairs together to make a four-patch unit. Make 100 four-patch units.

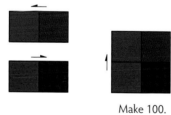

Make 100.

2. Sew three of the four-patch units together. Press the seam allowances toward the center unit. Make 20 of these units.

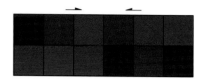

Make 20.

3. Sew beige 8⅜" triangles to opposite sides of the remaining four-patch units. The bottom of the triangle will line up with the bottom of the four-patch unit and the point of the triangle will be slightly longer than the four-patch unit. Press the seam allowances toward the triangles. Make 40 of these units.

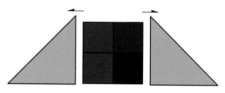

Make 40.

4. Lay out two units from step 3 together with a unit from step 2 as shown and sew the units together. Press the seam allowances toward the units from step 3.

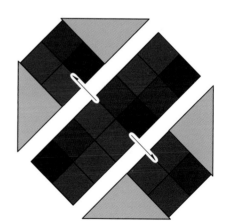

5 Sew a beige 4½" triangle to each corner of the block. Press the seam allowances toward the corner triangles. Make 20 blocks.

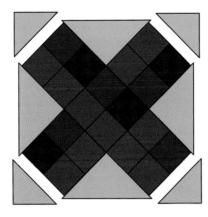

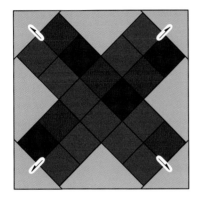

Make 20.

6 Trim each block to measure 14½" x 14½". Be sure to leave ¼" for seam allowance beyond the points so they will match up when you sew the blocks together.

Assembling the Quilt Top

1 Arrange the blocks into five rows of four blocks each.

2 Sew the blocks together, aligning the seams as you sew. Press the seam allowances open to eliminate bulk. Sew the rows together. Press the seam allowances open.

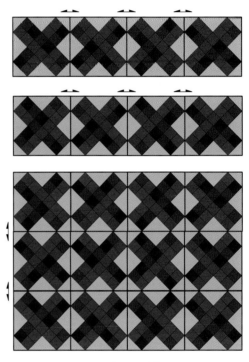

Quilt assembly

Finishing the Quilt

For detailed information on finishing techniques, including layering, basting, and quilting, go to ShopMartingale.com/HowtoQuilt for free downloadable instructions. Use the red 2½"-wide strips to bind the quilt.

Whirligigs

Remember days spent blowing on pinwheels and watching whirligigs turn in the summer breeze while you ran barefoot through Grandma's garden? Recapture those memories with some whirligigs of your own to be enjoyed throughout summer and beyond.

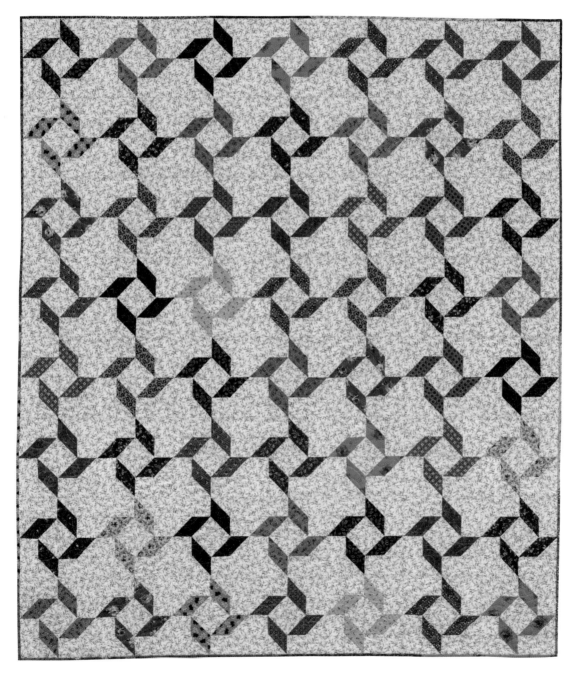

FINISHED QUILT: 56½" x 64½"
FINISHED BLOCK: 8" x 8"

Designed by Kim Diehl; pieced by Evelyne Schow and Pat Hansen; machine quilted by Cynthia Fuelling

Materials

Yardage is based on 42"-wide fabric. Fat quarters are 18" x 21".

4⅜ yards of cream print for background
7 fat quarters of assorted brown prints for blocks and binding
7 fat quarters of assorted pink prints for blocks and binding
4 yards of fabric for backing
63" x 71" piece of batting

Cutting

From *each* of the 7 assorted brown and 7 assorted pink print fat quarters, cut:
16 rectangles, 2½" x 4½" (224 total)
Enough 2½"-wide random lengths to make a 250" length of binding when joined end to end

From the cream print, cut:
56 strips, 2½" x 42"; crosscut into:
448 squares, 2½" x 2½"
224 rectangles, 2½" x 4½"

Piecing the Whirligig Blocks

1. Lightly draw a diagonal line on the wrong side of each of the 448 cream 2½" squares.

2. Select four matching brown 2½" x 4½" rectangles. Layer a prepared cream 2½" square over one end of each rectangle. Stitch the pairs together exactly on the drawn lines. Press and trim. Repeat on the opposite end of each rectangle.

Make 4.

3. Join a cream 2½" x 4½" rectangle to each of the pieced rectangles from step 2 to form a block unit. Press the seam allowances toward the cream rectangle.

Make 4.

4. Lay out four units as shown to make a Whirligig block. Join the pieces in each horizontal row. Press the seam allowances to the left in the top row and to the right in the bottom row. Join the rows. Press the center seam allowances open.

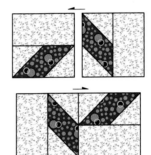 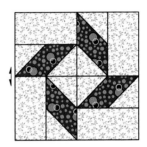

5. Repeat steps 2–4 for a total of 28 assorted pink blocks and 28 assorted brown blocks measuring 8½" square, including the seam allowances.

Assembling the Quilt Top

1. Lay out four brown blocks and three pink blocks in alternating positions. Join the blocks to make a row. Press the seam allowances toward the brown blocks. Repeat for a total of four A rows.

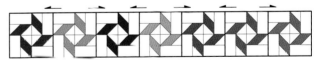

Row A.
Make 4.

2 Referring to step 1, use four pink blocks and three brown blocks to make a row. Repeat for a total of four B rows.

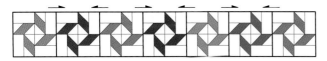

Row B.
Make 4.

3 Referring to the quilt photo on page 142, lay out four A rows and four B rows in alternating positions. Join the rows. Press the seam allowances in one direction. The pieced quilt top should measure 56½" x 64½", including the seam allowances.

Finishing the Quilt

For detailed information on finishing techniques, including layering, basting, and quilting, go to ShopMartingale.com/HowtoQuilt for free downloadable instructions. Use the pink and brown 2½"-wide strips to bind the quilt.

Quilt assembly

Jo's Jammies

Some quilts just make you want to curl up in your pajamas with a good book and a bowl of popcorn. The warm colors make this one the perfect choice to cuddle up with.

FINISHED QUILT: 64½" x 78½"

FINISHED BLOCK: 9½" x 9½"

Designed and pieced by Jeanne Large and Shelley Wicks; machine quilted by Wendy Findlay

Materials

Yardage is based on 42"-wide fabric. Fat quarters are 18" x 21".

6 fat quarters of assorted gold prints for Star blocks and pieced 2nd border

6 fat quarters of assorted green prints (Choose 3 fat quarters for Star block backgrounds and pieced 2nd border; 1 fat quarter for side setting triangles and pieced 2nd border; 1 fat quarter for alternate blocks; and 1 fat quarter for corner setting triangles.)

5 fat quarters of assorted dark-red prints (Choose 3 fat quarters for Star block backgrounds and pieced 2nd border; 1 fat quarter for side setting triangles and pieced 2nd border; and 1 fat quarter for corner setting triangles.)

1⅓ yards of black tone on tone for 1st and 3rd borders and binding

1¼ yards of dark-red print for outer border

2 fat quarters of assorted rust prints for side setting triangles and pieced 2nd border

1 fat quarter of dark-brown print for Star Blocks

1 fat quarter of dark-gold print for side setting triangles

1 fat quarter of brown print for alternate blocks

4¾ yards of fabric for backing

73" x 87" piece of batting

Cutting

To keep organized, sort fabric into piles according to the different sections of the quilt before cutting.

From *each* of the 6 assorted gold fat quarters, cut:

1 strip, 3½" x 21"; crosscut into 2 squares, 3½" x 3½" (12 total)

1 strip, 4¼" x 21"; crosscut into 4 squares, 4¼" x 4¼" (24 total). Cut the squares into quarters diagonally to yield 16 triangles (96 total).

3 strips, 2½" x 21" (18 total)

From the dark-brown fat quarter, cut:

3 strips, 4¼" x 21"; crosscut into 12 squares, 4¼" x 4¼". Cut the squares into quarters diagonally to yield 48 triangles.

From *each* of the 3 assorted dark-red and 3 assorted green fat quarters for Star block backgrounds and pieced 2nd border, cut:

2 strips, 3½" x 21"; crosscut into 8 squares, 3½" x 3½" (48 total)

1 strip, 4¼" x 21"; crosscut into 2 squares, 4¼" x 4¼" (12 total). Cut the squares into quarters diagonally to yield 8 triangles (48 total).

2 strips, 2½" x 21" (12 total)

From *each* of the 3 green, brown, and dark-red fat quarters for alternate blocks, cut:

1 strip, 9½" x 21"; crosscut into 2 squares, 9½" x 9½" (6 total)

2 strips, 2½" x 21" (6 total)

From *each* of the 5 assorted dark-red, green, dark-gold, and rust fat quarters for side setting triangles, cut:

1 strip, 10½" x 21"; crosscut into 1 square, 10½" x 10½" (5 total). Cut the square in half diagonally to yield 2 triangles (10 total).

2 strips, 2½" x 21" (10 total)

From the green fat quarter for corner setting triangles, cut:

1 strip, 8½" x 21"; crosscut into 2 squares, 8½" x 8½". Cut the squares in half diagonally to yield 4 triangles.

3 strips, 2½" x 21"

From the black tone on tone, cut:

3 strips, 2" x 42"

10 strips, 1½" x 42"

8 strips, 2½" x 42"

From the dark-red print, cut:

7 strips, 5½" x 42"

Making the Blocks

1 Arrange two matching gold triangles, one dark-brown triangle, and one of the green or red Star block background triangles as shown. Sew the triangles into pairs. Press the seam allowances toward the gold triangles. Sew the pairs together to make an hourglass unit. Press the seam allowances in one direction. Repeat to make four matching hourglass units.

Make 4
matching units.

2 Arrange four hourglass units from step 1, four matching green or red 3½" background squares, and one matching gold 3½" square into three horizontal rows as shown. Sew the pieces in each row together. Press the seam allowances toward the squares. Sew the rows together. Press the seam allowances toward the top and bottom rows. Make a total of 12 Star blocks.

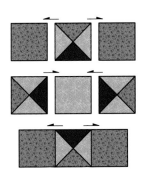 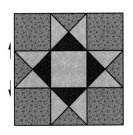

Make 12.

Assembling the Quilt Top

1 Refer to the diagram at right to arrange the Star blocks; the green, brown, and dark-red 9½" square alternate blocks; the dark-red, green, dark-gold, and assorted rust 10½" side setting triangles; and green corner setting triangles into diagonal rows as shown. Sew the blocks and side setting triangles in each row together. Press the seam allowances toward the alternate blocks and side setting triangles. Sew the rows together. Press the seam allowances away from the center row. Add the corner triangles last. Press the seam allowances toward the corner triangles.

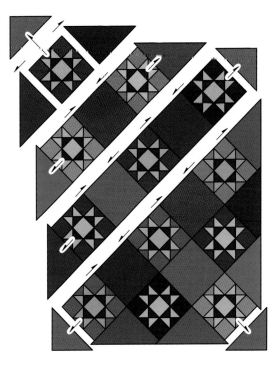

2 Trim around the outside edge of the quilt, ¼" from the block points to remove the excess setting triangle fabric. Your quilt center must measure 38½" x 51½" in order for the pieced second border to fit.

3 Sew three of the black 1½" x 42" first-border strips together end to end to make one long strip. From this strip, cut two strips, 1½" x 51½". Sew these strips to the sides of the quilt top. Press the seam allowances toward the border. Sew the black 2" x 42" first-border strips together end to end to make one long strip. From this strip, cut two strips, 2" x 40½". Sew these strips to the top and bottom of the quilt top. Press the seam allowances toward the border.

4 To make the pieced second border, randomly select three 2½" x 21" strips and sew them together along the long edges to make a strip set. Press the seam allowances in one direction. Repeat to make a total of 16 strip sets. You'll have one 2½" x 21" strip left over. Crosscut the strip sets into 106 segments, 2½" wide.

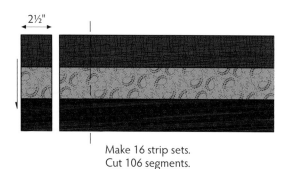

2½"

Make 16 strip sets.
Cut 106 segments.

5 Refer to the quilt assembly diagram at right to randomly sew 27 segments from step 4 together along the long edges. Press the seam allowances in one direction. Repeat to make a total of two second-border strips. Sew these strips to the sides of the quilt top. Press the seam allowances toward the first border. In the same manner, join 26 segments from step 4 along the long edges and press the seam allowances in one direction. Repeat to make a total of two second-border strips. Sew these strips to the top and bottom of the quilt top. Press the seam allowances toward the first border.

6 Sew the remaining black 1½" x 42" third-border strips together end to end to make one long strip. From this strip, cut two strips, 1½" x 66½", and two strips, 1½" x 54½". Sew the 1½" x 66½" strips to the sides of the quilt top. Press the seam allowances toward the third border. Sew the 1½" x 54½" strips to the top and bottom of the quilt top. Press the seam allowances toward the third border.

7 Sew the dark-red 5½" x 42" fourth-border strips together end to end to make one long strip. From this strip, cut two strips, 5½" x 68½", and two strips, 5½" x 64½". Sew the 5½" x 68½" strips to the sides of the quilt top. Press the seam allowances toward the fourth border. Sew the 5½" x 64½" strips to the top and bottom of the quilt top. Press the seam allowances toward the fourth border.

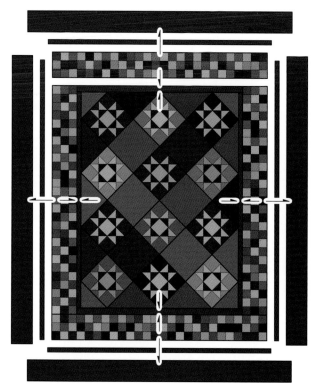

Quilt assembly

Finishing the Quilt

For detailed information on finishing techniques, including layering, basting, and quilting, go to ShopMartingale.com/HowtoQuilt for free downloadable instructions. Use the black 2½"-wide strips to bind the quilt.

Canyonlands

An abstract interpretation of birds in flight results in a stunningly modern quilt. The 12" square blocks make this an incredibly versatile quilt design, allowing for easy customization and resizing. It's also a pattern that would look just as lovely in a coordinated color palette as it would completely scrappy.

FINISHED QUILT: 60½" x 84½"

FINISHED BLOCK: 12" x 12"

Designed and pieced by John Q. Adams; quilted by Angela Walters

Materials

Yardage is based on 42"-wide fabric. Fat quarters are 18" x 21".

4½ yards of tan solid for blocks and quilt background
16 fat quarters of 8 assorted prints for blocks
⅔ yard of fabric for binding
5⅜ yards of fabric for backing
68" x 92" piece of batting

Cutting

From the *crosswise* grain of the tan solid, cut:
9 strips, 3½" x 42"; cut into 92 squares, 3½" x 3½"
6 strips, 9" x 42"; cut into 46 rectangles, 4½" x 9"

From the *lengthwise* grain of the remaining tan solid, cut:
1 strip, 12½" x 48½"
3 squares, 12½" x 12½"
10 rectangles, 6½" x 12½"

From the assorted prints, cut a *total* of:*
92 squares, 6½" x 6½"

From the binding fabric, cut:
8 strips, 2½" x 42"

You should be able to cut 6 squares from each fat quarter.

Assembling the Blocks

The quilt is made of two different blocks, a Double Starling block and a Single Starling block.

Block A—Double Starling

1 Draw a diagonal line from corner to corner on the wrong side of two tan 3½" squares. Place a marked square on the upper-right corner of a print square, right sides together and raw edges aligned. Sew on the marked line. Trim the excess corner fabric, leaving a ¼" seam allowance, and press the resulting triangle open.

2 Along the left edge of the print square, measure 3" up from the bottom-left corner and make a light pencil mark. Using a ruler, make a cut from this pencil mark to the bottom-right corner of the square.

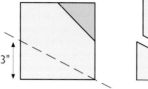

3 Cut a tan 4½" x 9" rectangle in half diagonally, from the top-left to the bottom-right corner.

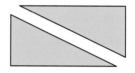

4 Sew one triangle from step 3 to the angled edge of the unit as shown. The triangle was cut a bit oversize for easier cutting and piecing. Press the seam allowances toward the tan triangle. Trim the unit to 6½" square.

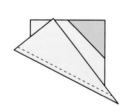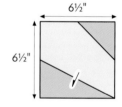

5 Repeat steps 1 and 2 to make the other half-block unit. Cut a tan 4½" x 9" rectangle in half diagonally, from the top-right to the bottom-left corner. Repeat step 4, sewing one triangle to the angled edge of the unit as shown to complete the unit. This unit is a mirror image of the first unit.

6 Lay out two mirror-image units made with the same print so that the print forms a V shape. Join the units to make a 6½" x 12½" starling unit.

Press the seam allowances open. Repeat the steps to make a total of 36 units.

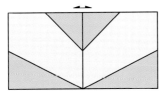

Make 36.

7 Join two starling units to make block A. The block should measure 12½" x 12½". Press the seam allowances open. Make a total of 18 of block A.

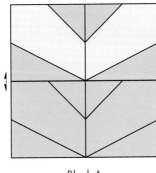

Block A.
Make 18.

Block B—Single Starling

1 Follow steps 1–6 of "Block A—Double Starling" to make a starling unit. Make 10 units.

2 Sew a tan 6½" x 12½" rectangle to the bottom of five of the units to make the B1 blocks. Press the seam allowances toward the tan rectangle.

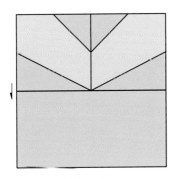

Block B1.
Make 5.

3 Sew a tan 6½" x 12½" rectangle to the top of each remaining starling unit to make five B2

blocks. Press the seam allowances toward the tan rectangle.

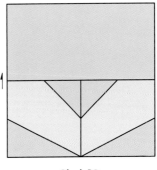

Block B2.
Make 5.

Assembling the Quilt Top

1 Lay out the A, B1, and B2 blocks, along with the tan 12½" squares and tan 12½" x 48½" strip, as shown in the quilt assembly diagram below. Join the blocks into rows; press the seam allowances in opposite directions from row to row.

2 Join the rows to complete the quilt top. Press the seam allowances in one direction. Trim and square up the quilt top as needed.

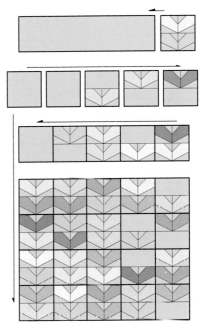

Quilt assembly

Finishing the Quilt

For detailed information on finishing techniques, including layering, basting, and quilting, go to ShopMartingale.com/HowtoQuilt for free downloadable instructions. Use the 2½"-wide strips to bind the quilt.

Frolic

Designer Rebecca Silbaugh admits that making a Log Cabin quilt was high on her bucket list. But rather than starting with a traditional center square, she pieced wonky Nine Patch centers for a style more reminiscent of reclaimed wood than modular housing, as the "logs" aren't always even.

FINISHED QUILT: 72½" x 72½"
FINISHED BLOCK: 12" x 12"
Designed and made by Rebecca Silbaugh

Materials

Yardage is based on 42"-wide fabric. Fat quarters are 18" x 21".

18 fat quarters of assorted light prints for blocks
18 fat quarters of assorted bold prints for blocks
⅝ yard of fabric for binding
4½ yards of fabric for backing
80" x 80" piece of batting

Cutting

From *each* of the light fat quarters, cut:
5 strips, 2" x 21"; crosscut into:
    2 rectangles, 2" x 11½" (36 total)
    2 rectangles, 2" x 10" (36 total)
    2 rectangles, 2" x 6½" (36 total)
    2 rectangles, 2" x 5" (36 total)
    4 rectangles, 2" x 2½" (72 total)
    4 rectangles, 1½" x 2" (72 total)
2 strips, 1½" x 21"; crosscut into:
    2 rectangles, 1½" x 8½" (36 total)
    2 rectangles, 1½" x 7½" (36 total)

From *each* of the bold fat quarters, cut:
1 strip, 2½" x 21"; crosscut into:
    2 squares, 2½" x 2½" (36 total)
    4 rectangles, 1½" x 2½" (72 total)
    2 squares, 2" x 2" (36 total)
    2 squares, 1½" x 1½" (36 total)
2 strips, 2" x 21"; crosscut into:
    2 rectangles, 2" x 10" (36 total)
    2 rectangles, 2" x 8½" (36 total)
4 strips, 1½" x 21"; crosscut into:
    2 rectangles, 1½" x 12½" (36 total)
    2 rectangles, 1½" x 11½" (36 total)
    2 rectangles, 1½" x 7½" (36 total)
    2 rectangles, 1½" x 6½" (36 total)

From the binding fabric, cut:
8 strips, 2¼" x 42"

Making the Blocks

1 For each wonky Nine Patch block, you'll need the following pieces from one bold print: one 1½" square, one 2" square, one 2½" square, and two 1½" x 2½" rectangles. From the light prints, randomly select two 1½" x 2" rectangles and two 2" x 2½" rectangles. Lay out the pieces in three rows as shown. Sew the pieces together in rows. Press the seam allowances toward the bold fabrics. Sew the rows together and press the seam allowances away from the center. The block should measure 5" x 5". Make 36 blocks.

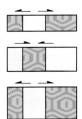

Make 36.

2 For efficiency in sewing the blocks together, stack the remaining rectangles in the order they will be used, with the largest rectangle on the bottom and the smallest rectangle on the top. Stack the rectangles in the following order:

Bold: 1½" x 12½"
Bold: 1½" x 11½"
Light: 2" x 11½"
Light: 2" x 10"
Bold: 2" x 10"
Bold: 2" x 8½"
Light: 1½" x 8½"
Light: 1½" x 7½"
Bold: 1½" x 7½"
Bold: 1½" x 6½"
Light: 2" x 6½"
Light: 2" x 5"

3 Randomly select a light 2" x 5" rectangle and sew it to the left side of a wonky Nine Patch block. Press the seam allowances toward the rectangle.

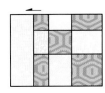

4 Randomly select a light 2" x 6½" rectangle and sew it to the top of the block. Press the seam allowances toward the rectangle.

5 Continue in the same way, adding rectangles around the center block in a clockwise direction. The light prints should always be added to the top and left of the center block, and the bold prints should always be added to the right and bottom. Press the seam allowances toward each newly added rectangle. Make 36 blocks.

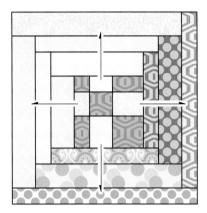

Make 36.

Assembling the Quilt Top

1 Lay out thc blocks in six rows of six blocks each, rotating the blocks to achieve the desired look and making sure the colors are balanced and well mixed. Refer to the quilt photo on page 152 and the assembly diagram below for placement guidance. Sew the blocks together in rows. Press the seam allowances in opposite directions from row to row.

2 Join the rows and press the seam allowances in one direction.

Finishing the Quilt

For detailed information on finishing techniques, including layering, basting, and quilting, go to ShopMartingale.com/HowtoQuilt for free downloadable instructions. Use the 2¼"-wide strips to bind the quilt.

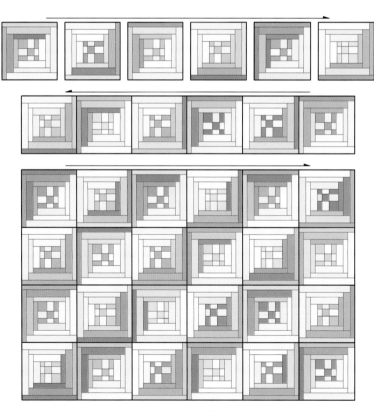

Quilt assembly

The Big Book of Fat-Quarter Quilts

Three Steps Forward

Whether you're building your quilting skills or you're a seasoned quilter, you'll find Three Steps Forward is an uplifting design. The easy-to-make Jacob's Ladder block, pieced with squares and half-square-triangle units, will elevate your confidence in no time.

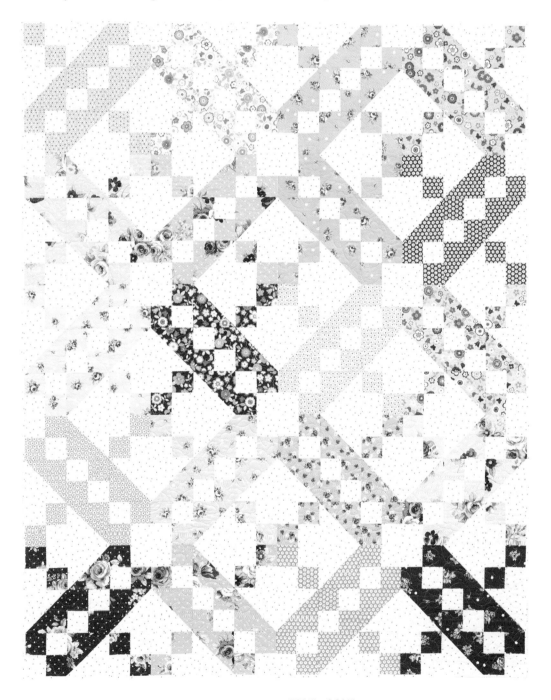

FINISHED QUILT: 72½" x 90½"
FINISHED BLOCK: 18" x 18"

Designed and pieced by Vickie Eapen; machine quilted by Al Kuthe

Materials

Yardage is based on 42"-wide fabric. Fat quarters are 18" x 21".

20 fat quarters of assorted florals for blocks
4⅜ yards of white print for blocks and binding
6 yards of fabric for backing
78" x 96" piece of batting

Cutting

From *each* of the floral fat quarters, cut:
2 strips, 3½" x 21"; crosscut into 10 squares,
   3½" x 3½" (200 total)
1 strip, 7" x 21"; crosscut into 2 squares, 7" x 7"
   (40 total)

From the white print, cut:
19 strips, 3½" x 42"; crosscut into 200 squares,
   3½" x 3½"
8 strips, 7" x 42"; crosscut into 40 squares, 7" x 7"
9 strips, 2¼" x 42"

Making the Blocks

1 Sew each floral 3½" square to a white-print 3½" square to make a two-patch unit. Press the seam allowances toward the floral squares. Sew two matching two-patch units together as shown to make a four-patch unit. The unit should measure 6½" x 6½". Repeat to make 20 sets of five matching units (100 total).

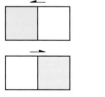

Make 20 sets of 5.

2 Draw a diagonal line from corner to corner on the wrong side of each white 7" square. Layer a marked square with a floral 7" square, right sides together, and stitch ¼" from the line on both sides. Cut the square apart on the line, pressing the seam allowances toward the green triangles. Trim each unit to 6½" x 6½". Make 20 sets of four matching units.

Make 20 sets of 4.

3 Using pieces from the same floral fabric, arrange five four-patch units and four half-square-triangle units into three horizontal rows as shown. Sew the units in each row together. Press the seam allowances in alternating directions from row to row. Sew the rows together. Press the seam allowances in one direction. Repeat to make a total of 20 blocks.

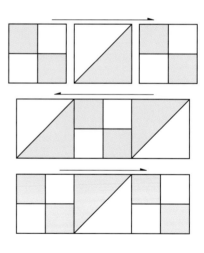

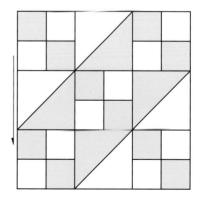

Make 20.

Assembling the Quilt Top

1. Arrange the blocks into five horizontal rows of four blocks each. Rotate every other block 90° so that the four-patch units form a diagonal line across the quilt as shown.

2. Sew the blocks in each row together. Press the seam allowances in opposite directions from row to row. Sew the rows together. Press the seam allowances in one direction.

Finishing the Quilt

For detailed information on finishing techniques, including layering, basting, and quilting, go to ShopMartingale.com/HowtoQuilt for free downloadable instructions. Use the white 2¼"-wide strips to bind the quilt.

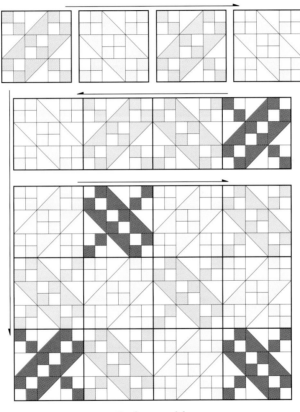

Quilt assembly

Garden Lattice

The contrast of bright persimmon red and cool jade green creates a fresh and fun quilt that brings to mind summertime blooms. Hints of black and cream add a sophisticated touch to the color scheme, and the simple lattice layout adds balance to the eclectic mix of prints.

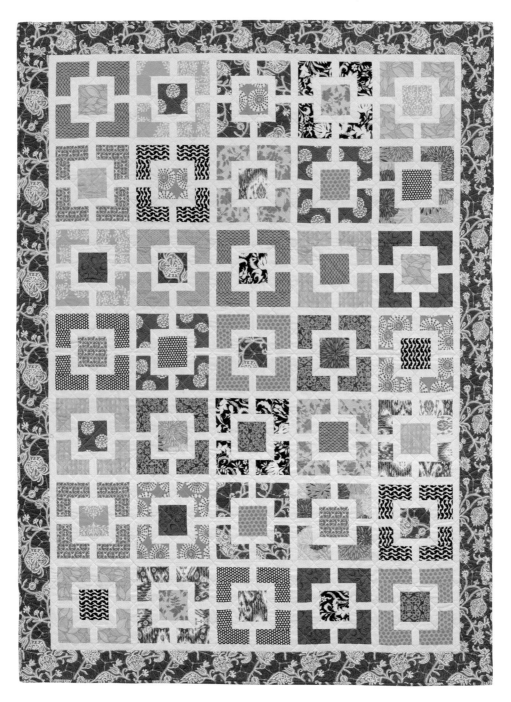

FINISHED QUILT: 64½" x 86½"
FINISHED BLOCK: 10" x 10"
Designed and made by Cindy Lammon

Materials

Yardage is based on 42"-wide fabric. Fat quarters are 18" x 21".

16 fat quarters of assorted red, green, and black prints for blocks

2⅝ yards of cream solid for blocks, sashing, and inner border

1⅞ yards of red print for blocks, outer border, and binding

5⅞ yards of fabric for backing

70" x 92" piece of batting

Cutting

From the cream solid, cut:

3 strips, 4½" x 42"; crosscut into 70 rectangles, 1½" x 4½"

3 strips, 6½" x 42"; crosscut into 70 rectangles, 1½" x 6½"

6 strips, 2½" x 42"; crosscut into 140 rectangles, 1½" x 2½"

1 strip, 10½" x 42"; crosscut into 26 sashing rectangles, 1½" x 10½"

17 strips, 1½" x 42"; crosscut 1 of the strips into 2 sashing rectangles, 1½" x 10½"

From *each* of the assorted red, green, and black fat quarters, cut:

4 strips, 2½" x 21" (64 total); crosscut each strip into:
2 rectangles, 2½" x 5" (128 total)
2 rectangles, 2½" x 3" (128 total)
2 squares, 4½" x 4½" (32 total)

From the red print, cut:

3 squares, 4½" x 4½"

8 rectangles, 2½" x 3"

8 rectangles, 2½" x 5"

8 strips, 4½" x 42"

8 strips, 2½" x 42"

Making the Blocks

1 Sew cream 1½" x 4½" rectangles to opposite sides of an assorted print 4½" square; press. Sew cream 1½" x 6½" rectangles to the top and bottom of the square; press as indicated.

2 Choose four 2½" x 3" rectangles and four 2½" x 5" rectangles from the same print. Sew a cream 1½" x 2½" rectangle between two 2½" x 3" rectangles; press. Make two. Sew these units to the sides of the unit from step 1.

 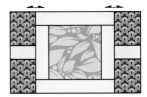

Make 2.

3 Sew a cream 1½" x 2½" rectangle between two 2½" x 5" rectangles; press. Make two. Sew these units to the top and bottom of the unit from step 2.

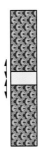 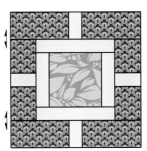

Make 2.

4 Repeat steps 1–3 to make a total of 35 blocks using the remaining fat-quarter pieces for 34 blocks and the red-print square and rectangles for one block.

Assembling the Quilt Top

1 Refer to the quilt assembly diagram below to arrange the blocks in seven horizontal rows of five blocks each, alternating the blocks with the cream 1½" x 10½" sashing rectangles. Sew the blocks and sashing rectangles in each row together. Press the seam allowances open.

2 Cut four cream 1½" x 42" strips in half crosswise. Sew each half-strip to one end of eight cream 1½" x 42" strips. Trim each of the resulting strips to 54½". Place one of these sashing strips between each of the rows and at the top and bottom of the rows. Sew the block rows and sashing strips together. Press the seam allowances open.

3 Sew two cream 1½" x 42" strips together end to end to make one long strip. Make two. Trim each of the resulting strips to 78½". Sew these strips to the sides of the quilt top. Press the seam allowances open.

4 Sew two red-print 4½" x 42" strips together end to end. Make four. From the pieced strips, cut two strips to the length of the quilt top. Sew the strips to the sides of the quilt top. Press the seam allowances toward the outer border. Trim the remaining two strips to the width of the quilt top. Sew these strips to the top and bottom of the quilt top. Press the seam allowances toward the outer border.

Finishing the Quilt

For detailed information on finishing techniques, including layering, basting, and quilting, go to ShopMartingale.com/HowtoQuilt for free downloadable instructions. Use the red 2½"-wide strips to bind the quilt.

Quilt assembly

Cayucos

Sometimes a good quilt design springs simply from working with your favorite fabrics and colors. This versatile pattern would be equally stunning made from all solids or with your favorite reproduction prints.

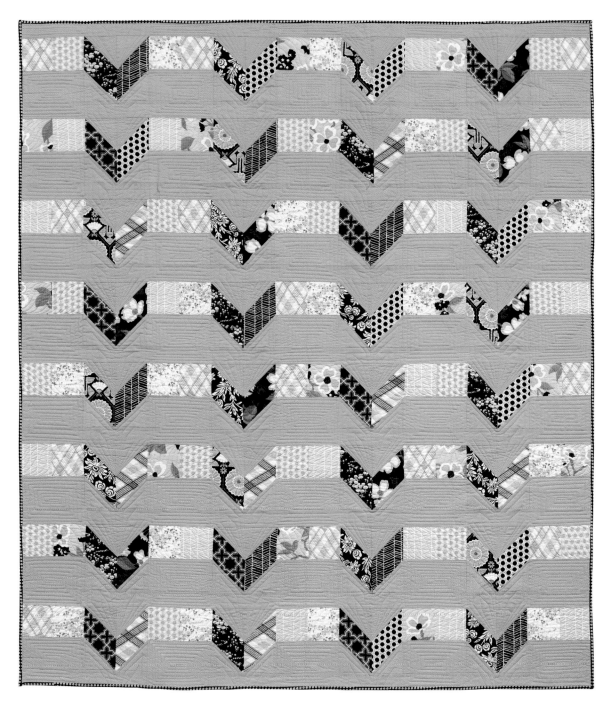

FINISHED QUILT: 72½" x 82½"
FINISHED BLOCK: 4" x 8"

Designed by John Q. Adams; pieced by Rebecca Makas; quilted by Angela Walters

Materials

Yardage is based on 42"-wide fabric. Fat quarters are 18" x 21".

5 yards of blue solid for blocks and sashing
13 fat quarters of assorted prints for blocks
⅔ yard of fabric for binding
5¼ yards of fabric for backing
80" x 90" piece of batting

Cutting

From the blue solid, cut:
26 strips, 4½" x 42"; cut into:
    128 squares, 4½" x 4½"
    40 rectangles, 4½" x 8½"
    18 strips, 2½" x 42"

From the assorted print fat quarters, cut a *total* of:
80 squares, 4½" x 4½"
64 rectangles, 4½" x 8½"*

From the binding fabric, cut:
7 strips, 2½" x 42"

*If you're using a directional fabric, take care to cut the rectangles so that they are oriented vertically.

Making the A Blocks

Lay out two print squares and one blue rectangle as shown. Join the squares and press the seam allowances toward the darker square. Sew the rectangle to the squares to complete the block. Press the seam allowances toward the blue rectangle. The block should measure 8½" x 8½". Make a total of 40 of block A.

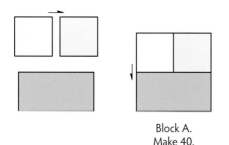

Block A.
Make 40.

Making the B Blocks

1 Draw a diagonal line from corner to corner on the wrong side of each blue square. Place a marked square on one end of print rectangle, right sides together, as shown. Sew on the marked line. Trim the excess corner fabric, leaving a ¼" seam allowance, and press the resulting triangle open.

2 Place a marked square on the diagonally opposite end of the unit from step 1 as shown. Sew on the marked line. Trim the excess corner fabric, leaving a ¼" seam allowance, and press the resulting triangle open. Make 32 units.

Make 32.

3 Repeat steps 1 and 2 to make a mirror-image unit as shown. Make 32 units.

Make 32.

Alternating Seams

Each sashing strip will have a vertical seam where the two pieces were joined. Rotate the strip on every other row to alternate the placement of the joining seams.

4 Join one unit from step 2 and one unit from step 3 as shown to complete the block. The block should measure 8½" x 8½". Press the seam allowances open. Make a total of 32 of block B.

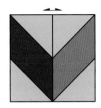

Block B.
Make 32.

Assembling the Quilt Top

1 To make the sashing strips, join two 2½"-wide blue strips end to end to make a long strip. Press the seam allowances open. Make a total of nine long strips. Trim each strip to measure 72½" long.

2 Sew five A blocks and four B blocks together as shown in the quilt assembly diagram below to make a block row. Press the seam allowances in one direction. The row should measure 72½" long. Make eight rows.

3 Sew the block rows and long sashing strips together, alternating them as shown. Press the seam allowances toward the sashing strips. Trim and square up the quilt top as needed.

Finishing the Quilt

For detailed information on finishing techniques, including layering, basting, and quilting, go to ShopMartingale.com/HowtoQuilt for free downloadable instructions. Use the 2½"-wide strips to bind the quilt.

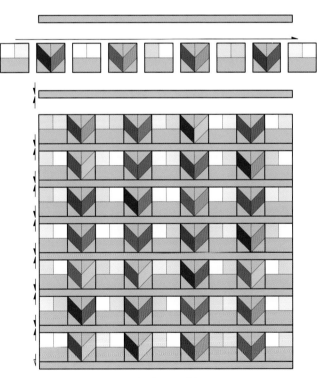

Quilt assembly

Fruit Basket

Full of juicy, zesty colors, this fun and easy quilt is like a basket overflowing with mouthwatering delights. Use a fruity print, or any other great focus fabric, and let it spill all over the place, too!

FINISHED QUILT: 59¼" x 84¾"

FINISHED BLOCK: 12" x 12"

Designed and made by Cheryl Brown

Materials

Yardage is based on 42"-wide fabric. Fat quarters are 18" x 21".

1⅔ yards of bright fruit-themed print for block centers and outer borders

⅞ yard of bright-green fabric for sashing

⅝ yard of bright-pink fabric for blocks

⅝ yard of bright-orange fabric for blocks

12 fat quarters of assorted bright prints (yellow, pink, red, and green) for blocks

⅝ yard of orange stripe for binding

5½ yards of fabric for backing

64" x 89" piece of batting

Cutting

From the fruit-themed print, cut:

4 strips, 6½" x 42"; crosscut into 24 squares, 6½" x 6½"

7 strips, 4" x 42"

From the assorted bright fat quarters, cut a *total* of:

120 strips, 1½" x 21"

From the bright-pink fabric, cut:

5 strips, 3½" x 42"; crosscut into 48 squares, 3½" x 3½"

From the bright-orange fabric, cut:

5 strips, 3½" x 42"; crosscut into 48 squares, 3½" x 3½"

From the bright-green fabric, cut:

20 strips, 1¼" x 42"; crosscut *10 of the strips* into 28 strips, 1¼" x 12½"

From the orange stripe, cut:

8 strips, 2¼" x 42"

Making the Blocks

1 Randomly sew together six 1½"-wide assorted bright strips along their long edges to make a strip set; press. Make 20. Crosscut the strip sets into 96 segments, 3½" wide.

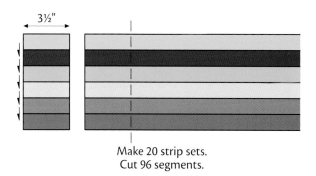

Make 20 strip sets.
Cut 96 segments.

2 Sew a segment from step 1 to each side of a 6½" square as shown to make a center unit; press. Make 24 center units.

Make 24.

3 Sew a pink square to each end of a segment from step 1 as shown to make 24 pink units; press. Sew an orange square to each end of a segment from step 1 to make 24 orange units; press.

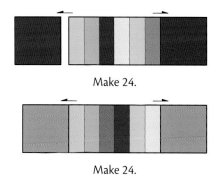

Make 24.

Make 24.

4 Sew pink units to the top and bottom of 12 of the center units from step 2 as shown; press. Make 12 pink blocks.

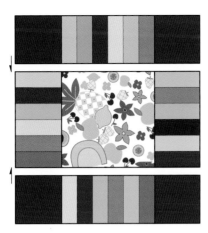

Pink block.
Make 12.

5 Sew orange units to the top and bottom of each remaining center unit as shown; press. Make 12 orange blocks.

Orange block.
Make 12.

Assembling the Quilt Top

1 Arrange seven 1¼" x 12½" green sashing strips, three pink blocks, and three orange blocks, alternating the blocks as shown. Sew the blocks and sashing strips together to make a row; press. Make four rows.

Make 4.

2 Measure the length of each of the four block rows. If they differ, calculate the average and consider this the length. Sew two 1¼"-wide green strips together end to end to make a long sashing strip. Make five. Trim each long strip to the correct length.

3 Sew the block rows and the five long sashing strips together, alternating them as shown in the quilt assembly diagram. Press the seam allowances toward the sashing strips.

4 Sew the 4"-wide fruit-print strips together end to end to make one long strip. Measure, cut, and sew the strips to the sides and then the top and bottom of the quilt for the outer border.

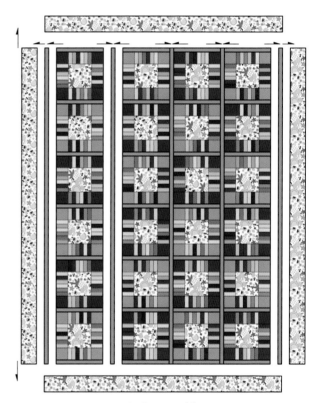

Quilt assembly

Finishing the Quilt

For detailed information on finishing techniques, including layering, basting, and quilting, go to ShopMartingale.com/HowtoQuilt for free downloadable instructions. Use the orange-striped 2¼"-wide strips to bind the quilt.

In Formation

Begin by selecting two complementary colorways. Use those as your launching point for gathering a pleasing gradation of solid-color fabrics, and then watch this bold quilt take flight.

FINISHED QUILT: 45½" x 45½"

FINISHED BLOCK: 4½" x 9"

Designed and made by Julie Herman

Materials

Yardage is based on 42"-wide fabric. Fat quarters are 18" x 21".

2⅓ yards of off-white solid for background and binding

6 fat quarters of assorted light-peach to dark-tan solids for blocks

4 fat quarters of assorted light- to medium-green solids for blocks

3⅛ yards of fabric for backing

51" x 51" piece of batting

Cutting

From *each* of the 10 solid fat quarters, cut:

5 rectangles, 5" x 9½", using cutting diagram below (50 total)

From the off-white solid, cut:

13 strips, 5" x 42"; crosscut into 100 squares, 5" x 5"

5 strips, 2" x 42"

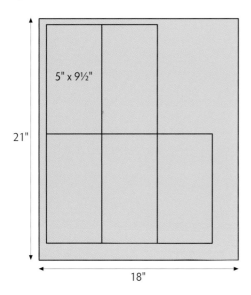

Making the Blocks

1 Draw a diagonal line on the wrong side of each off-white square. Place a marked square on one end of a solid-colored rectangle, right sides together, and sew along the marked line as shown. Trim away the corner fabric, leaving a ¼" seam allowance. Press the seam allowances open.

 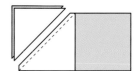

2 Place a second marked square on the opposite end of the rectangle, right sides together. Sew along the marked line and trim as before. Press the seam allowances open. Make a total of 50 Flying Geese blocks.

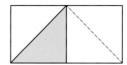 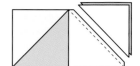

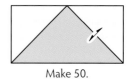

Make 50.

Assembling the Quilt Top

1 Lay out the Flying Geese blocks in five vertical rows of 10 blocks each as shown. Follow the diagram carefully to ensure proper color placement and to orient the blocks correctly. Sew the blocks into vertical rows; press the seam allowances open.

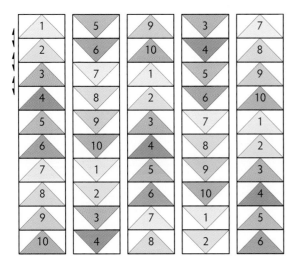

2 Sew the rows together and press the seam allowances open.

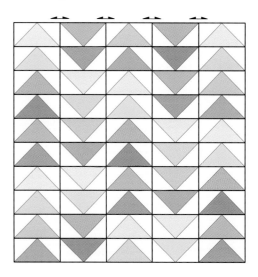

Finishing the Quilt

For detailed information on finishing techniques, including layering, basting, and quilting, go to ShopMartingale.com/HowtoQuilt for free downloadable instructions. Use the off-white 2¼"-wide strips to bind the quilt.

X Marks the Spot

Sometimes it's fun to give up control and let randomness rule the day. Here, Elizabeth placed blocks haphazardly rather than positioning each color carefully. If loss of control makes you fret, you could stagger your blocks by color to create a stunning visual flow.

FINISHED QUILT: 52½" x 63"

FINISHED BLOCK: 10½" x 10½"

Designed and made by Elizabeth Dackson

Materials

Yardage is based on 42"-wide fabric. Fat quarters are 18" x 21".

15 fat quarters of assorted prints for blocks
2 yards of white solid for blocks
⅝ yard of navy solid for binding
3½ yards of fabric for backing
61" x 71" piece of batting

Cutting

From *each* of the assorted print fat quarters, cut:
2 squares, 3" x 3" (30 total)
8 rectangles, 3" x 5½" (120 total)
4 squares, 2¾" x 2¾"; cut the squares in half diagonally to yield 8 triangles (120 total)

From the white solid, cut:
30 squares, 8⅜" x 8⅜"; cut the squares into quarters diagonally to yield 120 triangles

From the navy solid, cut:
6 strips, 2½" x 42"

Piecing the Blocks

Use a scant ¼" seam allowance and press seam allowances open after sewing each seam.

1   Pair a print triangle with a matching 3" x 5½" rectangle. With right sides together, align the long edge of the triangle with a short end of the rectangle, centering the rectangle on the triangle. Sew the pieces together and press. Make four matching units.

Make 4.

2   Sew a white triangle to one side of a unit from step 1, aligning the short edge of the triangle with the long edge of the rectangle. Press and repeat for the opposite side of the unit. Make two.

 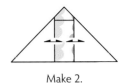

Make 2.

3   Sew the remaining two units from step 1 to opposite sides of a contrasting print 3" square as shown to make the block center.

4   Sew a unit from step 2 to each side of the center unit. Press carefully and measure your block. It should measure 11" x 11". Trim as needed to square up the block.

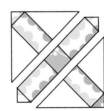 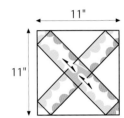

11"

11"

5   Repeat steps 1–4 to make a total of 30 blocks.

Assembling the Quilt Top

1 Arrange the blocks into six rows of five blocks each.

2 Once you're happy with the layout, sew the blocks in each row together. Press the seam allowances open as you go. Sew the rows together in pairs, and then sew the pairs together. Press.

Finishing the Quilt

For detailed information on finishing techniques, including layering, basting, and quilting, go to ShopMartingale.com/HowtoQuilt for free downloadable instructions. Use the navy 2½"-wide strips to bind the quilt.

Quilt assembly

The Big Book of Fat-Quarter Quilts

Hidden Baskets

Can you see the baskets? Look again . . . the bottoms of the baskets are white. This ultrasimple block creates a complicated-seeming quilt and looks great made with any style of fabric.

FINISHED QUILT: 50½" x 63"
FINISHED BLOCK: 12½" x 12½"

Designed and pieced by Vickie Eapen; machine quilted by Al Kuthe

Materials

Yardage is based on 42"-wide fabric. Fat quarters are 18" x 21".

10 fat quarters of assorted prints for blocks*
1½ yards of white solid for blocks
½ yard of mint-green print for binding
3½ yards of fabric for backing
57" x 69" piece of batting

Vickie used 13 fat quarters for a bit more scrappiness, but 10 fat quarters is sufficient.

Cutting

If you're using fat quarters for the assorted prints, refer to the cutting diagram at right to make the best use of your fabric.

From *each* of the assorted prints, cut:

5 squares, 3½" x 3½" (50 total)
2 rectangles, 3" x 10½" (20 total)
2 rectangles, 3" x 8" (20 total)
4 rectangles, 3" x 5½" (40 total)
6 squares, 3" x 3" (60 total)

From the white solid, cut:

4 strips, 3" x 42"; crosscut into 40 squares, 3" x 3"
6 strips, 3" x 42"; crosscut into 40 rectangles, 3" x 5½"
5 strips, 3½" x 42"; crosscut into 50 squares, 3½" x 3½"

From the mint-green print, cut:

6 strips, 2¼" x 42"

Making the Blocks

1 Draw a line from corner to corner on the wrong side of the white 3½" squares. Layer each marked square on a print 3½" square, right sides together. Sew ¼" from both sides of the drawn line. Cut on the drawn line to yield two half-square-triangle units. Make two half-square-triangle units from each pair (10 sets of 10 matching units). Press the seam allowances toward the print triangles. Trim each unit to 3" x 3".

Make 10 sets of 10.

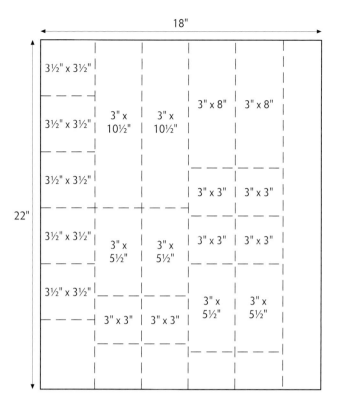

2 Using pieces from the same print, arrange five half-square-triangle units from step 1, one print 3" x 10½" rectangle, one print 3" x 8" rectangle, two print 3" x 5½" rectangles, three print 3" squares, two white 3" x 5½" rectangles, and two white 3" squares into five horizontal rows as shown. Sew the pieces in each row together. Press the seam allowances in the directions indicated. Sew the rows together. Do not press the seam allowances yet.

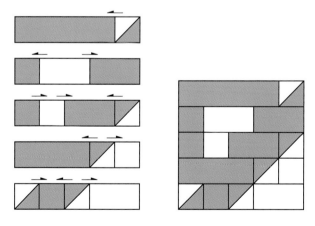

3 Repeat step 2 to make a total of 20 blocks.

Assembling the Quilt Top

1 Arrange the blocks into five horizontal rows of four blocks each. When you're satisfied with the block placement, press the block seam allowances so that they alternate directions from block to block in each row.

2 Sew the blocks in each row together. Press the seam allowances in alternate directions from row to row. Sew the rows together. Press the seam allowances in one direction.

Finishing the Quilt

For detailed information on finishing techniques, including layering, basting, and quilting, go to ShopMartingale.com/HowtoQuilt for free downloadable instructions. Use the mint-green 2¼"-wide strips to bind the quilt.

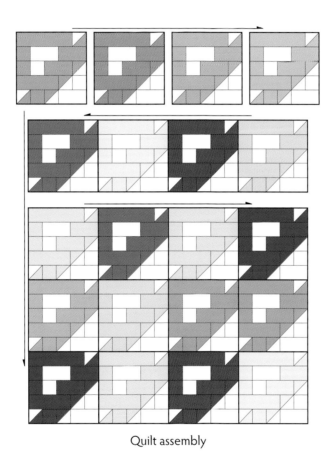

Quilt assembly

Resting Line

Architects and industrial designers are fond of saying, "form follows function." That was the watchword for the creation of this quilt. Design something neutral, something colorful, something that will coordinate with whatever sheets are being used. And, last but not least, make it big enough to cover a queen-size bed!

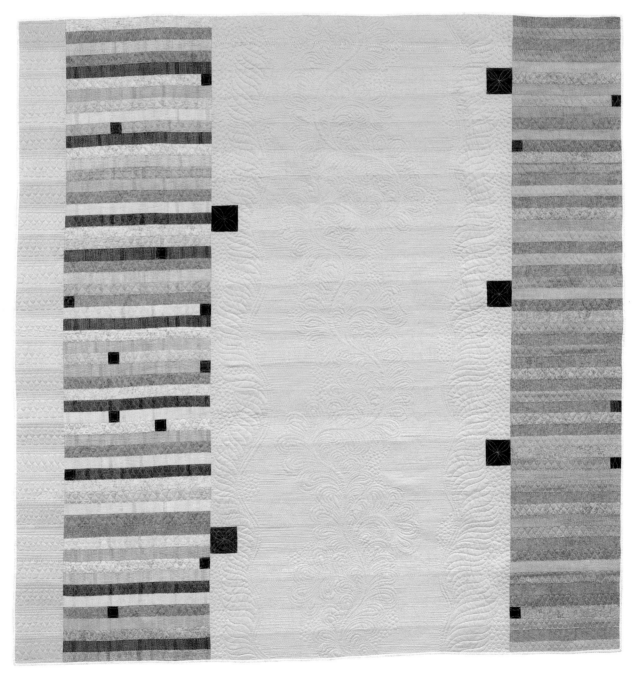

FINISHED QUILT: 83½" x 84½"

Designed and made by Natalie Barnes; quilted by Angela Walters

Materials

Yardage is based on 42"-wide fabric. Fat quarters are 18" x 21".

1⅓ yards *each* of 3 light-tan fabrics for background*

7 fat quarters of assorted bright prints (yellow, pink, blue, orange, red, purple, green) for left column

6 fat quarters of assorted muted prints (green, purple, pink, orange, blue, khaki) for right column

1 fat quarter of dark fabric for squares

¾ yard of fabric for binding

7⅝ yards of fabric for backing

90" x 91" piece of batting

*If any of your fabrics are less than 42" wide after removing the selvages, you can still use them. Simply make the middle section (C) slightly narrower.

Cutting

From *each* of the 3 light-tan fabrics, cut:

10 strips, 4" x 42" (30 total; 1 is extra). From the strips, crosscut:
  5 strips into 5 strips, 4" x 38½"
  5 strips into 24 rectangles, 4" x 7½"

From *each* of the 7 fat quarters for the left column, cut:

8 strips, 2" x 21" (56 total). From the strips, crosscut:
  6 strips into 6 strips, 2" x 13¼", and 6 rectangles, 2" x 6¾"
  6 strips into 6 strips, 2" x 19½"

From *each* of the 6 fat quarters for the right column, cut:

1 strip, 2" x 21" (6 total)

From the *remainder* of the 6 fat quarters, cut a total of:

53 strips, 2" x 14½" (2 are extra)*
7 strips, 2" x 13" (2 are extra)*

From the dark fat quarter, cut:

1 strip, 4" x 21", crosscut into 5 squares, 4" x 4"
2 strips, 2" x 21"; crosscut into 17 squares, 2" x 2"

From the binding fabric, cut:

9 strips, 2¼" x 42"

*Cut these strips across the 16" length that remains after cutting the 2" x 21" strips.

Making the Blocks

1 Sew a dark 2" square to a 2" x 19½" strip to form a 2" x 21" strip. Press the seam allowances toward the square. Make six.

Make 6.

2 Sew a dark 2" square, a 2" x 13¼" strip, and a 2" x 6¾" rectangle together as shown to form a 2" x 21" strip. Press the seam allowances toward the square. Make six.

Make 6.

3 Sew one strip from step 1 and one strip from step 2 together with three 2" x 21" strips as shown to make a block. Press the seam allowances in one direction. Make six of these blocks for section B.

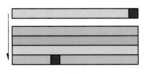

Make 6.

4 Sew a dark 4" square to a neutral 4" x 38½" strip. Press the seam allowances toward the dark square. Make five for section C.

Make 5.

5 Sew a dark 2" square to a 2" x 13" strip to form a 2" x 14½" strip. Press the seam allowances toward the square. Make five for section D.

Make 5.

Assembling the Quilt Top

Refer to the assembly diagram below for these steps.

1 Sew 24 tan 4" x 7½" rectangles together to make section A. Press the seam allowances toward what will be the bottom of the column.

2 To make section B, select 26 strips, 2" x 21", and sew them together randomly with the blocks from step 3 of "Making the Blocks." Mix in a few of the strips cut from the right-column fabrics. Press the seam allowances toward the top.

3 Sew the five strips from step 4 of "Making the Blocks" together randomly with 19 tan 4" x 42" strips to make section C. Press the seam allowances downward.

4 To make section D, select 51 strips, 2" x 14½", and sew them together randomly with the five units from step 5 of "Making the Blocks." Press the seam allowances upward.

Keep It Straight

While sewing long strips together, alternate the sewing direction from strip to strip. Pin along the length of the pieces you are sewing, matching the ends. This will ensure that the strips remain straight and square.

5 Sew sections A and B together and sections C and D together. Note that seven of the 1½"-wide strips will equal three of the 3½"-wide strips. Pin at these seams, and at the top and bottom of each section. You may need to re-press some of the seam allowances so they butt together. Remove pins as you sew the sections together. Press seam allowances toward section A and section C.

6 Pin section A/B to C/D. Place the bulk of the top in your lap. Begin sewing, removing pins as you stitch. As you sew, place the quilt top on your sewing table, to the left of your machine, so the weight of the top does not pull on your seam as you sew the final pieces together. Press the seam allowances toward section C.

Finishing the Quilt

For detailed information on finishing techniques, including layering, basting, and quilting, go to ShopMartingale.com/HowtoQuilt for free downloadable instructions. Use the 2¼"-wide strips to bind the quilt.

Section A	Section B	Section C	Section D

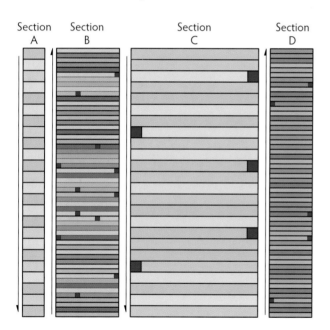

Broken V

Half-square triangles are the building blocks of many fabulous quilts, and they're fun to quilt too! A total of 168 half-square-triangle units are joined in matching pairs to create Double Diamond blocks that form an asymmetrical design. Play around with the basic unit and see what other designs you can create!

FINISHED QUILT: 60½" x 70½"
FINISHED BLOCK: 10" x 10"
Designed and made by Christa Watson

Materials

Yardage is based on 42"-wide fabric. Fat quarters are 18" x 21".

14 fat quarters of assorted solids for blocks
3 yards of gray solid for blocks
⅝ yard of light-purple solid for binding
4 yards of fabric for backing
66" x 76" piece of batting

Cutting

From *each* of the assorted solid fat quarters, cut:
2 strips, 6" x 21"; crosscut into 6 squares, 6" x 6"
   (84 total)

From the gray solid, cut:
14 strips, 6" x 42"; crosscut into 84 squares, 6" x 6"

From the light-purple solid, cut:
7 strips, 2¼" x 42"

Piecing the Blocks

1 Mark a diagonal line from corner to corner on the wrong side of each gray square.

2 With right sides together, lay a marked gray square over a colored square. Sew ¼" from both sides of the marked line. Cut the squares apart on the drawn line to make two half-square-triangle units. Repeat with the remaining gray and solid squares to make a total of 168 half-square-triangle units. Do not press the seam allowances yet. Keep pairs of matching units together.

3 Press the seam allowances of each unit open, and then trim each unit to 5½" x 5½", keeping the seamline centered diagonally.

On the Fast Track

Chain sew the units, sewing ¼" to the right of the marked line of each unit first. Remove the sewn units from the machine, but don't cut the threads between the units. Turn them around and feed the chain through your machine so you are again sewing ¼" to the right of the marked line of each unit. Remove the units from the machine and clip the threads between each unit.

4 Join two matching half-square-triangle units as shown to make unit A. Repeat to make a total of 28. Press the seam allowances open.

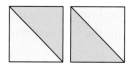 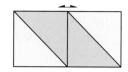

Unit A.
Make 28.

5 Join two matching half-square-triangle units as shown to make unit B. Repeat to make a total of 56. Press the seam allowances open.

  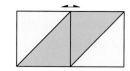

Unit B.
Make 56.

6 Join two A units as shown to make block A. Repeat to make a total of 14. Press the seam allowances open.

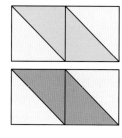 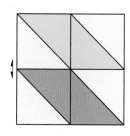

Block A.
Make 14.

7 Join two B units as shown to make block B. Repeat to make a total of 28. Press the seam allowances open.

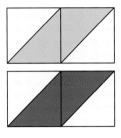 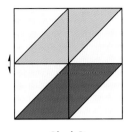

Block B.
Make 28.

Assembling the Quilt Top

1 Refer to the quilt assembly diagram below to lay out the blocks in six vertical rows of seven blocks each, using the A blocks in the first two rows and the B blocks in the remaining rows.

2 Sew the blocks in each row together. Press the seam allowances open. Join the rows to complete the quilt top. Press the seam allowances open.

3 Stitch ⅛" from the edges on all four sides to prevent the edge seams from splitting open.

Finishing the Quilt

For detailed information on finishing techniques, including layering, basting, and quilting, go to ShopMartingale.com/HowtoQuilt for free downloadable instructions. Use the light-purple 2¼"-wide strips to bind the quilt.

Quilt assembly

Don's Goose

Sometimes a quilt perfectly captures the spirit of a loved one, such as this design made in honor of Jeanne's dad, Don. For Jeanne and her family, the warm colors and flying geese evoke memories of a wonderful man whose life was full of friends, family, and love.

FINISHED QUILT: 56" x 72"
FINISHED BLOCK: 8" x 8"

Designed and pieced by Jeanne Large and Shelley Wicks; machine quilted by Wendy Findlay

Materials

Yardage is based on 42"-wide fabric. Fat quarters are 18" x 21".

12 fat quarters of assorted beige fabrics for blocks
9 fat quarters of assorted brown and gold fabrics for blocks
6 fat quarters of assorted red fabrics for blocks
1½ yards of dark brown fabric for border and binding
3⅝ yards of fabric for backing
64" x 80" piece of batting

Cutting

Use a variety of the fat quarters for each cut you make to ensure a scrappy look in your finished quilt.

From the 12 assorted beige fat quarters, cut a *total* of:

48 strips, 2¾" x 20"; crosscut each strip into 6 squares, 2¾" x 2¾" (288 total)
6 strips, 4" x 20"; crosscut each strip into 4 squares, 4" x 4". Cut the squares in half diagonally to yield 2 triangles (48 total).

From the 15 assorted red, brown and gold fat quarters, cut a *total* of:

24 strips, 5" x 20"; crosscut each strip into 6 rectangles, 2¾" x 5" (144 total)
16 strips, 5⅝" x 20"; crosscut each strip into 3 squares, 5⅝" x 5⅝" (48 total). Cut the squares in half diagonally to yield 2 triangles (96 total).
6 strips, 4" x 20"; crosscut each strip into 4 squares, 4" x 4". Cut the squares in half diagonally to yield 2 triangles (48 total).

From the dark-brown fabric for border and binding, cut:

7 strips, 4½" x 42"
7 strips, 2½" x 42"

Piecing the Blocks

1 Lightly draw a diagonal line on the wrong side of each beige 2¾" square.

2 Layer one of the marked squares on one end of a 2¾" x 5" rectangle as shown. Sew from corner to corner directly on the drawn line. Fold the top corner back and align it with the corner of the rectangle beneath it; press. Trim away the excess layers of fabric beneath the top triangle, leaving a ¼" seam allowance. Repeat to make a total of 144 units.

In the same manner, layer a beige square on the opposite end of the rectangle as shown and stitch, press, and trim to make a flying-geese unit. Designers Jeanne and Shelley like the look of mostly matching beige fabrics on each side of a flying-geese center, plus a couple of flying geese with a mismatched pair of beige prints. Make 144.

Make 144.

3 Join three flying-geese units along their long sides as shown. Press the seam allowances to one side. Repeat for a total of 48 units.

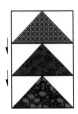

Make 48.

4 Sew a 5⅝" triangle to each long side of each unit from step 3. The end points of the triangles will be slightly longer than the flying-geese units. Evenly distribute the excess triangle fabric at each end of the flying-geese units as shown. Press the seam allowances toward the triangles just added.

5 Sew a red, brown, or gold 4" triangle to the top of each unit from step 4 and a beige 4" triangle to the bottom of each unit, adjusting the end points as you did in step 4. Press the seam allowances toward the triangles just added. Trim each block to measure 8½" x 8½".

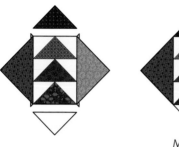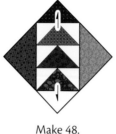

Make 48.

Assembling the Quilt Top

1 Arrange the blocks into eight rows of six blocks each, rotating the blocks to form the design as shown.

2 Sew the blocks together into rows; press the seam allowances open. Sew the rows together; press the seam allowances open.

Help for Crowded Corners

When multiple points come together at a corner, it's beneficial to press the seam allowances open to prevent large lumps from forming at the corners.

Adding the Borders

1 Sew the dark-brown 4½" x 42" strips together end to end to make one long continuous strip. From this strip, cut two strips, 56½" long, and two strips, 64½" long.

2 Sew the 64½"-long strips to the sides of the quilt; press. Sew the 56½"-long strips to the top and bottom of the quilt; press.

Finishing the Quilt

For detailed information on finishing techniques, including layering, basting, and quilting, go to ShopMartingale.com/HowtoQuilt for free downloadable instructions. Use the dark-brown 2½"-wide strips to bind the quilt.

Annabelle

Miniature stars are added to some of the blocks and scattered throughout the layout, injecting extra charm and keeping the quilt from being too simple. Using a mix of light-value and tone-on-tone prints for the background, rather than just one light fabric, also gives the design a personality boost.

FINISHED QUILT: 96½" x 96½"

FINISHED BLOCK: 12" x 12"

Designed and made by Rebecca Silbaugh

Materials

Yardage is based on 42"-wide fabric. Fat quarters are 18" x 21".

26 fat quarters of assorted light prints for blocks
5⅔ yards of red print for blocks
⅞ yard of fabric for binding
9 yards of fabric for backing
104" x 104" piece of batting

Cutting

From *each* of 13 light fat quarters, cut:
3 strips, 5" x 21"; crosscut into:
    10 squares, 5" x 5" (130 total; 10 are extra)
    1 square, 4½" x 4½" (13 total)

From *each* of the remaining 13 light fat quarters, cut:
2 strips, 5" x 21"; crosscut into 8 squares, 5" x 5"
    (104 total)
1 strip, 4½" x 21"; crosscut into 4 squares, 4½" x 4½"
    (52 total; 1 is extra)
1 strip, 2" x 21"; crosscut into 8 squares, 2" x 2"
    (104 total)

From the red print, cut:
28 strips, 5" x 42"; crosscut into 224 squares, 5" x 5"
5 strips, 4½" x 42"; crosscut into 38 squares,
    4½" x 4½"
2 strips, 2½" x 42"; crosscut into 26 squares,
    2½" x 2½"
6 strips, 2" x 42"; crosscut into 104 squares, 2" x 2"
4 strips, 1½" x 42"; crosscut into 104 squares,
    1½" x 1½"

From the binding fabric, cut:
10 strips, 2¼" x 42"

Making the Blocks

1. Mark a diagonal line from corner to corner on the wrong side of each light 2" square. Pair each marked light square right sides together with a red 2" square. Sew ¼" from each side of the drawn line. Cut the squares apart on the drawn line, and press the seam allowances open. Make 208 half-square-triangle units. Square up each unit to 1½" x 1½".

Make 208.

2. Randomly select two half-square-triangle units from step 1 and sew them together to resemble a flying-geese unit. Press the seam allowances open. Make 104 units.

Make 104.

3. Lay out four units from step 2, four red 1½" squares, and one red 2½" square in three rows as shown. Join the pieces in rows and then join the rows to make a Star block. Press the seam allowances as indicated. Make 26 blocks.

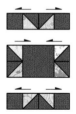

Make 26.

4. Mark a diagonal line from corner to corner on the wrong side of each light 5" square. Randomly pair each marked square right sides together with a red 5" square and stitch ¼" from each side of the drawn line. Cut the squares apart on the drawn line. Press the seam allowances open. Make 448 half-square-triangle units. Square up each unit to measure 4½" x 4½".

Make 448.

5 Lay out one Star block, seven half-square-triangle units from step 4, and one light 4½" square in three rows as shown. Sew the pieces together in rows. Press the seam allowances in opposite directions from row to row. Sew the rows together. Press the seam allowances open. Make 26 blocks.

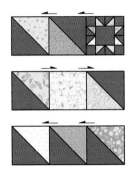 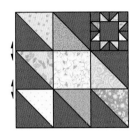

Make 26.

6 For the remaining blocks, lay out one red 4½" square, seven half-square-triangle units from step 4, and one light 4½" square in three rows as shown. Sew the pieces together in rows. Press the seam allowances in opposite directions from row to row. Sew the rows together. Press the seam allowances open. Make 38 blocks.

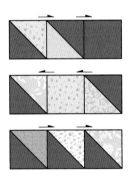 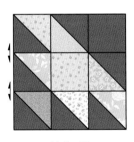

Make 38.

Assembling the Quilt Top

1 Lay out the blocks in eight rows of eight blocks each, randomly mixing in the Star blocks.

2 Sew the blocks together in rows. Press the seam allowances in opposite directions from row to row. Sew the rows together. Press the seam allowances in one direction.

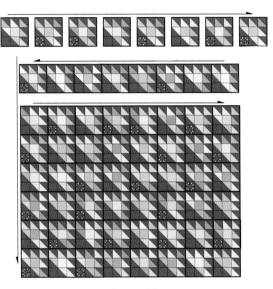

Quilt assembly

Finishing the Quilt

For detailed information on finishing techniques, including layering, basting, and quilting, go to ShopMartingale.com/HowtoQuilt for free downloadable instructions. Use the 2¼"-wide strips to bind the quilt.

Boo

Halloween presents a wonderful opportunity to pass on holiday traditions and create items to delight kids—like this spook-tacularly fun quilt!

FINISHED QUILT: 36½" x 47½"

FINISHED BLOCK: 5" x 9"

Designed and made by Barbara Brandeburg

Materials

Yardage is based on 42"-wide fabric. Fat quarters are 18" x 21".

1⅝ yards of black fabric for blocks, outer border, and binding

6 fat quarters of assorted green fabrics for block backgrounds and inner border

1 fat quarter of white fabric for ghosts and candy corn

Large scraps of 2 orange fabrics for pumpkins, candy corn, and cat facial details

Scraps of 2 yellow fabrics for candy corn and pumpkin stems

Scrap of light green for witch facial details

Scrap of black solid for pumpkin and ghost facial details

1⅝ yards of fabric for backing

41" x 52" piece of batting

⅜ yard of fusible web

Cutting

Store the pieces for each block in a plastic bag labeled with the block name. Patterns for the witch hat and witch hat background are on page 193.

From the green fat quarter for the Candy Corn block backgrounds, cut:
8 rectangles, 1½" x 7½"
8 rectangles, 1½" x 5½"

From the green fat quarter for the Pumpkin block backgrounds, cut:
8 rectangles, 1½" x 8"
8 rectangles, 1½" x 1¾"
4 rectangles, 2" x 5½"
4 rectangles, 1" x 3½"

From the green fat quarter for the Ghost block backgrounds, cut:
4 rectangles, 2" x 5½"
8 squares, 2" x 2"
8 rectangles, 1¼" x 6½"
4 rectangles, 1½" x 2½"
4 squares, 1" x 1"

From the green fat quarter for the Cat block backgrounds, cut:
4 rectangles, 2" x 3½"
4 rectangles, 1½" x 8½"
4 rectangles, 1½" x 8"
4 rectangles, 1½" x 5½"

From the green fat quarter for the Witch block backgrounds, cut:
4 witch hat backgrounds
4 witch hat backgrounds reversed
4 rectangles, 1½" x 5½"
8 rectangles, 1½" x 4½"
4 rectangles, 1" x 5½"

From the remainder of the assorted green fat quarters, cut a *total* of:
7 strips, 1½" x 20"

From the black fabric, cut:
5 strips, 2½" x 42"
2 strips, 5" x 38½"
2 strips, 5" x 36½"
4 rectangles, 3½" x 6½" (cat)
8 squares, 1½" x 1½" (cat)
4 rectangles, 1" x 4½" (cat)
4 rectangles, 3½" x 4½" (witch)
4 rectangles, 1" x 5½" (witch)
4 witch hats (witch)
8 rectangles, 1" x 1¼" (ghost)

From the white fat quarter, cut:
4 rectangles, 3½" x 6½" (ghosts)
4 rectangles, 2½" x 3½" (candy corn)

From the orange scraps, cut a *total* of:
4 squares, 3½" x 3½" (candy corn)
4 rectangles, 3½" x 6½" (pumpkins)

From the yellow scraps, cut a *total* of:
4 rectangles, 2½" x 3½" (candy corn)
4 rectangles, 1" x 1½" (pumpkin stems)

Making the Blocks

Press all seam allowances open as you add each piece.

Candy Corn Blocks

1 Sew a white 2½" x 3½" rectangle to the top of each orange 3½" square. Join a yellow 2½" x 3½" rectangle to the bottom of each orange square.

2 Sew green 1½" x 7½" rectangles to the sides, and then sew green 1½" x 5½" rectangles to the top and bottom of the units.

Pumpkin Blocks

1 Sew green 1½" x 1¾" rectangles to the sides of each yellow 1" x 1½" rectangle to make the stem unit. Sew a stem unit to the top of each orange 3½" x 6½" rectangle. Add a green 1" x 3½" rectangle to the top of the stem units.

2 Sew green 1½" x 8" rectangles to the sides, and then sew a green 2" x 5½" rectangle to the bottom of the units.

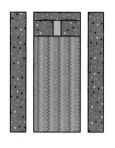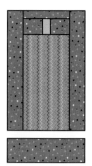

Ghost Blocks

1 Sew black 1" x 1¼" rectangles to the sides of each green 1" square. Sew a green 1½" x 2½" rectangle to the bottom of each unit. Sew green 2" squares to the sides to complete the shoe units.

2 Sew green 1½" x 6½" rectangles to the sides of each white 3½" x 6½" rectangle. To each of these units, join a shoe unit to the bottom and a green 2" x 5½" rectangle to the top.

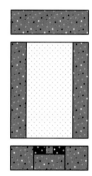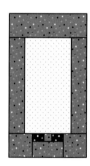

Cat Blocks

1. Place a black 1½" square on the lower-left corner of each green 2" x 3½" rectangle, right sides together. Sew diagonally across the square as shown. Cut off the outer triangle, leaving a ¼" seam allowance. Press the seam allowances open. Repeat on the lower-right corner of each rectangle to complete the ear units.

2. Sew an ear unit to the top of each black 3½" x 6½" rectangle. For each of these units, sew a green 1½" x 8" rectangle to the right side and a black 1" x 4½" rectangle to the bottom.

3. Sew a green 1½" x 8½" rectangle to the left side of each unit. Sew a green 1½" x 5½" rectangle to the bottom of each unit.

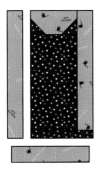 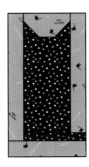

Witch Blocks

1. Sew a green witch background piece and a reversed witch background piece to the sides of each black hat piece.

2. Sew a black 1" x 5½" rectangle to the bottom of the hat. Join a green 1" x 5½" rectangle to the top to complete the hat units.

3. Sew green 1½" x 4½" rectangles to the sides of each black 3½" x 4½" rectangle. Sew a green 1½" x 5½" rectangle to the bottom of each unit. Join the hat units to the top of these units.

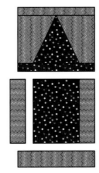 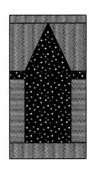

Adding the Appliqués

Using the patterns on page 193, prepare the shapes for your preferred method of appliqué. From the black scrap, make eight pumpkin eyes, four pumpkin noses, four pumpkin mouths, eight ghost eyes, and four ghost mouths. From the remaining orange fabric for the pumpkins, make eight cat eyes and four cat noses. From the scrap of light green, make eight witch eyes and four witch mouths. Refer to the photo on page 188 to position the shapes on the appropriate blocks. Secure in place. If desired, appliqué the edges of each piece with a narrow buttonhole stitch and coordinating thread.

Assembling the Quilt Top

1 Sew the blocks into four rows of five blocks each as shown. Sew the rows together.

2 Sew the assorted green 1½" x 20" strips together end to end in random order to make one long piece. From this piece, cut two border strips, 36½" long, and two border strips, 27½" long. Sew the 36½"-long strips to the sides of the quilt, and then sew the 27½"-long strips to the top and bottom of the quilt.

3 Sew the black 5" x 38½" strips to the sides of the quilt, and sew the black 5" x 36½" strips to the top and bottom of the quilt.

Quilt assembly

Finishing the Quilt

For detailed information on finishing techniques, including layering, basting, and quilting, go to ShopMartingale.com/HowtoQuilt for free downloadable instructions. Use the black 2½"-wide strips to bind the quilt.

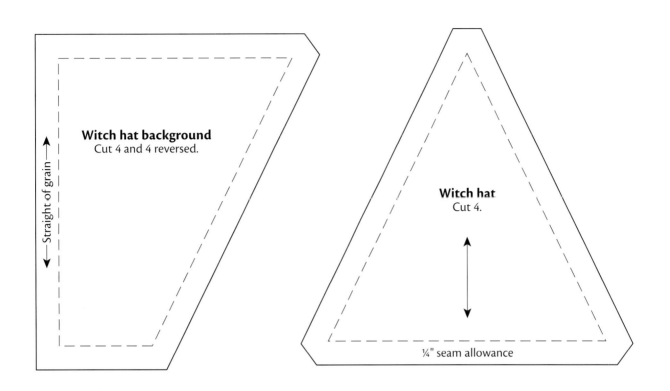

Witch hat background
Cut 4 and 4 reversed.

Straight of grain

Witch hat
Cut 4.

¼" seam allowance

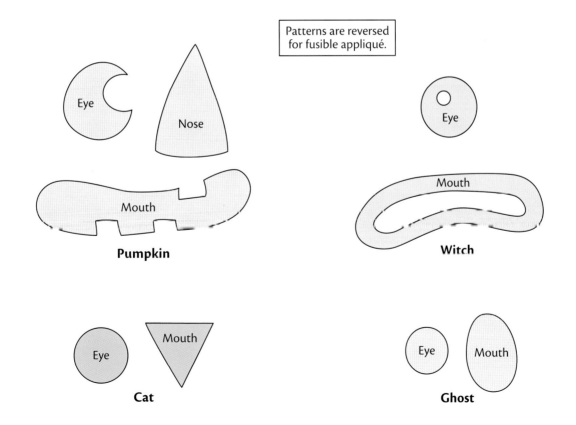

Patterns are reversed
for fusible appliqué.

Eye

Nose

Mouth

Pumpkin

Eye

Mouth

Witch

Eye

Mouth

Cat

Eye

Mouth

Ghost

On a Prairie Corner

Childhood memories are a fertile source of inspiration. Designers Jeanne and Shelley vividly recall drives in the country, watching the landscape change with the seasons. Their favorite was early fall with the crops slowly changing colors and the ditches full of wildflowers called brown-eyed Susans.

FINISHED QUILT: 48½" x 54½"

Designed and made by Jeanne Large and Shelley Wicks; machine quilted by Wendy Findlay

Materials

Yardage is based on 42"-wide fabric. Fat quarters are 18" x 21".

10 fat quarters of assorted medium-beige fabrics for blocks

1 yard of dark-beige print for blocks

⅞ yard of dark-brown print for inner border and binding

½ yard of green print for stem and leaf appliqués

¼ yard of brown print for basket and handle appliqués

1 fat quarter of dark-gold print for large sunflower appliqués

1 fat quarter of medium-gold print for large sunflower appliqués

1 fat quarter of dark-gold print for daisy appliqués

7" x 13" rectangle of black tone on tone for flower-center appliqués

3¼ yards of fabric for backing

57" x 63" piece of batting

1⅞ yards of 18"-wide lightweight paper-backed fusible web

Cutting

From the dark-beige print, cut:

5 strips, 3½" x 42"; crosscut into 45 squares, 3½" x 3½"

3 strips, 3½" x 42"; crosscut into 6 strips, 3½" x 21"

From *each* of the medium-beige fat quarters, cut:

1 strip, 6½" x 21" (10 total); crosscut into 5 rectangles, 3½" x 6½" (50 total; 5 are extra)

2 strips, 3½" x 21" (20 total; 1 is extra); crosscut *each* of 13 strips into 5 squares, 3½" x 3½" (65 total; 1 is extra)

From the dark-brown print, cut:

5 strips, 2" x 42"

6 strips, 2½" x 42"

Piecing the Panels

1 Sew a dark-beige 3½" square to one end of a medium-beige 3½" x 6½" rectangle. Press the seam allowances toward the square. Repeat to make a total of 45 units.

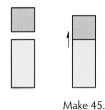

Make 45.

2 Sew 15 units from step 1 together along the long edges, alternating the direction of every other unit as shown. Press the seam allowances in one direction. The strip should measure 45½" long. Repeat to make a total of three wide panels.

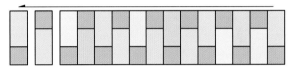

Make 3.

3 Join a medium-beige 3½" x 21" strip to a dark-beige 3½" x 21" strip along the long edges to make a strip set. Press the seam allowances toward the dark-beige strip. Repeat to make a total of six strip sets. Crosscut the strip sets into 30 segments, 3½" wide.

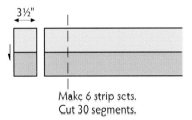

3½"

Make 6 strip sets.
Cut 30 segments.

4 Sew 15 segments from step 3 together along the long edges, alternating the direction of every other unit as shown. Press the seam allowances in the opposite direction of the wide panels. The strip should measure 45½" long. Repeat to make a total of two narrow panels.

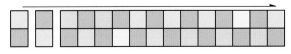

Make 2.

Assembling the Quilt Top

1 Refer to the quilt assembly diagram below to alternately arrange the wide and narrow panels in vertical rows, making sure the colors alternate across the quilt. Sew the panels together along the long edges. Press the seam allowances toward the narrow panels. The quilt center should now measure 39½" x 45½".

2 Sew the dark-brown 2" x 42" inner-border strips together end to end to make one long strip. From this strip, cut two strips, 2" x 45½", and two strips, 2" x 42½". Sew the 2" x 45½" strips to the sides of the quilt center. Press the seam allowances toward the inner border. Sew the 2" x 42½" strips to the top and bottom of the quilt center. Press the seam allowances toward the inner border.

Secure the Borders

It's helpful to backstitch at the beginning and end of the inner-border seams so that they hold securely while you add the appliqué.

3 Using the patterns on pages 197–201, prepare shapes for your preferred method of appliqué from the fabrics indicated. Prepare approximately 110" of bias stem from the green print.

4 Using the photo on page 194 as a guide, pin the bias stems in place. Arrange the appliqué shapes on the quilt top and secure in place. If desired, use matching thread to blanket-stitch around each shape by hand or machine.

5 Join 16 medium-beige squares end to end to make an outer-border strip. Press the seam allowances in one direction. Repeat to make a total of four strips. Sew border strips to opposite sides of the quilt top. Press the seam allowances toward the outer border. Sew the remaining border strips to the top and bottom of the quilt top. Press the seam allowances toward the outer border.

Finishing the Quilt

For detailed information on finishing techniques, including layering, basting, and quilting, go to ShopMartingale.com/HowtoQuilt for free downloadable instructions. Use the dark-brown 2½"-wide strips to bind the quilt.

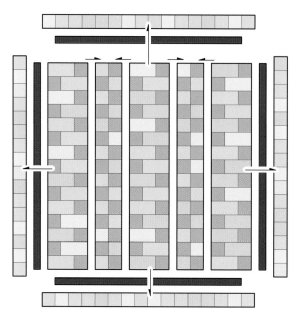

Quilt assembly

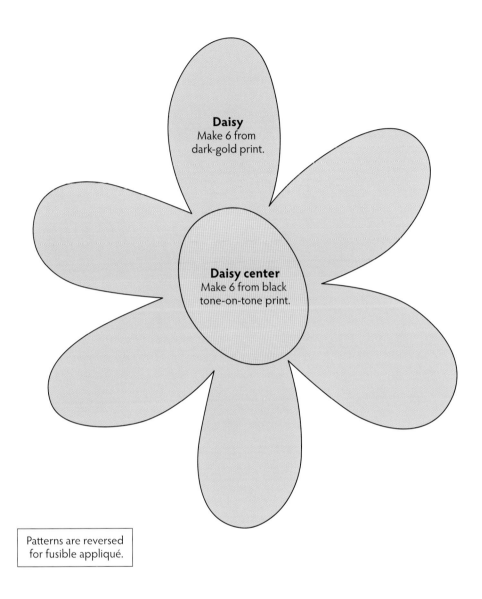

Daisy
Make 6 from
dark-gold print.

Daisy center
Make 6 from black
tone-on-tone print.

Patterns are reversed
for fusible appliqué.

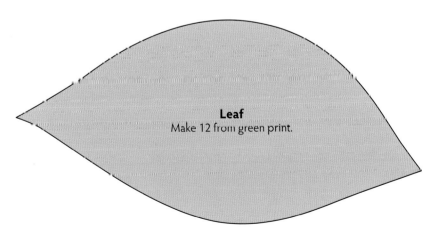

Leaf
Make 12 from green print.

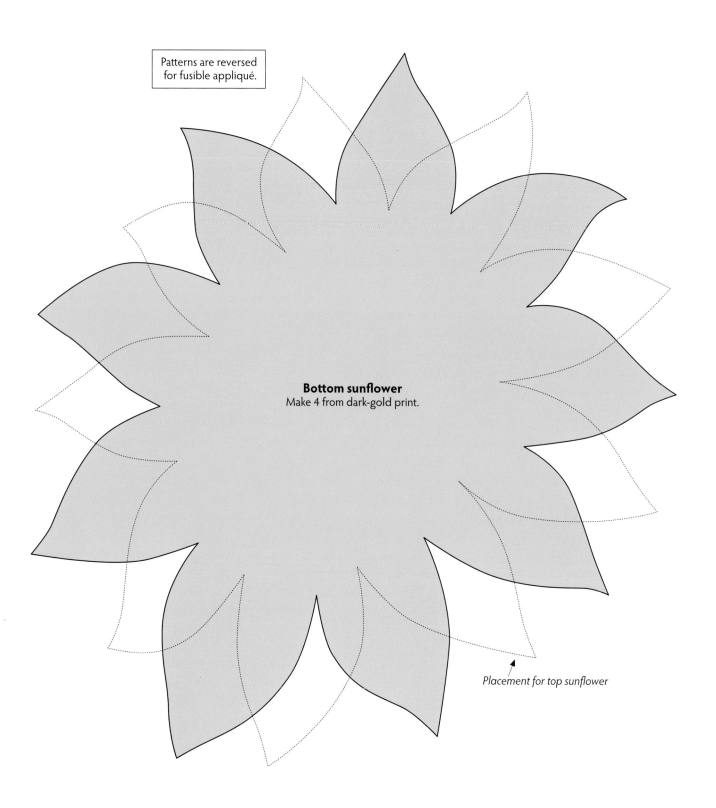

Patterns are reversed for fusible appliqué.

Bottom sunflower
Make 4 from dark-gold print.

Placement for top sunflower

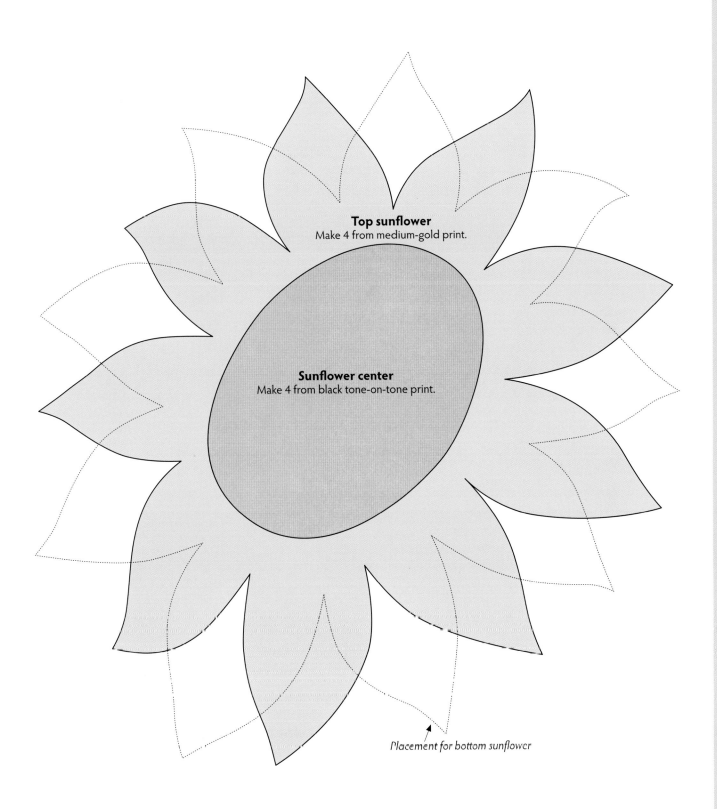

Top sunflower
Make 4 from medium-gold print.

Sunflower center
Make 4 from black tone-on-tone print.

Placement for bottom sunflower

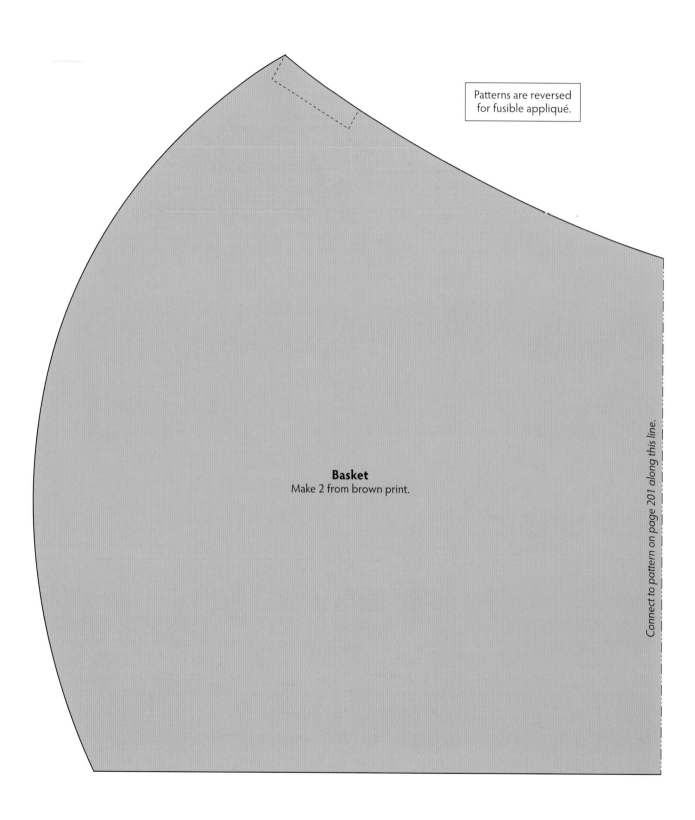

Patterns are reversed for fusible appliqué.

Basket
Make 2 from brown print.

Connect to pattern on page 201 along this line.

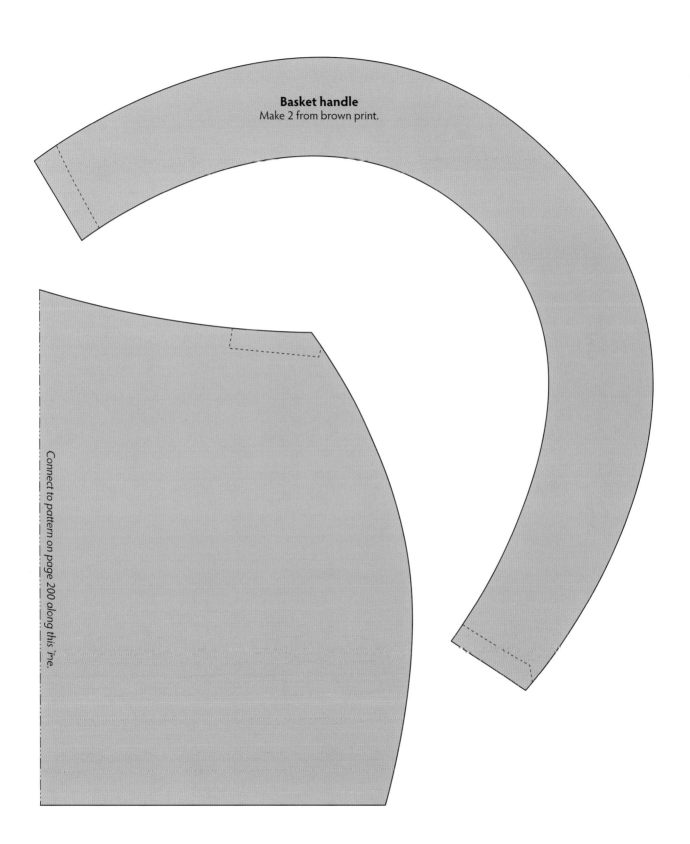

Basket handle
Make 2 from brown print.

Connect to pattern on page 200 along this line.

Spin Patch

Any quilt block can be supersized, so how about plumping up a pieced pinwheel? The blocks are a whopping 24"—you'll be pleased at how quickly this design comes together.

FINISHED QUILT: 65½" x 65½"

FINISHED BLOCK: 24" x 24"

Designed and pieced by Vickie Eapen; machine quilted by Al Kuthe

Materials

Yardage is based on 42"-wide fabric. Fat quarters are 18" x 21".

4 yards of coal solid for blocks, border, and binding
6 fat quarters of different cream prints for blocks
5 fat quarters of different red prints for blocks
4 fat quarters of different navy prints for blocks
3 fat quarters of different green prints for blocks
2 fat quarters of different yellow prints for blocks
1 fat quarter of a gray print for blocks
4 yards of fabric for backing
72" x 72" piece of batting

Cutting

From the gray fat quarter, cut:
4 squares, 4½" x 4½"

From *each* of the 2 yellow fat quarters, cut:
1 strip, 4½" x 42"; crosscut into 4 squares, 4½" x 4½"
    (8 total)

From *each* of the 3 green fat quarters, cut:
1 strip, 4½" x 42"; crosscut into 4 squares, 4½" x 4½"
    (12 total)

From *each* of the 4 navy fat quarters, cut:
1 strip, 4½" x 42"; crosscut into 4 squares, 4½" x 4½"
    (16 total)

From *each* of the 5 red fat quarters, cut:
1 strip, 4½" x 42"; crosscut into 4 squares, 4½" x 4½"
    (20 total)

From *each* of the 6 cream prints, cut:
1 strip, 4½" x 42"; crosscut into 2 rectangles, 4½" x 5"
    (12 total)

From the coal solid, cut:
2 strips, 24½" x 42"; crosscut into 2 pieces, 24½" x 25"
7 strips, 2¼" x 42"

From the *lengthwise* grain of the remainder of the coal solid, cut:
1 strip, 11½" x 65½"
1 strip, 6½" x 65½"
1 strip, 10½" x 48½"
1 strip, 7½" x 48½"

Making the Blocks

1 Arrange the gray, yellow, green, navy, and red squares and the cream rectangles into six horizontal rows as shown. Be sure you use one of each yellow, green, navy, and red print on each diagonal half of the unit and that the fabrics are in reverse order on each half. Proper placement is critical for the success of the block construction. Sew the pieces in each row together. Press the seam allowances in alternating directions from row to row. Sew the rows together. Press the seam allowances in one direction. Repeat to make a second identical unit. The units should measure 24½" x 25".

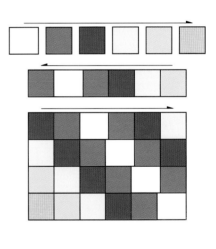

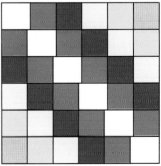

Make 2.

2 On the wrong side of each unit from step 1, draw a diagonal line from corner to corner through the cream rectangles.

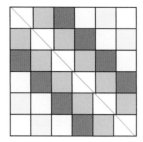

3 Place each of the marked units from step 2 right sides together with a coal 24½" x 25" piece. Sew ¼" from each side of the drawn line. Cut apart on the drawn line. Press the seam allowances toward the coal triangles. Trim each block to 24½" x 24½".

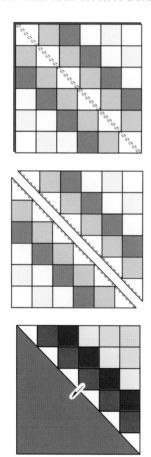

Assembling the Quilt Top

1 Arrange the blocks as shown. Sew the blocks in each row together. Press the seam allowances in alternating directions. Sew the rows together. Press

the seam allowances in one direction. The quilt center should measure 48½" x 48½".

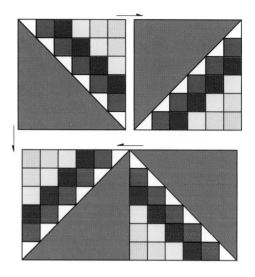

2 Sew the coal 7½" x 48½" strip to the top of the quilt center and the coal 10½" x 48½" strip to the bottom. Press the seam allowances toward the borders. Join the coal 11½" x 65½" strip to the right side of the quilt center and the coal 6½" x 65½" strip to the left side. Press the seam allowances toward the borders.

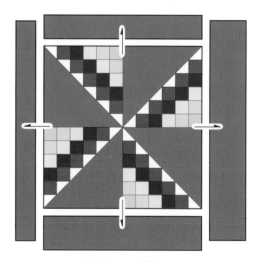

Quilt assembly

Finishing the Quilt

For detailed information on finishing techniques, including layering, basting, and quilting, go to ShopMartingale.com/HowtoQuilt for free downloadable instructions. Use the coal 2¼"-wide strips to bind the quilt.

Heartfelt

A quilt is a warm, gentle way to offer comfort when words fail—such as in times of grief. Pay tender tribute to a lost loved one's personality and tastes through color choices or the use of old garments as scraps for the patchwork.

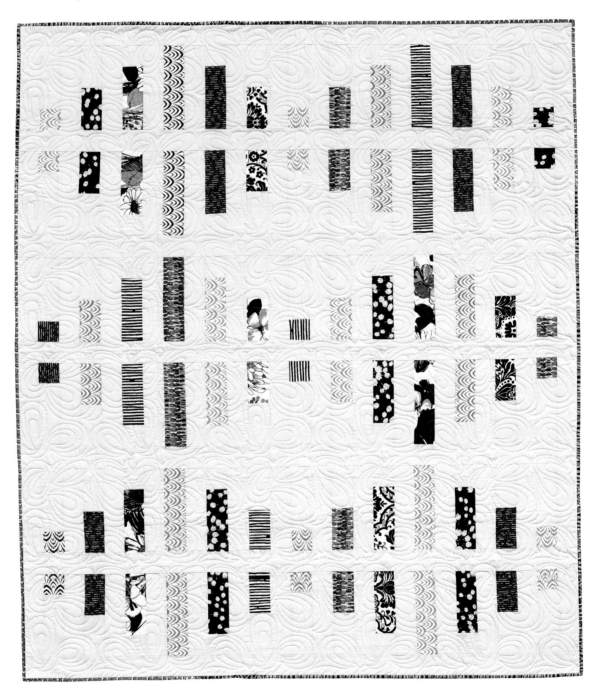

FINISHED QUILT: 54½" x 62½"
FINISHED BLOCK: 8" x 54"
Designed by Rachel Griffith; pieced by Molly Culley; quilted by Darla Padilla

Materials

Yardage is based on 42"-wide fabric. Fat quarters are 18" x 21".

6 fat quarters of assorted prints for blocks
3 yards of cream solid for blocks and sashing
⅝ yard of fabric for binding
3½ yards of fabric for backing
59" x 67" piece of batting

Cutting

From *each* of the fat quarters, cut:
4 strips, 2½" x 21"; crosscut into:
    4 squares, 2½" x 2½" (24 total; 6 are extra)
    4 strips, 2½" x 4½" (24 total)
    4 strips, 2½" x 6½" (24 total)
    2 strips, 2½" x 8½" (12 total)

From the cream solid, cut:
39 strips, 2½" x 42"; crosscut 29 of the strips into:
    84 strips, 2½" x 8½"
    18 strips, 2½" x 6½"
    24 strips, 2½" x 4½"
    24 squares, 2½" x 2½"

From the binding fabric, cut:
7 strips, 2¼" x 42"

Making the Rows

1. Join a print 2½" square to a cream 2½" x 6½" strip. Press the seam allowances toward the square. Make 18 units.

Make 18.

2. Join each print 2½" x 4½" strip to one end of a cream 2½" x 4½" strip. Press the seam allowances toward the assorted strip. Make 24 units.

Make 24.

3. Join each print 2½" x 6½" strip to a cream 2½" square. Press the seam allowances toward the assorted strip. Make 24 units.

Make 24.

4. Lay out three units from step 1, four units from step 2, four units from step 3, two assorted print 2½" x 8½" strips, and 14 cream 2½" x 8½" strips as shown. Join the strips to complete a Wavelength row. Press the seam allowances toward the cream strips. The row should measure 8½" x 54½". Make a total of six rows, referring to the photo on page 205 for placement guidance.

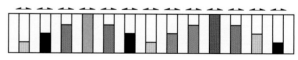

Make 6.

Assembling the Quilt Top

1 Sew the remaining cream 2½" x 42" strips together end to end. From the pieced strip, cut seven cream 54½"-long sashing strips.

2 Lay out the Wavelength rows and the sashing strips in horizontal rows, rotating the Wavelength rows and alternating them with the sashing strips as shown.

3 Sew the rows together to complete the quilt top. Press the seam allowances toward the sashing strips.

Finishing the Quilt

For detailed information on finishing techniques, including layering, basting, and quilting, go to ShopMartingale.com/HowtoQuilt for free downloadable instructions. Use the 2¼"-wide strips to bind the quilt.

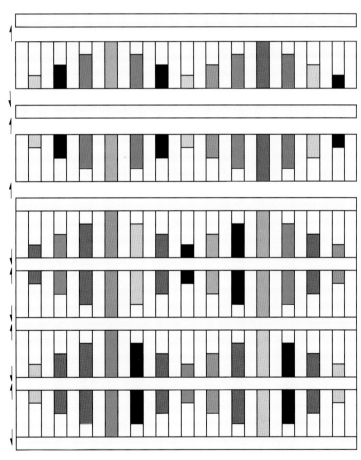

Quilt assembly

Sugar Sweet

This adorable crib-size quilt exudes charm and sweetness, and is the perfect sister project to Sugar (page 58). The quilts feature coordinating tulip-inspired quilt blocks and the same bright floral fabrics. Here, the blocks are smaller and paired with a darling checkerboard border.

FINISHED QUILT: 38" x 56"

FINISHED BLOCK: 7½" x 7½"

Designed and made by Amber Johnson

Materials

Yardage is based on 42"-wide fabric. Fat quarters are 18" x 21".

2 yards of white solid for blocks and pieced outer border

6 fat quarters of assorted bright prints for blocks and pieced outer border

¼ yard of aqua floral for inner border

½ yard of pink floral for binding

2⅝ yards of fabric for backing

46" x 64" piece of white batting

Cutting

From the white solid, cut:

6 strips, 2½" x 21"

14 strips, 2" x 42"; crosscut into:
 174 squares, 2" x 2"
 48 rectangles, 2" x 3½"

3 strips, 8" x 42"; crosscut into 13 squares, 8" x 8"

From *each* of the bright fat quarters, cut:

1 strip, 2½" x 21" (6 total)

32 squares, 2" x 2" (192 total; 8 are extra)

From the aqua floral, cut:

2 strips, 2" x 38"

From the pink floral, cut:

6 strips, 2½" x 42"

Assembling the Blocks

Try the method described here for making several half-square-triangle units from the same fabrics.

1 On the wrong side of each white 2½" x 21" strip, mark eight squares, 2½" x 2½". Draw a diagonal line from corner to corner on each square, alternating directions as shown so that the diagonal lines are connected along the strip.

Marked lines

2 Place a marked strip on top of a print 2½" x 21" strip with right sides together and pin. Stitch a scant ¼" from both sides of the drawn lines. Cut on all the drawn lines. Press the seam allowances toward the print triangles. You'll have 16 identical half-square-triangle units. Trim each one to measure 2" x 2". Repeat with the remaining 2½" x 21" strips to make a total of 96 half-square-triangle units.

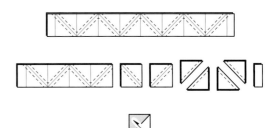

Make 96.

3 Sew a white 2" square to the left side of a half-square-triangle unit. Make four identical units. Then make four units reversed, with the half-square-triangle unit rotated and the square on the opposite side as shown. Press the seam allowances toward the squares.

Make 4 of each.

4 Sew a matching print 2" square to the right side of a half-square-triangle unit. Make four identical units. Make four units reversed, with the half-square-triangle unit rotated and the square on the opposite side as shown. Press the seam allowances toward the squares.

Make 4 of each.

5 Sew the units from steps 3 and 4 together in pairs as shown to make a "tulip." Make four and four reversed. Press the seam allowances open. The tulips should measure 3½" x 3½".

Make 4 of each.

6 Arrange two tulips, two reversed tulips, four white 2" x 3½" rectangles, and one matching print 2" square in rows as shown. Sew the pieces into rows, and then sew the rows together. Press the seam allowances toward the rectangles. The block should measure 8" x 8". Make two identical blocks. Repeat from step 3 to make two blocks from each bright print, for a total of 12 blocks.

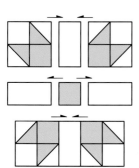 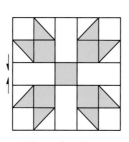

Make 2 of each print.

Assembling the Quilt Top

1 Arrange the 12 blocks and 13 white 8" squares in five rows, alternating the pieced blocks and squares as shown.

2 Sew the blocks into rows. Press the seam allowances toward the white squares. Sew the rows together and press the seam allowances open. The quilt center should measure 38" x 38".

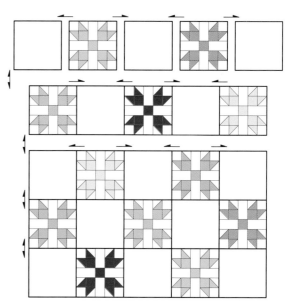

Quilt assembly

Adding the Borders

1. For the inner border, pin and sew the aqua 2" x 38" strips to the top and bottom of the quilt center. Press the seam allowances toward the aqua border.

2. To make the outer border, sew together 12 print 2" squares and 13 white 2" squares to form one border strip. Press the seam allowances toward the bright squares. Make six A border strips. Sew together 13 print squares and 12 white squares to form a border strip. Press the seam allowances toward the print squares. Make four B border strips.

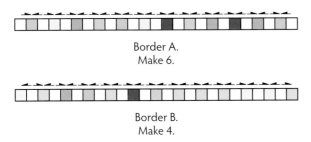

Border A.
Make 6.

Border B.
Make 4.

3. Sew together three A border strips and two B border strips in alternating positions, pinning at the seam intersections. Press the seam allowances open. Make two border sections. Sew one section to the top and one section to the bottom of the

quilt center. Press the seam allowances toward the aqua inner border.

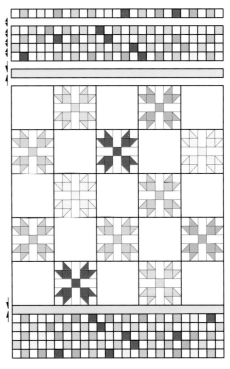

Adding borders

Finishing the Quilt

For detailed information on finishing techniques, including layering, basting, and quilting, go to ShopMartingale.com/HowtoQuilt for free downloadable instructions. Use the pink 2½"-wide strips to bind the quilt.

Patchwork Dreams

Simple squares in varying sizes create an interesting rectangular patchwork block, which repeats in rows separated by brightly colored sashing. Keep in mind that each fat quarter will be cut into both large and small squares. See the box on page 213 for tips on choosing large-scale prints.

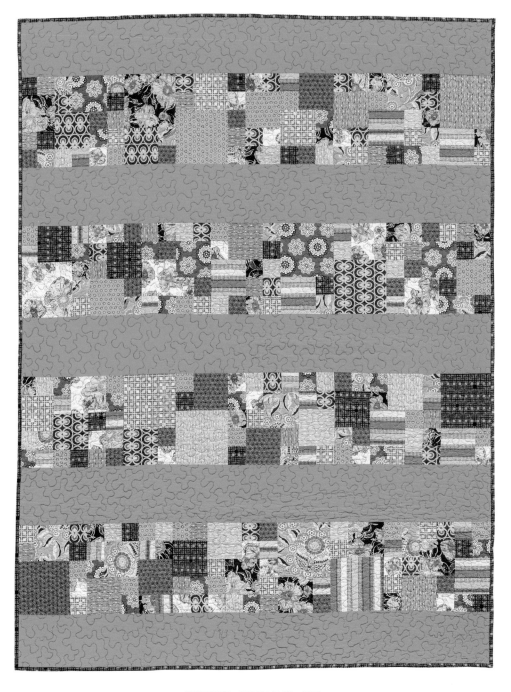

FINISHED QUILT: 54" x 70"
FINISHED BLOCK: 10" x 18"
Designed and made by Elizabeth Dackson

Materials

Yardage is based on 42"-wide fabric. Fat quarters are 18" x 21".

12 fat quarters of assorted prints for patchwork
1½ yards of emerald solid for sashing
⅝ yard of small-scale print for binding
3½ yards of fabric for backing
62" x 78" piece of batting

Auditioning Prints

Some large-scale prints work quite well when cut into small pieces. An easy way to get a feel for this is by covering the fabric with your hands, leaving just a 2" or 2½" square open between your thumbs and forefingers. This lets you see the visual impression made by a small area of the print. You can also cut an opening in a blank piece of paper and move it around on the fabric.

Cutting

From *each* of the assorted print fat quarters, cut:
1 square, 6½" x 6½" (12 total)
4 squares, 4½" x 4½" (48 total)
20 squares, 2½" x 2½" (240 total)

From the emerald solid, cut:
7 strips, 6½" x 42"

From the small-scale print, cut:
7 strips, 2½" x 42"

If Bigger Is Better

Have your heart set on a queen-size quilt? You'll need to make 30 blocks, set 5 x 6, for a 90" x 102½" finished size.

Materials

30 fat quarters of assorted prints for patchwork
3½ yards of solid for sashing
⅞ yard of fabric for binding
8½ yards of fabric for backing
98" x 110" piece of batting

Piecing the Blocks

This block is pieced in columns. For each block you will need 20 print 2½" squares, four print 4½" squares, and one print 6½" square. Be sure to select a variety of prints for each block. Use a scant ¼" seam allowance and press seam allowances open after sewing each seam.

1 To make the left column, sew six print 2½" squares together into three pairs. Sew one pair to the top edge of a print 4½" square. Sew the two remaining pairs together to create a four-patch unit. Sew the four-patch unit to the bottom of the 4½" square.

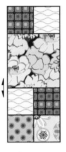

Left column

2 For the center column, sew 12 print 2½" squares together into six pairs. Sew one pair to each side of a print 4½" square. Sew two pairs together to create a four-patch unit. Sew this unit to the right side of another print 4½" square. Sew two pairs of squares together to create a chain of four squares. Assemble the units into a column.

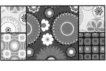
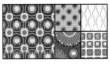

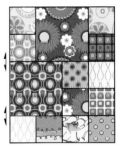

Center column

3 For the right column, sew two print 2½" squares together. Sew this pair to the right side of a print 4½" square. Sew this unit to the bottom of a print 6½" square.

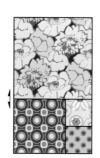

Right column

4 Sew the left and center columns together, and then add the right column.

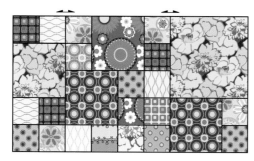

5 Repeat steps 1–4 to make a total of 12 blocks.

Assembling the Quilt Top

1 Arrange your blocks into four rows of three blocks each. Elizabeth rotated every other block to create more movement and variety in the quilt. Once you're happy with the layout, sew the blocks in each row together, pressing seam allowances open as you go.

2 Join the seven 6½" x 42" emerald strips together to make one long strip. Press the seam allowances open. Cut into five lengths, 6½" x 54½", for the sashing rows.

3 Sew the sashing rows together with the block rows, alternating them as shown in the quilt assembly diagram. Press.

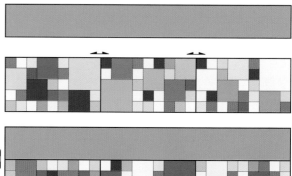

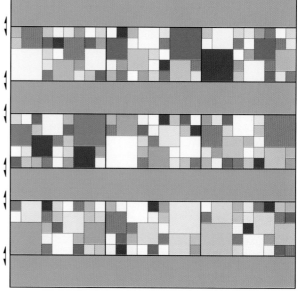

Quilt assembly

Finishing the Quilt

For detailed information on finishing techniques, including layering, basting, and quilting, go to ShopMartingale.com/HowtoQuilt for free downloadable instructions. Use the print 2½"-wide strips to bind the quilt.

Farsighted

Everyone gets a little homesick at times, but wrapping up in a quilt can be so comforting. These fabrics are bright and busy but the design is simple, and would make any college student feel right at home.

FINISHED QUILT: 60½" x 60½"

Designed and pieced by Rachel Griffith; quilted by Darla Padilla

Materials

Yardage is based on 42"-wide fabric. Fat quarters are 18" x 21".

8 fat quarters of assorted light prints
8 fat quarters of assorted dark prints
⅝ yard of fabric for binding
3⅞ yards of fabric for backing
65" x 65" piece of batting

Cutting

From the assorted light fat quarters, cut a *total* of:
4 squares, 15½" x 15½"
4 squares, 15⅞" x 15⅞"

From the assorted dark fat quarters, cut a *total* of:
4 squares, 15½" x 15½"
4 squares, 15⅞" x 15⅞"

From the binding fabric, cut:
7 strips, 2¼" x 42"

Assembling the Quilt Top

1 Draw a diagonal line from corner to corner on the wrong side of the light 15⅞" squares. Layer each marked square right sides together with a dark 15⅞" square and stitch ¼" from the drawn line on both sides. Cut the squares apart on the drawn line, and press the seam allowances toward the dark triangles. Make eight half-square-triangle units measuring 15½" x 15½".

Make 8.

2 Lay out the half-square-triangle units and assorted 15½" squares in four rows, alternating the units and squares as shown below. Sew the pieces together into rows. Press the seam allowances in opposite directions from row to row.

3 Sew the rows together. Press the seam allowances in one direction.

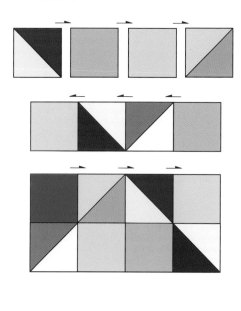

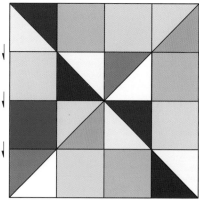

Quilt assembly

Finishing the Quilt

For detailed information on finishing techniques, including layering, basting, and quilting, go to ShopMartingale.com/HowtoQuilt for free downloadable instructions. Use the 2¼"-wide strips to bind the quilt.

Funky Christmas

Funky—modern and stylish in an unconventional way. That's a perfect description for this take on a traditional quilt block, made fun and funky by the use of nontraditional color choices.

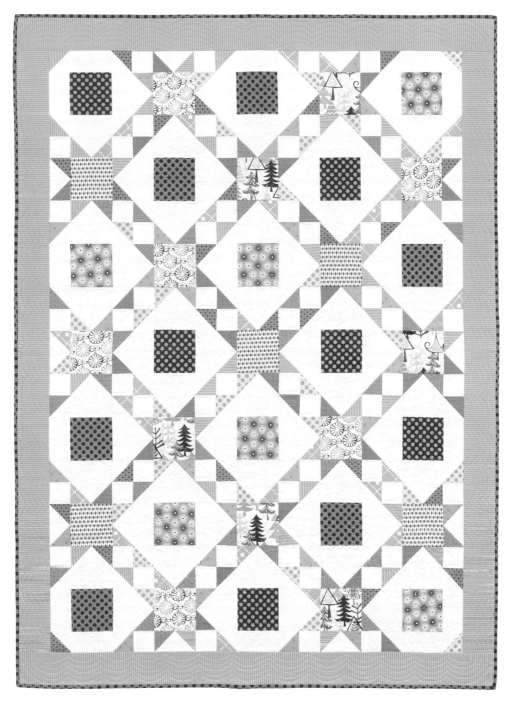

FINISHED QUILT: 58½" x 78½"

FINISHED BLOCK: 10" x 10"

Designed and made by Cindy Lammon

Materials

Yardage is based on 42"-wide fabric. Fat quarters are 18" x 21".

2⅞ yards of white solid for background
1 yard of aqua-and-white stripe for borders
7 fat quarters of assorted aqua prints for blocks
3 fat quarters of assorted red-and-pink prints
    for blocks
3 fat quarters of assorted Christmas prints for blocks
⅔ yard of red-and-pink polka dot for binding
5¼ yards of fabric for backing
65" x 85" piece of batting

Cutting

From the white solid, cut:
8 strips, 5½" x 42"; crosscut into 104 rectangles,
    3" x 5½"
6 strips, 3" x 42"; crosscut into 68 squares, 3" x 3"
3 strips, 10½" x 42"; crosscut into 36 rectangles,
    3" x 10½"

From *each* of the 7 aqua print fat quarters, cut:
5 strips, 3" x 21" (35 total); crosscut into 30 squares,
    3" x 3" (210 total; 2 are extra)

**From *each* of the 3 Christmas print fat quarters,
cut:**
2 strips, 5½" x 21" (6 total); crosscut into 6 squares,
    5½" x 5½" (18 total; 1 is extra)

From *each* of the 3 red-and-pink fat quarters, cut:
2 strips, 5½" x 21" (6 total); crosscut into 6 squares,
    5½" x 5½" (18 total)

From the aqua-and-white stripe, cut:
7 strips, 4½" x 42"

From the red-and-pink polka dot, cut:
8 strips, 2½" x 42"

Making the Star Blocks

After sewing each seam, press the seam allowances as indicated by the arrows.

1. Draw a diagonal line from corner to corner on the wrong side of two aqua 3" squares. Layer a marked square on one end of a white 3" x 5½" rectangle, right sides together, and sew from corner to corner on the drawn line. Trim the excess corner fabric and press toward the resulting aqua triangle. In the same manner, add the second marked square to the other end of the rectangle. Repeat to make a total of 68 flying-geese units.

Make 68.

2. Arrange four flying-geese units, a Christmas print 5½" square, and four white 3" squares into three horizontal rows as shown. Sew the pieces in each row together; press. Join the rows to complete the block; press. Repeat to make a total of 17 Star blocks.

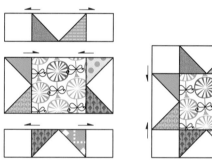

Make 17.

Making the Alternate Blocks

1. Sew white 3" x 5½" rectangles to the top and bottom of a red-and-pink 5½" square; press. Sew white 3" x 10½" rectangles to the sides of the unit. Repeat to make a total of 18 units.

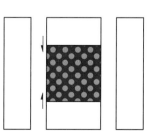
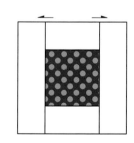

Make 18.

2 Draw a diagonal line from corner to corner on the wrong side of each of the remaining aqua 3" squares. Place a marked square on each corner of a unit from step 1, noting the direction of the marked line. Sew on the marked line. Trim ¼" from the stitching line; press. Repeat to make a total of 18 alternate blocks.

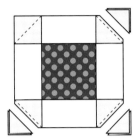 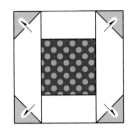

Make 18.

Assembling the Quilt Top

1 Refer to the quilt assembly diagram below to arrange the blocks in seven rows of five blocks each, alternating the two blocks in each row and from row to row. Sew the blocks in each row together. Press the seam allowances toward the alternate blocks. Join the rows. Press the seam allowances in one direction.

2 Join two aqua-and-white striped 4½"-wide strips together end to end to make one long strip. Repeat to make a total of two pieced strips. Trim both pieced strips to the length of the quilt top. Sew the strips to the sides of the quilt top. Press the seam allowances toward the border.

3 Sew the remaining three aqua-and-white strips together end to end to make one long strip. From the pieced strip, cut two strips to the width of the quilt top and sew them to the top and bottom of the quilt top. Press the seam allowances toward the border.

Finishing the Quilt

For detailed information on finishing techniques, including layering, basting, and quilting, go to ShopMartingale.com/HowtoQuilt for free downloadable instructions. Use the red-and-pink 2½"-wide strips to bind the quilt.

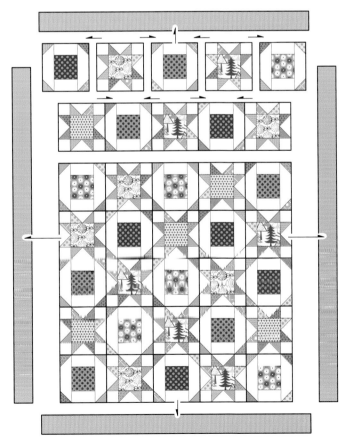

Quilt assembly

Checkerboard Dots

Circles on squares? How delightfully simple! But check out the visual interest created by a fascinating range of batik prints. Some of the circle shapes burst with geometric angles; some of the background squares bubble up with waves and pebble patterns. And they all glow with strikingly gorgeous color.

FINISHED QUILT: 48½" x 48½"

Designed and pieced by Julie Herman; machine quilted by Angela Walters

Materials

Yardage is based on 42"-wide fabric. Fat quarters are 18" x 21".

32 fat quarters of assorted batiks for backgrounds and circle appliqués

⅛ yard each of 6 assorted batiks for binding

3¼ yards of fabric for backing

54" x 54" piece of batting

2¾ yards of 16"-wide fusible web

Cutting

From the assorted batik fat quarters, cut a *total* of:

16 squares, 9½" x 9½"

16 rectangles, 6½" x 9½"

4 squares, 6½" x 6½"

Set aside the remaining fabric for appliqué circles.

From each ⅛-yard cut of an assorted batik, cut:

1 strip, 2¼" x 42" (6 total)

Assembling the Quilt

This design is scrappy, so don't overplan.

1. Lay out the 9½" batik squares, 6½" batik squares, and batik rectangles in six rows as shown.

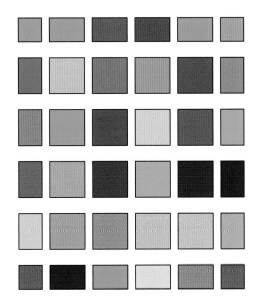

2. Sew the pieces together into rows. Press the seam allowances open. Sew the rows together and press the seam allowances open.

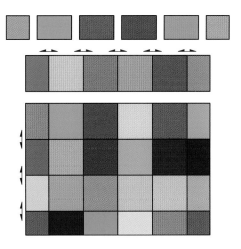

3. Using the pattern on page 222, trace 25 circles onto the paper side of the fusible web. Roughly cut out the circles, approximately ¼" outside the traced line. Fuse each circle to the wrong side of a different batik. Cut out each circle directly on the traced line.

4. Remove the paper backing and fuse the circles in place, centering them on top of the seam intersections as shown. Stitch the circles in place using a machine blanket stitch or a zigzag stitch.

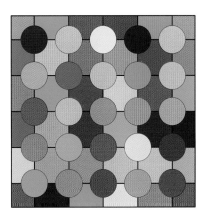

Finishing the Quilt

For detailed information on finishing techniques, including layering, basting, and quilting, go to ShopMartingale.com/HowtoQuilt for free downloadable instructions. Use the batik 2¼"-wide strips to bind the quilt.

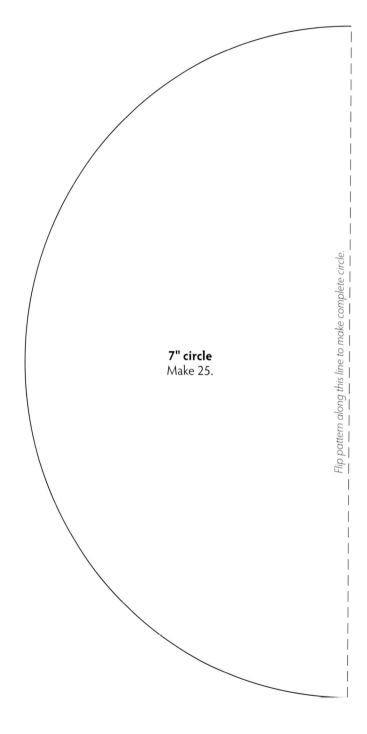

7" circle
Make 25.

Flip pattern along this line to make complete circle.

Vintage Cherries

Time to pull your favorite fat quarters from your stash. Although designed as a holiday project, this quilt is sure to be a winner throughout the year.

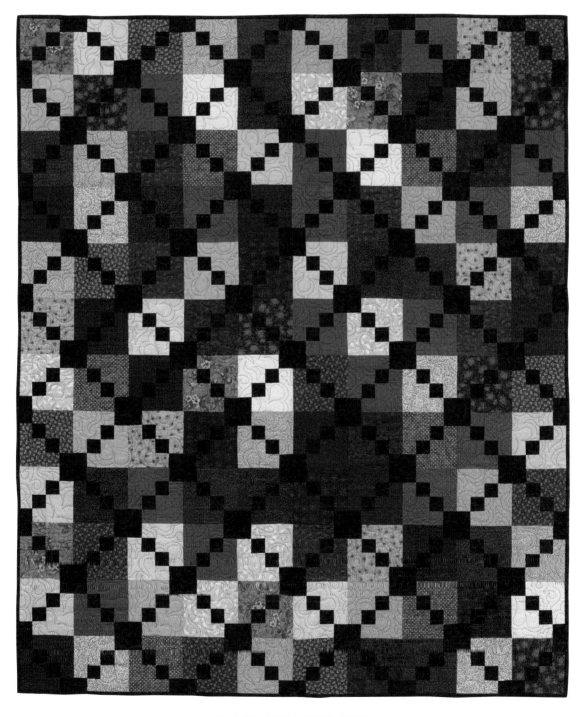

FINISHED QUILT: 60½" x 72½"

FINISHED BLOCK: 6" x 6"

Designed and made by Jeanne Large and Shelley Wicks; machine quilted by Laila Nelson

Materials

Yardage is based on 42"-wide fabric. Fat quarters are 18" x 21".

1⅝ yards of black tone on tone for blocks

24 fat quarters of assorted prints in pink, red, burgundy, brown, and beige for blocks

⅝ yard of black fabric for binding

4 yards of fabric for backing

70" x 82" piece of batting

Cutting

From the black tone on tone, cut:

24 strips, 2" x 42"; crosscut each strip into 2 strips, 2" x 21" (48 total)

From *each* of the 24 fat quarters, cut:

2 strips, 2" x 21" (48 total)

2 strips, 3½" x 21" (48 total); crosscut each strip into 5 squares, 3½" x 3½" (240 total)

From the black binding fabric, cut:

7 strips, 2½" x 42"

Making the Blocks

1 Sew a print 2" x 21" strip to a black 2" x 21" strip to make a strip set. Press the seam allowances toward the black fabric. Make a total of 48 strip sets. Crosscut each strip set into 10 segments, 2" wide (480 total).

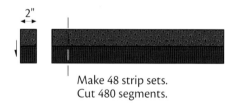

Make 48 strip sets.
Cut 480 segments.

2 Sew two matching segments together as shown to make a four-patch unit. Make 240 units.

Make 240.

3 Sew a matching print 3½" square to one side of each four-patch unit. Press the seam allowances toward the 3½" square. Sew two of these

sections together to make one block. Press the seam allowances to one side. Make 120 blocks.

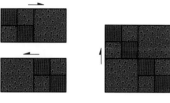

Make 120.

Quick Fix for Lumpy Corners

If you have a bulky corner or lots of points coming together, try pressing the seam allowances open rather than to one side. A little bit of spray starch also helps when dealing with stubborn seams.

Assembling the Quilt Top

1 Arrange the blocks into 12 rows of 10 blocks each, rotating the blocks to form the chain as shown.

2 Sew the blocks together into rows. Press the seam allowances in opposite directions from row to row. Sew the rows together. Press the seam allowances in one direction.

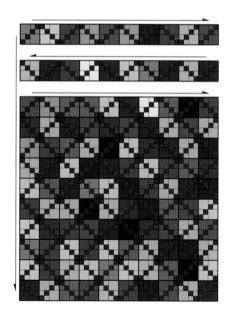

Finishing the Quilt

For detailed information on finishing techniques, including layering, basting, and quilting, go to ShopMartingale.com/HowtoQuilt for free downloadable instructions. Use the black 2½"-wide strips to bind the quilt.

Square City

You don't need to be an urban planner to appreciate Square City's neatly organized layout. Open spaces for large-scale prints exist side by side with tidy blocks, creating an aesthetically refreshing and uncluttered atmosphere.

FINISHED QUILT: 67" x 67"

FINISHED BLOCK: 9½" x 9½"

Designed and pieced by Julie Herman; machine quilted by Angela Walters

Materials

Yardage is based on 42"-wide fabric. Fat quarters are 18" x 21".

25 fat quarters of assorted prints for blocks and plain squares
1 yard of gray print for block centers
⅞ yard of large-scale stripe for bias binding
4⅜ yards of fabric for backing
73" x 73" piece of batting

Cutting

From the gray print, cut:
5 strips, 6" x 42"; crosscut 25 squares, 6" x 6"

From *each* of the assorted print fat quarters, cut:
1 square, 10" x 10" (25 total; 1 is extra)
4 strips, 1½" x 18"; crosscut into:
    2 rectangles, 1½" x 10" (50 total)
    4 rectangles, 1½" x 8" (100 total)
    2 rectangles, 1½" x 6" (50 total)

From the large-scale stripe, cut:
2¼"-wide bias strips to total 280" in length

Making the Blocks

1 Sew matching 1½" x 6" assorted rectangles to opposite sides of a gray square. Press the seam allowances open.

2 Sew 1½" x 8" rectangles that match the rectangles in step 1 to the two remaining sides of the gray square. Press the seam allowances open.

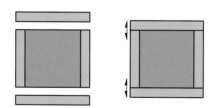

3 Sew matching 1½" x 8" assorted rectangles from a different print to opposite sides of the unit as shown. Press the seam allowances open.

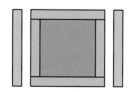
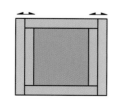

4 Sew 1½" x 10" rectangles that match the rectangles added in step 3 to the two remaining sides of the unit to complete the block. Press the seam allowances open. Repeat from step 1 to make a total of 25 blocks.

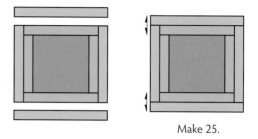

Make 25.

Assembling the Quilt Top

1 Lay out the blocks and the 10" assorted squares in seven rows of seven units each, alternating the plain squares and the blocks in each row and from row to row.

2 Sew the blocks and squares together in rows; press the seam allowances open. Sew the rows together and press.

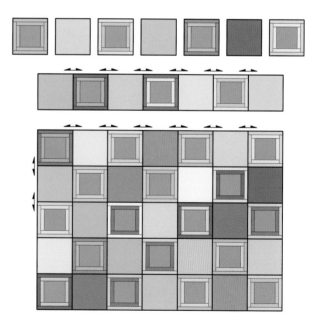

Finishing the Quilt

For detailed information on finishing techniques, including layering, basting, and quilting, go to ShopMartingale.com/HowtoQuilt for free downloadable instructions. Use the striped 2¼"-wide bias strips to bind the quilt.

Scraps and Strips

At last—a way to use your stash of assorted leftover strips! You simply sew strips to a muslin square, flip them open, and keep going until the muslin is covered. No worrying about seam allowances or sewing straight! When you're done, simply square up the block to the right size.

FINISHED QUILT: 50⅞" x 60"

Designed and made by Heather Mulder Peterson

Materials

Yardage is based on 42"-wide fabric. Fat quarters are 18" x 21".

11 fat quarters of assorted colors for blocks and pieced borders

1⅓ yards of muslin for block foundation

1⅓ yards of burgundy fabric for outer border

1⅛ yards of black fabric for sashing and inner border

⅛ yard of gold fabric for sashing squares

¾ yard of black plaid for binding

3¼ yards of fabric for backing

55" x 64" piece of batting

Cutting

From the assorted fat quarters, cut a *total* of:

130 pieces, from 1¾" to 2¼" wide x 8¾" long

100 pieces, 2⅛" x 3¾"

From the muslin, cut:

5 strips, 8½" x 42"; crosscut into 20 squares, 8½" x 8½"

From the black fabric, cut:

7 strips, 1⅛" x 42"; crosscut into 31 pieces, 1⅛" x 8"

6 strips, 2⅛" x 42"; crosscut into 104 squares, 2⅛" x 2⅛"

2 strips, 3" x 42"

2 strips, 2½" x 42"

From the gold fabric, cut:

12 squares, 1⅛" x 1⅛"

From the burgundy fabric, cut:

6 strips, 4½" x 42"

6 strips, 2⅛" x 42"; crosscut into 100 squares, 2⅛" x 2⅛"

4 squares, 3¾" x 3¾"

From the black plaid, cut:

2½"-wide bias strips to total 230" in length

Making the Blocks

Lay one of the colored strips right side up on a muslin foundation block. Lay another colored strip right side down on the first strip and sew. Before pressing, trim the seam allowance to ¼" if needed to help reduce bulk. Press the seam as directed by the arrow. Lay another colored strip right side down, angling if desired but watching to see that the strip below will be caught in the seam allowance. Sew and press. Continue across the block as shown and then trim the block to 8" x 8". Make 20 of these strip-pieced blocks.

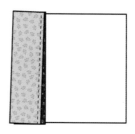 

 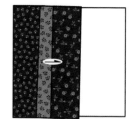

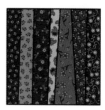

Make 20.

Assembling the Quilt Top

1 Sew the blocks together with the 1⅛" x 8" black strips and the 1⅛" gold squares as shown. Press the seam allowances toward the black sashing strips. Square up the quilt-top center to 32⅜" x 40½".

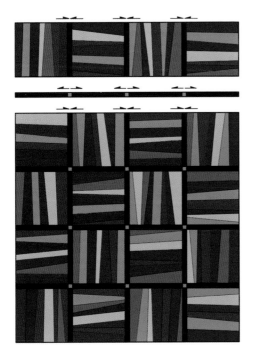

2 Cut the 2½"-wide black strips to a length of 40½" (piecing as needed) and sew them to the sides of the quilt top, pressing the seam allowances toward the black. Cut the 3"-wide black strips to a length of 36⅜" and sew these to the top and bottom of the quilt top, pressing the seam allowances toward the black. Square up the quilt top to 36⅜" x 45½".

3 Sew a 2⅛" black square to a 3¾" burgundy square as shown. Make four of these corner units and set them aside for step 5.

Make 4.

4 Sew the 2⅛" x 3¾" colored pieces into pairs, pressing the seam allowances open. Using the folded-corner technique, sew the 2⅛" black squares and burgundy squares to each unit as shown. Be careful that the center seam is between the black and burgundy triangles. Press the seam allowances toward the triangles.

5 Sew the units from step 4 into two rows of 14 units each and trim each row to a length of 45½". Press the seam allowances open to reduce bulk. Sew the strips to the sides of the quilt top as shown in the assembly diagram, and press the seam allowances toward the black borders. Sew the remaining units into two rows of 11 units each and trim each row to a length of 36¼". Sew the corner units from step 3 to the ends of each row, and then sew them to the top and bottom of the quilt top, pressing the seam allowances toward the black borders. Square up the quilt top to 42¾" x 52".

Side pieced border.
Make 2.

Top/bottom pieced border.
Make 2.

6 Sew the burgundy strips together end to end. Cut two strips, 52" long, and sew them to the sides of the quilt top. Press the seam allowances toward the outer border. Cut two strips, 50¾" long, and sew them to the top and bottom of the quilt top. Press the seam allowances toward the outer border.

Finishing the Quilt

For detailed information on finishing techniques, including layering, basting, and quilting, go to ShopMartingale.com/HowtoQuilt for free downloadable instructions. Use the black-plaid 2½"-wide bias strips to bind the quilt.

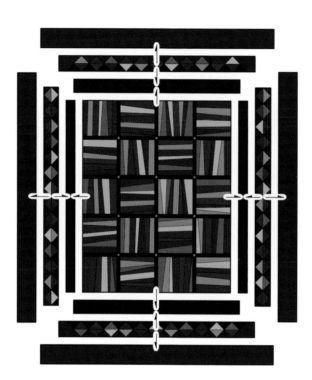

Holiday Stars

Stars are a great accent at any time of the year, but they truly lend themselves to holiday decorations. This project will add a touch of sparkle and charm to any room.

FINISHED QUILT: 46½" x 62½"
FINISHED BLOCK: 8" x 8"

Designed and pieced by Shelley Wicks and Jeanne Large; machine quilted by Shelley Wicks

Materials

Yardage is based on 42"-wide fabric. Fat quarters are 18" x 21". The materials list contains sufficient fabric to make the quilt. The actual quilt is more scrappy than what's called for. If you enjoy a scrappier look, feel free to add more fabrics.

9 fat quarters of assorted red fabrics for blocks and outer border

9 fat quarters of assorted green fabrics for blocks and outer border

⅓ yard of gold fabric for inner border

⅓ yard of gold fabric for star appliqués

½ yard of green fabric for binding

3 yards of fabric for backing

55" x 71" piece of batting

1 yard of lightweight fusible web for appliqués

Cutting

From *each* of the red fat quarters, cut:

1 strip, 4½" x 21"; crosscut each strip into 2 squares, 4½" x 4½" (18 total)

1 strip, 2½" x 21"; crosscut each strip into 4 rectangles, 2½" x 4½" (36 total; 2 are extra)

2 strips, 2½" x 21"; crosscut each strip into 2 rectangles, 2½" x 8½" (36 total; 2 are extra)

1 strip, 2½" x 21" (9 total)

From *each* of the green fat quarters, cut:

1 strip, 4½" x 21"; crosscut each strip into 2 squares, 4½" x 4½" (18 total; 1 is extra)

1 strip, 2½" x 21"; crosscut each strip into 4 rectangles, 2½" x 4½" (36 total)

2 strips, 2½" x 21"; crosscut each strip into 2 rectangles, 2½" x 8½" (36 total)

1 strip, 2½" x 21" (9 total)

From the gold inner-border fabric, cut:

5 strips, 1½" x 42"

From the green binding fabric, cut:

6 strips, 2½" x 42"

Piecing the Blocks

1 Sew matching red 2½" x 4½" rectangles to opposite sides of a green 4½" square. Press seam allowances toward the red. Make 17 units.

Make 17.

2 Sew matching red 2½" x 8½" rectangles to the top and bottom of a unit made in step 1. Press the seam allowances toward the red. Make 17 blocks with green centers.

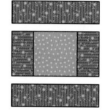
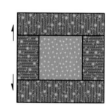

Make 17.

3 Following steps 1 and 2, reverse the color placement to make 18 blocks with red centers.

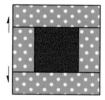

Make 18.

Assembling the Quilt Top

1 Arrange the blocks into seven rows of five blocks each. Starting with a green block in the top-right corner, alternate the red and green blocks. When you're satisfied with your arrangement, make sure that each block is also positioned so that the green blocks have the long strips on the top and bottom and the red blocks have the long strips on the sides. This makes for easier stitching!

2 Sew the blocks together into rows. Press the seam allowances in opposite directions from row to row. Sew the rows together. Press the seam allowances in one direction.

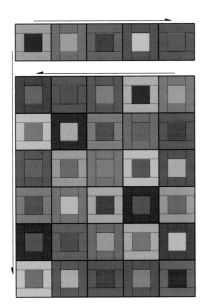

Press. Sew the 46½"-long strips to the top and bottom of the quilt. Press.

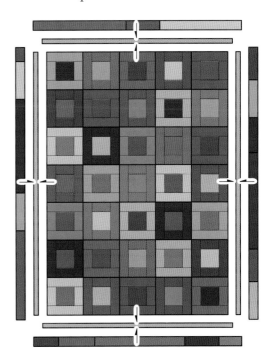

Adding the Borders

1 Sew the gold 1½" x 42" inner-border strips together end to end to make one continuous strip. From this strip, cut two strips, 56½" long, and two strips, 42½" long. Sew the 56½"-long strips to the sides of the quilt. Press. Sew the 42½"-long strips to the top and bottom of the quilt. Press.

2 To make the scrappy outer border, use the remaining 2½"-wide strips of red and green. Cut the strips into random lengths and sew them together end to end to make one continuous strip approximately 220" long. Press the seam allowances in one direction. From this strip, cut two strips, 58½" long, and two strips, 46½" long. Sew the 58½"-long strips to the sides of the quilt.

Appliquéing the Stars

1 Using the star patterns on page 234 and the gold fabric, prepare the following shapes for your favorite method of appliqué:

- 17 large stars

- 18 small stars

2 Using the photo on page 231 as a guide, randomly place and appliqué one star onto each block.

Finishing the Quilt

For detailed information on finishing techniques, including layering, basting, and quilting, go to ShopMartingale.com/HowtoQuilt for free downloadable instructions. Use the green 2½"-wide strips to bind the quilt.

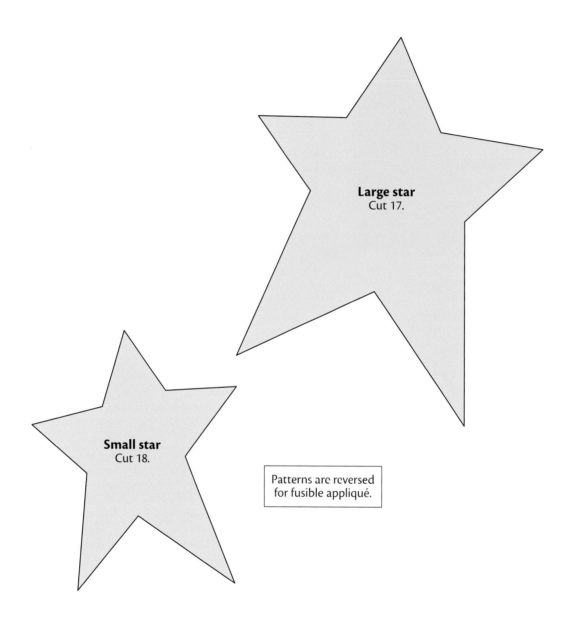

Large star
Cut 17.

Small star
Cut 18.

Patterns are reversed
for fusible appliqué.

Christmas Magic

Remember childhood holidays with boughs of evergreens and sprigs of mistletoe, earnest letters to Santa, and cookies on a plate by the twinkling tree? Recapture these moments as you stitch a little tabletop quilt bursting with the magic of Christmas.

FINISHED QUILT: 48½" x 48½"

FINISHED BLOCK: 6" x 6"

Designed, pieced, and machine appliquéd by Kim Diehl; machine quilted by Celeste Freiberg

Materials

Yardage is based on 42"-wide fabric. Fat quarters are 18" x 21"; fat eighths are 9" x 21".

2½ yards of tan print for blocks and borders

1 fat quarter *each* of 3 assorted red prints for blocks and outer border

1 fat quarter each of 2 assorted green prints for blocks and outer border

1 fat quarter *each* of 2 assorted brown prints for block, outer border, and branch appliqués

1 fat quarter of gold print for block, star appliqués, and outer border

1 fat quarter of blue print for block and outer border

1 fat quarter of cream print for snowman appliqués

1 fat quarter of green plaid for holly leaf appliqués

1 fat quarter of red stripe for outer pomegranate appliqués

1 fat eighth of contrasting red print for inner pomegranate appliqués

1 fat eighth of red print for bow appliqués

Scraps of light- and dark-blue prints for hat appliqués

Scraps of orange print for carrot nose appliqués

½ yard of green stripe for binding

3 yards of fabric for backing

54" x 54" piece of batting

3⁄16" bias bar

Water-soluble marker

20 black buttons in assorted sizes for snowmen

40 red buttons in assorted sizes for berries

#8 black perle cotton

Size 5 embroidery needle

Cutting

Cut all strips across the width of the fabric unless otherwise noted. Refer to page 240 for appliqué patterns A–J.

From the *lengthwise* grain of the tan print, cut:

2 strips, 9½" x 42½"

2 strips, 9½" x 24½"

2 squares, 6½" x 6½"

From the *remainder* of the tan print, cut:

1 strip, 6½" x 42"; crosscut into 6 squares, 6½" x 6½"

20 strips, 1½" x 42"; crosscut into:

    184 rectangles, 1½" x 2½"

    176 squares, 1½" x 1½"

4 squares, 1⅞" x 1⅞"; cut the squares in half diagonally to yield 8 triangles

From *each* of the 8 fat quarters for blocks, cut:

44 squares, 1½" x 1½" (352 total)

11 squares, 2½" x 2½" (88 total)

From the *remainder of 1* green fat quarter, cut:

8 squares, 1½" x 1½"

2 squares, 2⅞" x 2⅞"; cut the squares in half diagonally to yield 4 triangles

From the cream print, cut:

4 using pattern A

From the brown fat quarter for branches, cut:

8 strips, 1" x 18"

16 rectangles, 1" x 2¼"

8 rectangles, 1" x 1½"

From the scraps of dark-blue print, cut:

4 using pattern B

From the scraps of light-blue print, cut:

4 using pattern C

From the red print for bows, cut:

4 using pattern D

4 using pattern E

From the scraps of orange print, cut:

4 using pattern F

From the green plaid, cut:

20 using pattern G*

From the red stripe, cut:

24 using pattern H

From the contrasting red print, cut:

24 using pattern I

From the remainder of the gold-print fat quarter, cut:

16 using pattern J

From the green stripe, cut:

5 strips, 2½" x 42"

*For added flavor, a handful of the G appliqués were cut from the remainder of the green fat quarters used for the blocks.

Making the Blocks

1 Use a pencil to draw a diagonal line on the wrong side of 88 tan print 1½" squares.

2 Using the red, green, gold, blue, and brown print squares, select a matching set of four 1½" squares and one 2½" square. Use a pencil to draw a diagonal line on the wrong side of the 1½" squares.

3 With right sides together, layer a prepared red, green, gold, blue, or brown print 1½" square over one end of a tan print 1½" x 2½" rectangle as shown. Stitch the pair exactly on the drawn line. Layer a second prepared square of the same color over the remaining end of the rectangle as shown. Stitch, press, and trim as previously instructed. Repeat for a total of two pieced rectangles.

Make 2.

4 Join a pieced rectangle to one side of a matching print 2½" square. Press the seam allowance away from the pieced rectangle. Join a tan print 1½" square to one end of the remaining pieced rectangle as shown. Press the seam allowance toward the tan print. Join this pieced unit to the adjacent side of the 2½" square. Press the seam allowance toward the 2½" square.

 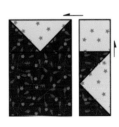

5 Layer a prepared tan print 1½" square over a unit from step 4. Stitch, press, and trim as previously instructed.

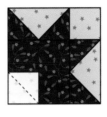 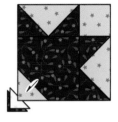

6 Repeat steps 2–5 for a total of 88 pieced units.

7 Select four matching units. Lay out the units in two horizontal rows to form a block. Join the units in each row. Press the seam allowances in alternating directions. Join the rows. Press the seam allowance to one side. Repeat for a total of three red print blocks, two green print blocks, and one each of blue, gold, and brown print blocks. Each block should measure 6½" square. Reserve the remaining units for later use.

 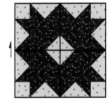
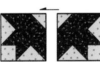

Make 8 total.

Assembling the Quilt Center

Lay out eight blocks and eight tan print 6½" squares in four horizontal rows as shown. Join the pieces in each row. Press the seam allowances toward the tan squares. Join the rows. Press the seam allowances in one direction. The pieced quilt center should now measure 24½" square.

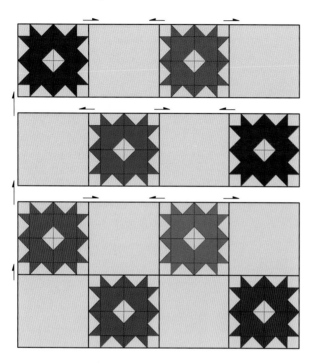

Adding and Appliquéing the Inner Border

1. Join tan 9½" x 24½" strips to the right and left sides of the quilt center. Press the seam allowances toward the tan strips. Join tan 9½" x 42½" strips to the remaining sides of the quilt center. Press the seam allowances toward the tan strips.

2. Lightly press a diagonal crease at each border corner, extending from the corner of the quilt center to the outer point of the inner border. Carefully fold a prepared A appliqué in half vertically and finger-press a crease. Line up the

crease of the snowman with the background crease, positioning it about 1¾" from each border edge; baste in place. Repeat with the remaining corners.

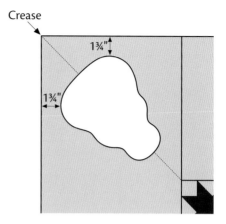

Crease

1¾"

1¾"

3. Appliqué each snowman into position.

4. Use a bias bar to prepare the brown strips and rectangles for the stems. (For more information on using bias bars, download free "How to Appliqué" instructions from ShopMartingale. com/HowtoQuilt.) Using the quilt photo as a guide, lay out one prepared 18" length, two 2¼" lengths, and one 1½" length on each side of the snowmen. (The branch pieces have been cut on the straight of grain, so they will be a bit gnarly and knobby when laid out, rather than smooth and flowing.) After ensuring that the raw ends of the short stems are tucked securely under the main branches, baste and stitch the appliqués. Repeat with the remaining corners of the quilt top.

5. Referring to the quilt photo, work from the bottom layer to the top to lay out and affix the remaining appliqués to the quilt top. If you find it difficult to prepare the small nose shapes for turned-edge appliqué, use fusible web instead, following the manufacturer's instructions. Fuse the pieces to the snowmen and satin stitch the raw edges with matching thread.

Piecing and Adding the Outer Border

1 Select 14 reserved units sewn from an assortment of prints. Join the units end to end to form a pieced border strip. Press the seam allowances in one direction. Repeat for a total of four pieced border strips.

Make 4.

2 Sew pieced border strips to the right and left sides of the quilt top. Carefully press the seam allowances toward the inner border, taking care not to apply heat to the appliqués.

3 Join a tan print 1⅞" triangle to one side of a green print 1½" square. Press the seam allowance toward the tan print. In the same manner, sew and press a second tan triangle to the adjacent side of the green square. Trim away the dog-ear points. Join this pieced triangle to a green print 2⅞" triangle as shown. Press the seam allowance toward the green print. Repeat for a total of four pieced square units.

Make 4.

4 Join a tan print 1½" x 2½" rectangle to a pieced square unit from step 3 as shown below. Press the seam allowances toward the rectangle. Join a green print 1½" square to one end of a tan print 1½" x 2½" rectangle. Press the seam allowance toward the tan print. Join this pieced rectangle to the adjacent side of the pieced square. Press the seam allowances toward the pieced rectangle. Repeat for a total of four Corner Post blocks.

Make 4.

5 Referring to the quilt photo, join a Corner Post block to the ends of the remaining pieced border strips. Press the seam allowances toward the Corner Post blocks. Join these border strips to the remaining sides of the quilt top. Carefully press the seam allowances toward the appliquéd snowman border. The pieced quilt top should now measure 48½" square.

Finishing the Quilt

For detailed information on finishing techniques, including layering, basting, and quilting, go to ShopMartingale.com/HowtoQuilt for free downloadable instructions. Use a water-soluble marker to draw dots on each snowman face as a guide for sewing French knots at the mouth and eyes. Use the size 5 embroidery needle and perle cotton to add the French knots, sliding the needle under the batting between each knot to prevent shadowing. Use the perle cotton to sew five black buttons in assorted sizes to each snowman body, again sliding the needle under the batting layer. Stitch five assorted red buttons to each branch, taking care to cover the raw stem ends and hide the thread lines underneath the batting. Use the green-striped 2½"-wide strips to bind the quilt.

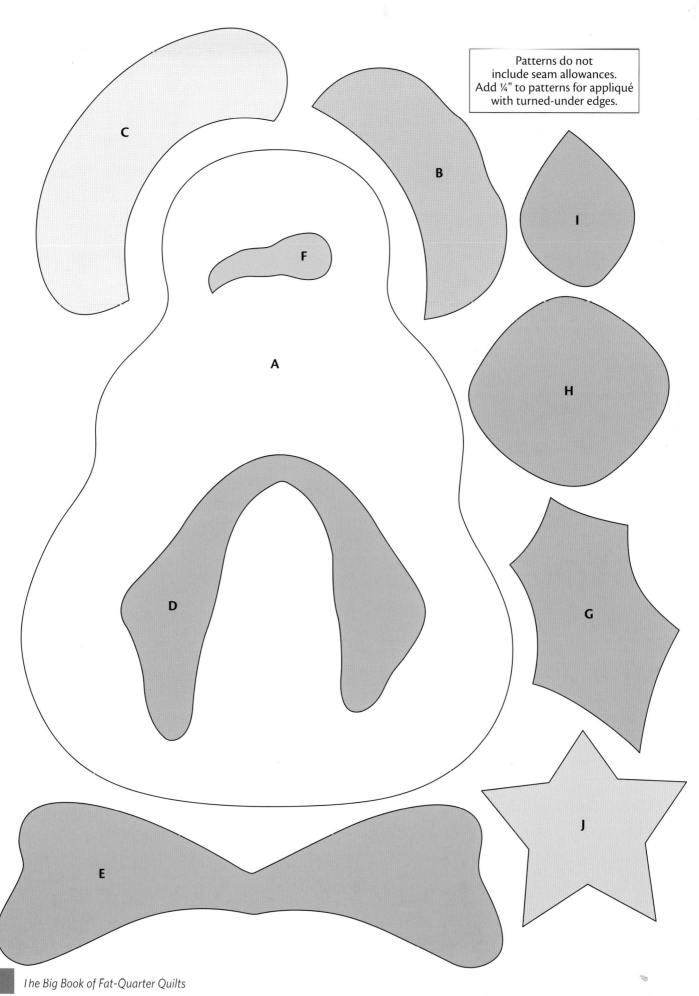

Patterns do not
include seam allowances.
Add ¼" to patterns for appliqué
with turned-under edges.